Clinical Supervision and Teacher Development

Preservice and Inservice Applications

Clinical Supervision and Teacher Development

Preservice and Inservice Applications

Fifth Edition

Keith A. Acheson

Meredith Damien Gall

John Wiley & Sons, Inc.

Acquisitions Editor   *Brad Hanson*
Marketing Manager   *Kevin Molloy*
Development Editor   *Joan Petrokofsky*
Senior Production Editor   *Valerie A. Vargas*
Cover Designer   *Madelyn Lesure*
Cover Image   *© CORBIS*
Production Management Services   *Suzanne Ingrao / Ingrao Associates*

This book was set in 10/12 Times Roman by Pine Tree and printed and bound by Malloy Lithographers. The cover was printed by Phoenix Color.

This book is printed on acid-free paper. ∞

Library of Congress Cataloging in Publication Data:
Acheson, Keith A., 1925–
    Clinical supervision and teacher development: preservice and inservice applications /
Keith A. Acheson, Meredith Damien Gall.—5th ed.
        p.   cm.
    Rev. ed. of: Techniques in the clinical supervision of teachers. 4th ed. ©1997.
    Includes bibliographical references and index.
    ISBN 0-471-39142-5 (pbk. : alk. paper)
    1. Student teaching. 2. Teachers—In-service training. 3. School supervision. 4.
Observation (Educational method) 5. Teachers' workshops. I. Gall, Meredith D., 1942–
    II. Acheson, Keith A., 1925– Techniques in the clinical supervision of teachers. III. Title.

LB2157.A3 A29 2003
370'71—dc21

                                                                    2002068992

ISBN 0-471-39142-5

Printed in the United States of America

10 9 8 7 6 5 4 3 2 1

Contents

viii Contents

Preface

This book is about the clinical supervision of teachers. Several texts on clinical supervision have been published in the last 15 years, but in general they have emphasized theory and research on clinical supervision. Our book is practical. We emphasize the techniques of clinical supervision, the "nuts and bolts" of how to work with teachers in order to help them improve their classroom teaching.

In preparing the text, we were guided by a set of objectives to help you, the supervisor, develop

- an understanding of the three phases of clinical supervision: planning conference, classroom observation, and feedback conference;
- knowledge and skill in using specific techniques in conferences with teachers and in observing their classroom teaching;
- understanding of issues and problems in clinical supervision;
- understanding of role differences of the supervisor as facilitator, evaluator, counselor, and curriculum adviser;
- positive attitudes toward clinical supervision as a method of promoting teacher growth; and
- insights into the roles that teachers and principals can play in using the techniques of clinical supervision.

The textbook format is better suited for helping you to attain knowledge and for understanding objectives than it is for helping you to achieve skill-related objectives. If you are typical of most educators, you did not learn how to teach by reading textbooks. You learned how to teach by practicing the act of teaching in actual classroom situations. (We hope you had a skillful supervisor to assist you!) Textbooks may have facilitated this process by suggesting specific techniques for you to try.

This same principle applies to acquiring skill as a clinical supervisor. We would like to think that this textbook is sufficient to train you to be a highly skilled supervisor. Our experience suggests otherwise. You will need to practice and receive feedback on each conference and observation technique if you are to incorporate them into your supervisory repertoire. It will help, too, if you have the opportunity to observe supervisors who can demonstrate these techniques.

Building principals, school district personnel, and teacher educators in colleges and universities may be required to do teacher supervision as part of their duties. These professional educators need to be skilled in the processes of clinical teacher supervision. If you currently supervise teachers or if you plan to do so in the future, this book was written with you in mind.

This book is organized into four units. Unit 1 provides background necessary for understanding techniques of clinical supervision. Unit 2 introduces the supervisory roles and uses of clinical supervision that occur in actual practice. Units 3 and 4 describe specific techniques for conducting feedback conferences and collecting observation data.

ACKNOWLEDGMENTS
First Edition 1980

Some of the ideas in this book were developed at Stanford University in the early 1960s, along with techniques for using videotape and other forms of feedback in the training of preservice and inservice teachers. People in that project who influenced the ideas, research, and applications were Robert Bush, Dwight Allen, Fred McDonald, Norman Boyan, Horace Aubertine, Bill Johnson, Jim Olivero, Frank MacGraw, Al Robertson, and Jimmy Fortune.

Both authors, along with John Hansen, worked on earlier versions of the techniques presented here as part of a project sponsored by the Far West Laboratory for Educational Research and Development. The support and suggestions of Walter Borg and Ned Flanders were especially helpful. The materials that grew out of the project were used in many workshops and were published by the Association of California School Administrators and, later, at Florida State University. Ed Beaubier and Art Thayer were instrumental during this phase of the materials' development, as was Ray Hull.

For two decades, research conducted at the University of Oregon by the authors, their colleagues, and students has influenced the attitudes and recommendations reflected in this book. We thank Peter Titze, Wes Tolliver, Michael Carl, Colin Yarham, Gary Martin, Jim Shinn, Judy Aubrecht, John Suttle, and Kathy Lovell. Several professional associations and state education departments have supported the development and dissemination of the ideas and procedures recounted here. We are especially grateful to the Confederation of Oregon School Administrators and Ozzie Rose, the Oregon State Department of Education and Ron Burge, the Nevada Association of School Administrators, the principals' and superintendents' associations in Washington State and British Columbia, the Nebraska Association for Supervision and Curriculum Development, the British Columbia Ministry of Education and Russ Leskiw, the National Academy of School Executives, and the many school districts that have conducted workshops and conferences using our materials and personnel.

The research of Dale Bolton at the University of Washington and Rob Spaulding at San Jose State has influenced our conclusions. Reports of our work have been presented at two conventions of the American Educational Research Association, in a paper written in collaboration with Paul Tucker and Cal Zigler, and, more recently, in a symposium with members of the Teacher Corps Research Adaptation Cluster. We also thank the administrators and teachers who reacted to earlier drafts of the materials in three annual workshops conducted on Orcas Island in Washington State.

Second Edition 1987

Since publication of the first edition of this book, the authors, our students, and our colleagues have continued to conduct research, interact with people in the field, and consider trends in supervision. What we see—not only in the United States but in other countries, as well—is a movement toward the kind of processes we described in the first edition.

This new edition adds material on teacher evaluation, collegial observation, research, and other aspects of supervision that are growing in importance.

We thank those people with whom we have worked in Alberta, British Columbia, Manitoba, and Saskatchewan, Canada; in Australia, Guam, Japan, Jordan, Mexico, Saudi Arabia, Singapore, and South Korea; and in Alaska, the District of Columbia, Kansas, Montana, Oregon, and Washington State.

The number of individuals to thank has grown geometrically; the number of annual workshops conducted on Orcas Island in Washington State has proceeded arithmetically to ten at the time of this writing. The participants have reacted to, enriched, and improved our expanding ideas.

Third Edition 1992

For the third edition we have updated the reports of research that pertain to the topics of our chapters and have added a new chapter on the analysis of teaching. We have adapted some parts to recognize the growing number of persons who use the techniques of clinical supervision in other roles: mentors, teacher coaches, peer consultants. We are seeing applications of the techniques in a variety of settings and institutions, for example, community colleges, medical schools, universities in Asia. The number of people we need to thank has grown out of proportion to the size of the book. The number of years at Orcas and nearby, friendly islands has reached fifteen at this writing. We mourn the loss of our friend, Walter Borg, who influenced our work in many ways.

Fourth Edition 1997

For the fourth edition we have updated some of the examples and reordered the chapters to reflect what we see as trends in the field. The shift toward shared leadership in schools has had an impact on supervision arrangements. Interest in collaborative activities for teachers has grown. This phenomenon is addressed in a new chapter, Peer Consultation. A prime source for our understanding of how this application of the techniques can take place is the Program for Quality Teaching of the British Columbia Teachers' Federation. We acknowledge the many persons who worked in the development and successful implementation of that program over the past 12 years.

Fifth Edition

In the fifth edition, we have changed the title of this text to *Clinical Supervision and Teacher Development: Preservice and Inservice Applications*, which more accurately reflects its content. We have added Author's Notes introducing each chapter in order to summarize and contextualize the chapter's themes. We have also simplified the organization of the book, rearranging and combining several of the later chapters from the fourth edition, so that there are four units rather than five. Answers to frequently addressed questions are now available on our website, new to this edition: *http://www.wiley.com/college/acheson*. We gratefully acknowledge the educators and supervisors who have helped us in this edition.

A Note to the Instructor

The content of this book can be taught in several formats. We recommend taking up observation techniques as early as possible, giving the participants opportunities to practice in a live setting whenever possible and to share experiences and data with other class members. Planning conferences can be introduced as a topic related to trying out different observation systems. An analysis of a planning conference is a reasonable assignment. Teachers should be selected for their willingness to let observers practice their skills. Observers who have student teachers assigned to them and principals who have a faculty to work with should have no difficulty finding opportunities to apply their new skills. After feedback conferences have been discussed, students should have a chance to work through several complete cycles with a teacher.

Simulated situations can be set up to allow participants to practice observing short lessons taught by classmates to their peers. Participants can also practice conference skills in role-playing sessions with classmates, using data supplied by the instructor; an observer for each pair of role players allows for subsequent debriefing and discussion. Tape recordings of conferences are useful in the analysis process, but we find that many teachers are reluctant to permit tape recording unless they understand clearly what use will be made of the tapes and feel that they will not be evaluated or embarrassed in the process.

A number of activities, exercises, and assignments can be used in conjunction with the printed materials and instructor presentations. Listing what class members feel to be the crucial competencies of teaching will stimulate interest in the aspects of teaching effectiveness discussed in Chapter 3.

Tape recordings of classroom interaction can be used to practice writing selected verbatim comments, questions, or responses. Films or videotapes showing nonverbal behaviors also can be useful. A prepared tape (or psychodrama) of a conference also gives class members something tangible to react to when studying conference techniques. Overhead projector transparencies of data from seating charts or other observation instruments can serve for analysis and discussion.

Teaching the skills for coding interaction requires some structured practice, however. We suggest using a tape recording that has been carefully coded by an expert so that class members can be given feedback when they practice.

Instructor presentations on topics such as research on teaching, supervision, or teacher evaluation can augment the material on these topics in this book. Small-group discussions in which participants share their experiences, data, and opinions have been valuable activities in our courses.

Unit One

Overview

OVERVIEW

Clinical supervision has as its goal the professional development of teachers, with an emphasis on improving teachers' classroom performance. Chapter 1 introduces the basic characteristics of clinical supervision and compares it with other forms of teacher supervision.

OBJECTIVES

The purpose of this unit is to help you develop an understanding of:

The basic processes and goals of clinical supervision

How clinical supervision differs from other forms of teacher supervision

The current state of research on the effectiveness of clinical supervision

Chapter 1

The Nature of Clinical Supervision

Author's Note

Clinical supervision had its roots in the Harvard Yard. Microteaching sprang up on the Stanford Farm. These two seedlings sprouted at about the same time (early 1960s). At the time, Gall (MDG) was an undergraduate and master's student at Harvard; Acheson was a graduate student at Stanford. In 1969 we first met at an assembly of R & D Center/ Educational Laboratory persons.

MDG was representing the Far West Laboratory for Educational Research and Development (FWLERD). KAA was representing the U.S. Office of Education, Bureau of Research, Division of R&D Centers and Laboratories while on leave from the University of Oregon (U of O). During the early 1970s we collaborated on a number of projects involving the lab and the university. One project was intended to become a "minicourse," but became a book, *Observations and Conferences with Teachers* (Acheson and Hansen, 1973, Association of California School Administrators).

In 1975 we traded locations for 6 months, after which MDG remained at U of O and KAA returned. This book was conceived during the next few years. It built on all of the above. In addition, participation in Teacher Corps activities enriched our understanding of what goes on "out there" as opposed to what is important "up here." Up here in the higher branches of education we often hear disdain for the lower branches. Out there we still hear disdain from upper branches toward lower branches, for example, grade 4 teachers who deplore what the teachers in the third grade achieved.

What clinical supervision can contribute to addressing the multitudinous problems we face in education will be addressed in chapters that follow. We use the term "clinical supervision" because that is how the method was labeled by its originators and how it is still referred to by most educators today. However, we do so with concern that "clinical" could suggest lying naked on a cold marble slab, while "supervision" connotes, for many who have been supervised, looking down on the creature on the slab, and inspecting warts and moles, rather than strengths and needs. In our view of clinical supervision, the teacher is always viewed as a professional who is actively seeking greater expertise, and the focus is on strength and needs.

We don't promise to answer all your individual questions to your satisfaction, but we have added a website to this edition that can respond to questions that arise frequently.

KAA

Of crucial importance, is to have a supervision that is fundamentally humane, one that is emancipated from the dogma and authoritarianism and vested interests of administration and just plain trouble-making that have typified much of the supervision we have known before.

—Robert Goldhammer[1]

INTRODUCTION

The spirit of clinical supervision is difficult to capture in words. Clinical supervision is a process, a distinctive style of relating to teachers. For this process to be effective, the clinical supervisor's mind, emotions, and actions must work together to achieve the primary goal of clinical supervision–the professional development of the preservice or inservice teacher.

Although we acknowledge the unitary nature of clinical supervision, our book is primarily analytical. It attempts to tease out and describe the components and techniques of clinical supervision. This analytical approach is intended to facilitate your development as a clinical supervisor. However, as with the analysis of any phenomenon, it is easy to lose the forest for the trees. Therefore, we start by presenting an episode from an actual case of clinical supervision so that you can see the process as a whole.

An Example

Arthur Harris, a university supervisor, was assigned to supervise Jim, a student teacher at a local middle school. Arthur had an initial meeting with Jim to get acquainted, discuss his role as a supervisor, and answer questions. He then met with the two teachers in whose classrooms Jim would work and with the school's principal. The two teachers gave Jim several weeks to observe their classes, become acquainted with the students, and prepare several social studies units.

Arthur viewed his initial role as providing support and encouragement to Jim. Once Jim had found his bearings, Arthur explained the procedures of clinical supervision and initiated a supervisory cycle by asking Jim to describe his lesson plan for the class on Africa that Arthur would observe later in the week (Conference Technique 7 in Chapter 7). Jim's plan was to organize the students into three groups and have each group read a different article about Rhodesia (a region of Africa now comprising Zambia and Zimbabwe). Then Jim wanted students in each group to state what they learned from the articles and answer questions about them.

Arthur and Jim agreed that it would be helpful to collect data on verbal interaction patterns in the lesson (Conference Technique 6 in Chapter 7). Two specific areas of focus were selected:

- the distribution of student talk during the lesson, which would be recorded on a seating chart (Observation Technique 7 in Chapter 10).
- Jim's responses to students' answers and ideas, which Arthur would record by script taping (Observation Technique 9 in Chapter 11).

Figure 1.1 shows a sample of the data collected by Arthur using each technique. When he and Jim met the following day for a feedback conference, Jim was able to use the data to reach his own conclusions about how the lesson went. Arthur initiated this process by asking, "What do these data tell you about your teaching?" (Conference Technique 9 in Chapter 8). Jim realized that he had not praised or elaborated on student ideas; he had simply acknowledged them. Also, Jim saw that he was successful in getting students to talk, but the distribution of talk was unbalanced: Students nearest the teacher, and one student in particular, did most of the speaking.

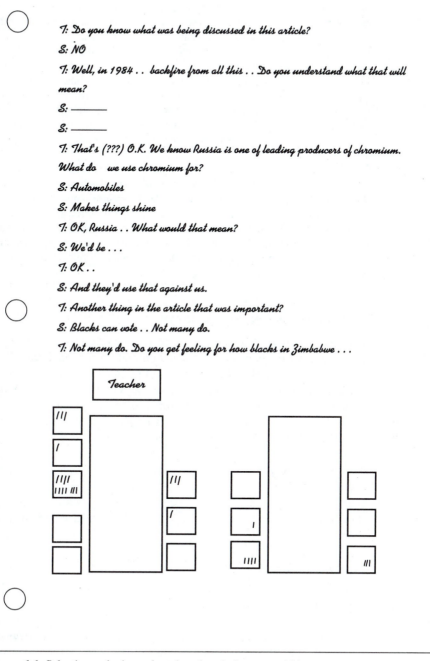

T: Do you know what was being discussed in this article?

S: NO

T: Well, in 1984 . . backfire from all this . . Do you understand what that will mean?

S: ——

S: ——

T: That's (???) O.K. We know Russia is one of leading producers of chromium. What do   we use chromium for?

S: Automobiles

S: Makes things shine

T: OK, Russia . . What would that mean?

S: We'd be . . .

T: OK . .

S: And they'd use that against us.

T: Another thing in the article that was important?

S: Blacks can vote . . Not many do.

T: Not many do. Do you get feeling for how blacks in Zimbabwe . . .

Figure 1.1 Selective verbatim and seating chart in lesson on Africa.

Arthur's next move in the feedback conference was to ask Jim how he would explain why these verbal patterns occurred (Conference Technique 10 in Chapter 8). Jim commented that he had heard in his methods courses about the importance of responding constructively to student ideas, but he had not made the connection to his own teaching behavior until now. As for the distribution of student talk, Jim stated he was simply unaware that the imbalance had occurred. He realized, though, that he probably called a number of times on the student who talked the most because he could depend on her to give good answers.

Arthur asked Jim what he might do based on these observations (Conference Technique 11 in Chapter 8). Jim said he would practice using praise in his next lessons and would make an effort to call on more students. Arthur suggested several ways that Jim might acknowledge student ideas and incorporate them in the lesson. He also suggested that a different arrangement of desks—perhaps a semicircle or circle—might encourage students to express more ideas and engage in discussion among themselves.

This brief example illustrates the three phases of the clinical supervision cycle: planning conference, classroom observation, and feedback conference. The example also makes clear that clinical supervision focuses on the teacher's actual classroom instruction and includes the teacher as an active participant in the supervisory process. In this respect, clinical supervision differs from typical courses and workshops: The instructor determines the curriculum, and its content is not grounded in the individual teacher's classroom reality. Courses and workshops have an important role in teacher education, but they are no substitute for the professional development that good clinical supervision promotes.

THE PITFALLS OF TEACHER SUPERVISION

Many teachers react defensively to supervision and do not find it helpful, even though it is a required part of their initial preparation and professional work. This generalization is supported by Arthur Blumberg's review of research on teacher supervision, from which he concluded that teachers view supervision "as a part of the system that exists but that does not play an important role in their professional lives, almost like an organizational ritual that is no longer relevant."[2] Blumberg's review covers research up until the early 1970s, but our experience suggests that his conclusion would still hold true today.

The prevalence of teacher resistance to supervision suggests that schools should abandon it entirely. A more hopeful conclusion is that teachers are hostile, not to supervision, but to the style of supervision they typically receive. Teachers might react positively to a supervisory style that is more responsive to their concerns and aspirations. The model of clinical supervision that we present in this book is based on this premise.

Teacher Resistance to Evaluation

In traditional inservice supervision, the supervisor—usually the school principal—initiates the supervisory process to evaluate the teacher's performance. The evaluation function may be mandated by state law, the local school board, or other authority.

This situation creates two problems at the start. First, supervision becomes equated with evaluation. Most people, including teachers, tend to be anxious when they know they are being evaluated, especially if negative evaluations threaten their jobs. The second problem is that supervision arises from a need of the supervisor, rather than from a need felt by the teacher.

Because traditional supervision tends to be unpleasant, interaction between supervisor and teacher is avoided or minimized. Unfortunately, this practice compounds the problem. The supervisor might show up unannounced at the teacher's classroom to observe what is happening. The teacher has no knowledge of what the supervisor might observe and evaluate. For example, is the supervisor interested in the teacher's classroom management or in his teaching activities? The supervisor, on the other hand, might not have planned what to observe and evaluate. The resulting observational data are highly subjective and vague. Nor is the follow-up to classroom visitation likely to improve matters. Typically the supervisor completes a rating checklist and writes an evaluative report on the teacher's performance, often without an opportunity for the teacher to confer with the supervisor about the observational data and evaluative criteria used in the report.

This highly directive form of supervision reflects the historical role of supervisors as school "inspectors." As far back as the early eighteenth century, lay committees in Boston were charged with inspecting schools periodically. The purpose of inspection was to determine whether instructional standards were being maintained. School inspection by lay committees continued until schools grew large enough to require more than one teacher in each school. The inspection function then became the responsibility of one of the teachers, who was known as the "principal teacher." Eventually the title was shortened to "principal." To the extent that supervision is perceived as inspection rather than as a source of professional development, teachers will resist it.

Communication Patterns in Supervision

Communication in traditional supervision tends not to be helpful for the teacher. The communication pattern is represented by the "nose-to-nose" characters on the left side of Figure 1.2. The supervisor emits advice or admonitions that go in one ear of the teacher and out the other, or right on by, or off an invisible shield that "defends" the teacher.

The "side-by-side" characters in Figure 1.2 represent a different style of communication in supervision. Both the supervisor and teacher look at objective data (such as a videotape of the teacher's lesson), analyze and interpret the data, and make decisions as colleagues rather than as adversaries. This communication style characterizes the model of clinical supervision described in this book.

Finding Time for Supervision

Finding time for supervision is another pitfall of teacher supervision. Several research studies have found that experienced teachers rarely, if ever, participate in clinical supervision designed to improve their instruction.[3] The situation is somewhat better in preservice teacher education, because a certain amount of supervision is typically mandated by state regulations. However, university supervisors often have heavy workloads, and consequently their opportunity to collect observational data and confer with student teachers is severely constrained.[4]

Time is not only an issue in teacher development, but also in school improvement and reform. For example, Michael Fullan and Matthew Miles concluded that, "every analysis of the problems of change efforts that we have seen in the last decade of research and practice [the 1980s] has concluded that time is the salient issue."[5] School districts often

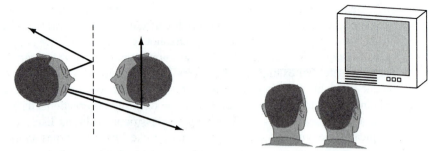

Figure 1.2 Nose-to-nose supervision versus side-by-side supervision.

rely on "one-shot" inservice workshops instead of sustained staff development (which might include clinical supervision and related methods), which is necessary for adoption and valid implementation of new practices.

There is no simple explanation for the insufficient time allocated for clinical supervision in preservice and inservice education. Undoubtedly, many factors are involved. One of them might be the fact that there is a large amount of turnover in the teaching profession. Half of the teachers in the United States leave the profession every 7 years.[6] Why invest in a teacher's development if there is a substantial likelihood that the teacher will not be a classroom instructor for the length of a typical career (25–30 years)? Of course, one might argue that more teachers would stay in the profession if they had access to good clinical supervision and other methods of professional development.

Let us assume for a moment that policy makers and administrators are willing to make a commitment to clinical supervision. It seems likely, then, that the use of time in schools and university teacher education programs will need to change. For example, inservice teachers might be given lighter teaching loads so that they have more time for clinical supervision and other methods of professional development. Preservice teachers might have longer programs of preparation or change the relative amount of time allocated for university course work and field experiences. These are only a few of the options that have been considered by educators who are interested in improving schools and teachers' work lives.[7]

A MODEL OF CLINICAL SUPERVISION

The preceding descriptions of teacher supervision are overdrawn, yet they characterize what some supervisors do some of the time. To the extent that the portrayals are accurate, they account for teachers' pervasive negative feelings about supervision. We wish to promote an alternative model of supervision that is interactive rather than directive, democratic rather than authoritarian, teacher-centered rather than supervisor-centered. This supervisory style is called clinical supervision.

We use the label *clinical supervision* because the model presented here is based directly on the methods developed and given that label by Morris Cogan and colleagues while coordinating the Master of Arts in Teaching program at the Harvard School of Education in the 1960s.[8] Clinical is meant to suggest a face-to-face relationship between teacher and supervisor and a focus on the teacher's actual behavior in the classroom. As Goldhammer puts it, "Given close observation, detailed observational data, face-to-face interaction between the supervisor and teacher, and an intensity of focus that binds the two together in an intimate professional relationship, the meaning of 'clinical' is pretty well filled out."[9] (Goldhammer's reference to "face-to-face'" communication is similar to the "side-by-side" communication depicted in Figure 1.2.)

The word *clinical* sometimes connotes pathology, which is inappropriate in the context of our model of clinical supervision. We certainly do not wish you to think that clinical supervision is a "remedy" applied by the supervisor to deficient or unhealthy behavior exhibited by the teacher.

To avoid this connotation, we considered using the term *teacher-centered supervision*. A nice feature of this label is that it parallels the method of "person-centered counseling" popularized by Carl Rogers, with which clinical supervision has much in common.[10] However, we settled on *clinical supervision* as the term to use in this book, because it continues the tradition of the group at the Harvard School of Education who originated this model of supervision.

The Processes of Clinical Supervision

Clinical supervision is a cyclical process with three major components. The supervisor:

1. meets with the teacher and plans for classroom observation.
2. observes a lesson systematically (and nonjudgmentally) and records information related to the objectives set during the planning conference; and
3. meets with the teacher to (a) analyze (together) the data recorded by the observer, (b) interpret the meaning of this information from the teacher's perspective, and (c) reach decisions about the next steps.

This process is shown graphically in Figure 1.3.

This cyclical process should be repeated at least several times during the course of the school year with experienced teachers, and more often with preservice teachers. The cycles of clinical supervision would intensify further for teachers on a plan of assistance or a student teacher who is experiencing significant difficulty in a field placement.

The Planning Conference

The supervisor begins the process of supervision by holding a conference with the teacher. In the conference, the teacher has an opportunity to state personal concerns, needs, and aspirations. The supervisor's role is to help the teacher clarify these perceptions so that both have a clear picture of the teacher's current instruction, the teacher's view of ideal instruction, and whether there is a discrepancy between the two. Next, supervisor and teacher explore new techniques that the teacher might try in order to move the instruction toward the ideal.

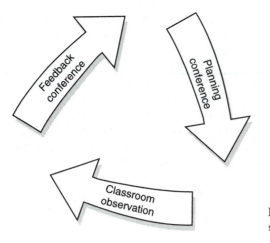

Figure 1.3 The three phases of the clinical supervision cycle.

Done properly, the planning conference establishes supervision as a process in which the teacher and supervisor have joint ownership. The teacher perceives the supervisor as someone with whom to share perceptions, thus breaking down the isolation of classroom teaching (i.e., most teachers teach alone). The supervisor likewise perceives the teacher as a partner in making sense of the teacher's classroom instruction and improving it.

Many teachers have a vague anxiety about the effectiveness of their teaching. They do not know whether they are doing a good job, whether a "problem" student can be helped, or whether their instruction can be improved. Teachers rarely have the opportunity to observe other teachers' classroom performance, which might provide a basis for reflecting on their own performance. Supervisors can meet this need by using a different approach—helping the teacher clarify goals, collecting observational data on classroom events, and analyzing the data for discrepancies. For teachers who are not aware of their goals or how they "come across" in the classroom, this process can be a useful guide.

The planning conference results in a cooperative decision by teacher and supervisor to collect observational data. For example, a teacher we know had a vaguely defined concern that he was turning off the brighter students in the class. In the planning conference, the teacher developed the hypothesis that perhaps he was spending the majority of his time with the slower students and ignoring the needs of the brighter students. Together, teacher and supervisor decided to do a verbal flow analysis (Observation Technique 7 in Chapter 10) of the teacher's discussion behavior. This analysis involves observation of the students with whom the teacher initiates interaction and how he responds to each student's ideas. The teacher and supervisor also decided it would be worthwhile for the teacher to collect class assignments over a 2-week period to determine their level of difficulty and challenge.

Classroom Observation

It is curious how rarely we collect data on different aspects of the teacher's classroom performance. In the field of sports, for example, athletes watch closely the statistical data that summarize observations of their performance—number of home runs in baseball, percentage of completed passes in football, final and intermediate times in track events, and so forth. Also, athletes are exposed constantly to videotape replays of their performance so that they can perfect their techniques. In such professions as medicine, business, and law, the practitioner has access to many indicators that directly reflect quality of performance—number of lives saved, cases settled in the client's favor, sales figures. Additionally, practitioners often hear expressions of satisfaction or dissatisfaction from their clients. We need to provide teachers with similar indicators of performance, based on direct or indirect observation.

Although complete objectivity is probably not attainable, that is the goal of classroom observation. Skillful clinical supervisors find a way to maintain a neutral stance in the data-collection process, so that the data speak for themselves. This process is facilitated if the teacher has a hand in selecting the observation instrument, or instruments, to be used.

The Feedback Conference

In the final phase of a clinical-supervision cycle, the teacher and supervisor meet to review the observational data, with the supervisor encouraging the teacher to make his or her own inferences about teaching effectiveness. For example, in viewing a videotape of their performance, teachers usually notice a number of areas in which they need to improve. They comment that they hadn't known how much they talk in class, that they tend to ignore or fail to acknowledge student comments, that they do not speak loudly enough, and the like. As the teacher reviews the observational data, the feedback conference often turns into a planning conference—with teacher and supervisor deciding cooperatively to collect further observational data or plan a self-improvement program.

This approach to providing feedback contrasts sharply with what is sometimes found in traditional supervision. Instead of starting with data and analyzing them before reaching decisions, the supervisor starts with a conclusion or preconception, interprets any evidence in the light of that prejudgment, and pursues the self-fulfilling hypothesis by selecting only data that fit. For example: "Two students were not paying attention" rather than "Twenty-eight were at task." Jerome Bruner has called this "functional fixedness"— proceeding on the basis of a single hypothesis that happens to be wrong.[11]

For many teachers, self-concept or confidence level is fragile enough that having their teaching analyzed in the backward fashion just described can have devastating effects. An extreme literary analogy is the film *Gaslight* in which a husband (played by Charles Boyer) deranges his wife (played by Ingrid Bergmann) by telling her she only thinks the lights are dimming when they actually are (through the efforts of the husband's confederate, played by a young Angela Lansbury). This analogy was used in a teacher dismissal arbitration to describe the overwhelmingly negative feedback provided by a principal and vice principal in a program of assistance for a teacher. The teacher previously had 18 years of positive reinforcement for his efforts.

The Goals of Clinical Supervision

The major goal of clinical supervision is to improve teachers' classroom instruction. Of course, teachers do other important kinds of work, such as serve on curriculum committees, confer with parents, and administer specialized programs. However, their core work—the work that distinguishes them from doctors, lawyers, engineers, accountants, and other professionals—is helping individuals learn. Learning can occur in different kinds of settings, but the teacher is a specialist in promoting learning within the complex environment of a classroom, which is situated in the complex organizational conditions of a school.

In our view, clinical supervision needs to focus on this core work of teachers and help them do it better. It is no easy task to promote learning, especially with the diversity of students found in present-day classrooms and the various curriculum mandates and regulations that constrain teachers' work.

The general goal of clinical supervision—to improve teachers' classroom instruction—can be analyzed into more specific goals as follows:

- *To Provide Teachers with Objective Feedback on the Current State of Their Instruction.* The essence of clinical supervision is to hold up a mirror so that teachers can see what they are actually doing while teaching. What teachers are doing can be quite different from what teachers think they are doing. For example, many teachers believe they are good at encouraging students to express their ideas until they listen to audiotapes of their lessons. Then they discover the extent to which they dominate the lesson. Typically, two-thirds of classroom talk is by the teacher. Receiving objective feedback is often sufficient stimulus for teachers to initiate a self-improvement process.

- *To Diagnose and Solve Instructional Problems.* Clinical supervisors use conference techniques and observational records to help teachers identify flaws in their instruction or better ways to accomplish an instructional goal. Teachers occasionally can do this on their own. Otherwise, the skilled intervention of a supervisor is necessary. A parallel situation exists in classroom instruction. Sometimes students can self-diagnose learning problems and take remedial steps on the basis of this information. At other times, students are stymied by their inability to learn a particular subject, and the teacher is needed to diagnose and remediate.

- *To Help Teachers Develop Skill in Using Instructional Strategies.* If the only purpose of clinical supervision were to help the teacher solve immediate problems and crises, its value would be severely limited. The supervisor would be needed each time the teacher had a "brush fire" to put out. This is not true. The skillful supervisor uses the clinical conference and observation data to help the teacher develop enduring patterns of behavior—what we call instructional strategies. These strategies are effective in promoting learning, motivating students, and managing the classroom. The observational techniques presented in the chapters of Unit 4 and the criteria for effective teaching in Chapter 3 reflect instructional strategies that most educators consider to be effective. Teachers can practice these strategies and can receive objective data on improvement resulting from practice.

- *To Evaluate Teachers for Promotion, Tenure, or Other Decisions.* This is the most controversial function of clinical supervision. Some supervisors avoid evaluation, but most supervisors are required by their employer (typically a school district or college of education) to evaluate the teacher's competence, usually at the end of the supervisory process. Although clinical supervision emphasizes the teacher's professional development, the objective data collected through systematic classroom observation provide one basis for evaluating the teacher's competence. As we discuss later in the chapter (and in Chapter 4), the "sting" of evaluation can be lessened if, as part of the clinical supervision process, the supervisor shares with the teacher the criteria and standards to be used in the evaluation report.

- *To Help Teachers Develop a Positive Attitude about Continuous Professional Development.* A major goal of clinical supervision is to help teachers realize that their professional development does not end with the completion of certification requirements. Teachers need to view themselves as professionals, which means, in part, that they engage in self-development and skill training as a career-long effort. The clinical supervisor can model this aspect of professionalism through a willingness to develop new supervisory skills. We discuss the role of clinical supervision in the larger context of professional development in the next chapter.

OTHER MODELS OF CLINICAL SUPERVISION

Since the seminal work of Morris Cogan and colleagues, other educators have developed new models of clinical supervision. Edward Pajak described, analyzed, and contrasted these models.[12] His summary of the models, organized into four families, is shown in Figure 1.4. None of them, including ours, is radically new; to one degree or another, they all build on the work of the original developers.

You will note that our model of clinical supervision is characterized as technical/didactic. This label emphasizes the fact that we believe that there is a knowledge base about effective teaching (see Chapter 3) that can be used to guide the supervisory process. In other words, at appropriate points in the supervisory process, the supervisor can make a teacher aware of effective techniques that the teacher might consider incorporating into his or her teaching repertoire. We do not assume that every classroom is unique and therefore the teacher must discover on his or her own a set of instructional principles for that situation.

We find much of value in all the models of clinical supervision listed in Figure 1.4. In our opinion, none of them is wrong or misdirected. It is a matter of emphasis. We endorse other models' emphasis on teacher reflection and self-discovery, but in our model we emphasize the knowledge base about effective teaching. We endorse other models' emphasis on education's role in social reform, but in our model we emphasize existing classroom reality and the pragmatic need to prepare teachers to succeed in that reality. We endorse other models' emphasis on the individuality of teachers and their instructional conditions, but in our model we emphasize the commonalities among teachers and their instructional conditions.

If our model of clinical supervision has any particular advantages, they involve practical relevance and comprehensiveness. As you engage in clinical supervision of teachers, we think you will find that all the observation and conferencing techniques we present can be used to good benefit. In other words, after studying each technique, you should be able to apply it, if you wish, to actual clinical supervision. Also, you will find that the

Family	Emphasis
Original Clinical Models	The models proposed by Goldhammer,[13] Mosher and Purpel,[14] and Cogan[15] offer an eclectic blending of empirical, phenomenological, behavioral, and developmental perspectives. These models emphasize the importance of collegial relations between supervisors and teachers, cooperative discovery of meaning, and development of individually unique teaching styles.
Humanistic/Artistic Models	The perspectives of Blumberg[16] and Eisner[17] are based on existential and aesthetic principles. These models forsake step-by-step procedures and emphasize open interpersonal relations and personal intuition, artistry, and idiosyncrasy. Supervisors are encouraged to help teachers understand the expressive and artistic richness of teaching.
Technical/Didactic Models	The work of Acheson and Gall, Hunter,[18] and Joyce and Showers[19] draws on process-product and effective teaching research from the 1970s. These models emphasize techniques of observation and feedback that reinforce certain "effective" behaviors or predetermined models of teaching to which teachers attempt to conform.
Developmental/Reflective Models	The models of Glickman,[20] Costa and Garmston,[21] Schön,[22] Zeichner and Liston,[23] Garman,[24] Smyth,[25] Retallick,[26] and Bowers and Flinders[27] are sensitive to individual differences and the organizational, social, political, and cultural contexts of teaching. These models call for supervisors to encourage reflection and introspection among teachers in order to foster professional growth, discover context-specific principles of practice, and promote justice and equity.

Figure 1.4 Models of clinical supervision

Source: Pajak, E. (1993). *Approaches to clinical supervision: Alternatives for improving instruction* (p. 312). Norwood, MA: Christopher-Gordon.

techniques are comprehensive in that they cover most, if not all, aspects of the supervisory process. (Pajak comments that, "Acheson and Gall provide an impressively broad array of strategies for recording behavior that generate both quantitative and qualitative data.")[28] However, we encourage you to study other models of clinical supervision in addition to ours. Each model is intellectually stimulating and will challenge you to think about teaching and supervision in new ways.

OTHER TYPES OF TEACHER SUPERVISION

The objectives of clinical supervision can be clarified by comparing it with other kinds of teacher supervision.

Counseling

Many teachers—especially student teachers and first-year teachers—have overt anxiety and insecurity about their ability to perform in the classroom. Some teachers experience temporary crises in their personal lives that interfere with classroom performance. Some teachers suffer from chronic emotional problems (e.g., depression or unprovoked outbursts of anger) that disrupt their teaching effectiveness.

Sensitive supervisors respond to teachers' anxiety, insecurity, and other personal problems by providing emotional support and reassurance. They make an effort to deal with more serious problems by referring the teacher to appropriate specialists. In carrying out these functions, the supervisor is performing the role of counselor. Clinical supervision may also incorporate these functions, but its focus is on the teacher's instructional performance rather than the teacher's personal problems.

Issues about career decisions can also arise in the context of supervision. Student teachers often wonder whether they are cut out to be teachers, or they might request assistance in seeking teaching positions. Experienced teachers sometimes feel undecided about whether to remain in the teaching profession, to seek a transfer to another school, or to teach a different content area and grade level. The supervisor who advises a teacher about such problems is performing a counseling function, which should not be confused with clinical supervision as we describe it in this book.

Curriculum Support

Teachers sometimes ask their supervisors for advice about curriculum materials they are using. Are the materials suitable? How should they be used? Are alternative materials available? A teacher might have other curriculum concerns as well: the amount of time to spend on each curriculum topic, procedures for organizing a course of study, or new curriculum policy and guidelines in the school district.

Supervision in the form of curriculum support can be very helpful to the teacher, but it should not be equated with clinical supervision. Clinical supervision focuses directly on the actual observable events of teaching. In contrast, curriculum support focuses on materials, objectives, and philosophy of instruction. These are major influences on teaching, but they are not the teaching act itself.

A Note of Caution

Counseling and curriculum support are important, legitimate functions of teacher supervision. Teachers do experience emotional problems and curriculum concerns that might impede their instructional effectiveness. However, a teacher conceivably might use these issues as an excuse to avoid dealing with difficulties in the act of teaching. For example, a teacher might feel uncomfortable about the fact that students in class are generally unruly. Yet, the teacher does not wish to confront this problem and does not want the supervisor to notice what is happening. Thus, the teacher steers the supervisory conference in the direction of problems and events that exist outside the classroom. (We know of instances where teacher and supervisor used their time together to talk about the problems of other teachers in the school.) When these situations occur, the clinical supervisor should listen sensitively to the teacher's comments, but then tactfully steer the conference back to the teacher's own classroom behavior.

THE ROLE OF CLINICAL SUPERVISOR

Any educator responsible for the professional development of teachers can use the techniques of clinical supervision. Methods instructors, practicum supervisors, supervisors of student teachers, cooperating teachers,[29] school administrators, curriculum specialists, and staff development specialists guide the professional development of teachers to varying degrees. All these educators can make use of clinical supervision techniques.

It has been estimated that as many as a quarter of a million persons in the United States provide inservice education to teachers on a full-time or part-time basis.[30] These educators include 80,000 education professors, supervisors, and consultants; 100,000 principals and vice principals; and perhaps 50,000 support personnel, such as reading instructors, media experts, and mental health specialists. To this number, we would add the tens of thousands of cooperating teachers and university supervisors who are involved in the preparation of new teachers each year.

Each of these professionals, at one time or another, is likely to hold conferences with individual teachers or visit their classrooms for the purpose of making observations. Anyone who interacts with teachers in these contexts will find it useful—perhaps even necessary—to employ the techniques of clinical supervision.

Are clinical techniques useful to those whose primary or only responsibility is the evaluation of teachers? The short answer to this question is, "Yes, under certain conditions." In Chapter 4, we discuss in depth this and other questions concerning the relationship between clinical supervision and teacher evaluation.

It might seem that we are promoting clinical supervision as a panacea to be used by all supervisors with all teachers. To a certain extent this is true. As you become familiar with the techniques of clinical supervision, you will find that they deal with basic processes—speaking, listening, observing, teaching—that occur in virtually professional interactions among educators. Thus, clinical supervision has a certain universality that makes it useful to educators in many roles.

The fact that educators in many roles do clinical supervision does not mean that they are trained to perform this function. For example, a national survey of teacher education programs found that fewer than 20 percent of their cooperating teachers had been trained in supervisory processes.[31] This is unfortunate, because research has found that cooperating teachers who do receive training improve their supervisory skills and are more eager to accept student teachers in their classroom.[32] This finding suggests that educators in other roles should receive training in clinical supervision, too, if they are called on to perform this function.

RESEARCH ON CLINICAL SUPERVISION

Researchers have conducted studies of the effects of clinical supervision on various outcomes. Carl Glickman and Theresa Bey reviewed this research and concluded that clinical supervision has positive effects on teachers and students.[33] Specifically, clinical supervision has been found to improve:

- teachers' ability to reflect on their instruction and engage in higher-order thinking.
- collegiality, openness, and communication between teachers and between teachers, supervisors, and principals.
- retention of teachers in the profession, while also reducing teacher anxiety and burnout.
- teachers' sense of autonomy, personal efficacy, and self-growth.
- teachers' attitudes toward the supervisory process.
- student achievement and attitudes.

As one might expect, these outcomes were affected by the quality of clinical supervision that was provided for teachers. Just because an intervention is labeled "clinical supervision" does not mean that a supervisor's behavior followed the model presented in this book or the other models shown in Figure 1.4. Researchers generally have obtained better outcomes when supervisors have been trained in techniques of clinical supervision or when clinical supervision has been used over an extensive period of time.

Case Study Research on Supervision

Jim Nolan, Brent Hawkes, and Pam Francis conducted a review of research involving six case studies of clinical supervision with inservice teachers.[34] The advantage of case studies as a research methodology is that they allow for greater depth of inquiry into complex phenomena such as clinical supervision. All the case studies revealed positive changes in teachers' ability to think productively about their instruction and improve their instruction. Among the improvements noted were these:

- A first-year biology teacher learned how to hold her students accountable for performing intellectually.
- A third-year social sciences teacher learned how to increase the number of students who participated in class discussions.
- An elementary teacher with 10 years of experience increased his students' at-task behavior.

- A physics teacher with 15 years of experience increased his students' participation in class activities.
- An elementary teacher with 22 years of experience improved her ability to meet individual student needs, implemented process-oriented curriculum, and adopted a student-centered classroom management style.

In reviewing this body of research, Nolan and colleagues looked for commonalities in supervisory behavior that facilitated these changes in teacher behavior. Five commonalities emerged from their analysis:

1. the development of a collegial relationship in which the teacher feels safe and supported.
2. teacher control over the products of supervision.
3. continuity in the supervisory process over time.
4. focused, descriptive records of actual teaching and learning events as the basis for reflection.
5. reflection by both the teacher and supervisor as the heart of the process of post-conferencing.[35]

These principles of effective supervision correspond very well to the model of clinical supervision described in this chapter. However, the principles are stated at a high level of generality. What we have done—particularly in Units 3 and 4—is to analyze them into specific techniques that can be learned and implemented with relative ease.

Teacher Attitudes toward Supervision

Research has been conducted to determine teachers' attitude toward the techniques of clinical supervision that we describe in this book. In a study by James Shinn, inservice teachers were asked to rate the ideal frequency with which they would like school principals to use various techniques of clinical supervision and their actual frequency of such use.[36] The results are shown graphically in Figure 1.5. The most significant finding is that teachers believe all the techniques of clinical supervision are worthwhile; each technique was rated as meriting occasional or frequent use. Another noteworthy finding is that, according to teachers, principals who had received training in the techniques used them more often than untrained principals did. Subsequent survey research has yielded similar findings.[37]

Gary Martin conducted a research study to determine whether training supervisors in the clinical-supervision model would affect teachers' acceptance of the model.[38] Martin surveyed a group of inservice teachers and supervisors trained in the observation techniques presented in Unit 4. A comparison group of teachers and supervisors had not received this training. Martin found that the trained teachers believed that their annual evaluation was more helpful to them than did the untrained teachers. Also, the trained teachers were more likely to accept evaluation as a basis for promotion and tenure decisions than were the untrained teachers.

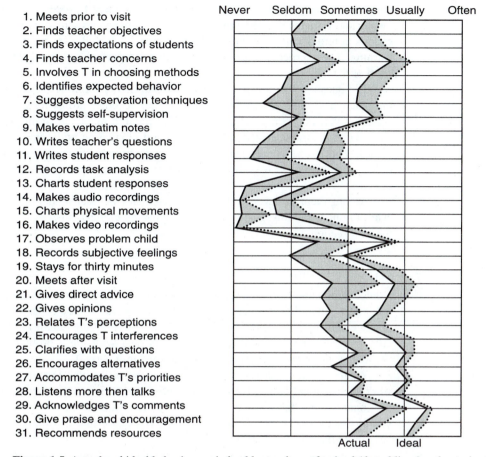

Never Seldom Sometimes Usually Often

1. Meets prior to visit
2. Finds teacher objectives
3. Finds expectations of students
4. Finds teacher concerns
5. Involves T in choosing methods
6. Identifies expected behavior
7. Suggests observation techniques
8. Suggests self-supervision
9. Makes verbatim notes
10. Writes teacher's questions
11. Writes student responses
12. Records task analysis
13. Charts student responses
14. Makes audio recordings
15. Charts physical movements
16. Makes video recordings
17. Observes problem child
18. Records subjective feelings
19. Stays for thirty minutes
20. Meets after visit
21. Gives direct advice
22. Gives opinions
23. Relates T's perceptions
24. Encourages T interferences
25. Clarifies with questions
26. Encourages alternatives
27. Accommodates T's priorities
28. Listens more then talks
29. Acknowledges T's comments
30. Give praise and encouragement
31. Recommends resources

Actual   Ideal

Figure 1.5 Actual and ideal behaviors as judged by teachers of trained (dotted lines) and untrained (solid lines) principals.

Source: From James L. Shinn, "Teacher Perceptions of Ideal and Actual Supervisory Procedures Used by California Elementary Principals" (Ph.D. diss., University of Oregon, 1976), p. 52.

A THEORETICAL BASIS FOR CLINICAL SUPERVISION

A theory is a particular type of explanation of observed phenomena: It uses a system of carefully defined concepts and a set of rules that specify the relationships between the concepts. Some theories are personal in nature (e.g., I might have my own theory of why Republicans and Democrats react differently to issues). Other theories—sometimes called *folk* theories—are held by groups that share a common culture or other characteristic. These theories tend to be informal and not rigorously tested (e.g., some types of folk medicine). Other theories—sometimes called *formal theories*—are constructed by trained scientists and are subjected to rigorous empirical tests that buttress or refute them. Einstein's theory of relativity is an example of a formal theory.

Clinical supervision appears to have developed as a folk theory about teacher education. If you look around at different professions and crafts, you find that they prepare new members, in varying degrees, through the time-honored process of apprenticeship and mentoring. Initiates into the profession or craft observe experts doing their work, and the experts in turn observe the initiates, provide feedback, and give suggestions for additional learning. These processes are found in clinical supervision as well. In fact, they are the heart of the method.

The question that arises is whether formal theory might serve any useful purpose in the practice of clinical supervision. If we look to other professions, the answer is a resounding yes. For example, the advances of modern medicine would not have been possible without formal, tested theories of blood circulation and genetics. Formal theories identify entities, processes, and relationships that are by no means obvious. They help us describe, predict, and explain observed phenomena in ways that can lead to improved practice.

Among theories developed by social scientists, we believe that one in particular is relevant to understanding, justifying, and improving clinical supervision. We describe it in the next section.

The Theory of Reflective Practice

Donald Schön and Chris Argyris have developed a theory about how professionals in various fields—including education—conduct their work.[39] They observed that problems of practice are often "messy" and not solvable by applying scientific principles or specific research findings. Skillful practitioners deal with these problems by engaging in "reflection-in-practice" (or, in shortened form, "reflection").

What does it mean for a professional to be reflective? Drawing on the theoretical work of Schön and others, Doreen Ross defines reflection as: "a way of thinking about educational matters that involves the ability to make rational choices and to assume responsibility for those choices."[40] Schön and Argyris claim that this thinking is of two types: "espoused theories" and "theories-in-use."

An espoused theory consists of the explanations that professionals give to others when asked to justify their actions to others and themselves. For example, a teacher might say, "I change my teaching activities frequently during a lesson, because my students have short attention spans." Activity change and attention span are the key concepts in the theory that this teacher *espouses* to explain and justify his teaching practice.

In contrast, a theory-in-use is the theory that actually governs a professional's practice. This is an important distinction, because as Schön and Argyris claim:

> . . . the theory that actually governs [a professional's] actions is his theory-in-use, which may or may not be compatible with his espoused theory; furthermore the individual may or may not be aware of the incompatibility of the two theories.[41]

If Schön and Argyris are correct, one task of clinical supervisors is to elicit teachers' thinking and determine whether their espoused theory of instruction is compatible with what they actually do in the classroom. With reference to the example we stated above, it is possible that a teacher might believe in the importance of varying instructional activities, but do little of it in the classroom (perhaps because of inadequate lesson preparation). Planning and feedback conferences, which we describe in Chapters 7 and 8, provide the opportunity for this type of critical examination of espoused and in-use theories.

Schön and Argyris note that theories-in-use are often tacit: "Theories-in-use tend to be tacit structures whose relation to action is like the relation of grammar-in-use to speech."[42] To make theories-in-use explicit, it is necessary to infer them from careful observations of the teacher's behavior. In fact, observation is a key element of clinical supervision. The four chapters of Unit 4 describe a wide range of classroom observation instruments.

One reason for making explicit a teacher's theory-in-use is to determine whether it is compatible with the teacher's espoused theory, as we stated above. But there is another, more compelling reason, as Schön and Argyris explain:

> *What, then, is the advantage of explicitly stating the theories-in-use we already hold? If unstated theories-in-use appear to enable the agent to perform effectively, there may be no advantage. But if the agent is performing ineffectively and does not know why or if others are aware of his ineffectiveness and he is not, explicitly stating his theory-in-use allows conscious criticism.*[43]

A major part of reflection, then, involves "conscious criticism" of one's teaching to determine whether the theory-in-use allows one to be effective with students. The supervisor facilitates this process by collecting observational data and encouraging the teacher to interpret them and consider new, more effective ways of teaching. Also, by being knowledgeable about effective teaching practices (the subject of Chapter 3), the supervisor can suggest practices that the teacher might not otherwise imagine.

How do teachers, or any professionals, go about becoming more effective in that their behavior (and the theories-in-use that underlie it) reliably produces desirable outcomes? Ross states the learning process of a reflective practitioner involves these elements:

- recognizing educational dilemmas.
- responding to a dilemma by recognizing both the similarities to other situations and the unique qualities of the particular situation.
- framing and reframing the dilemma.
- experimenting with the dilemma to discover the implications of various solutions.
- examining the intended and unintended consequences of an implemented solution and evaluating it by determining whether the consequences are desirable.[44]

These same elements are features of good clinical supervision. Working together, the teacher and supervisor identify "concerns and problems"—our terms for "dilemmas"—in the teacher's instruction (Conference Techniques 1 and 2 in Chapter 7). The supervisor then can help the teacher identify possibly more effective instructional techniques (Conference Technique 3 in Chapter 7 and Conference Techniques 10 and 11 in Chapter 8). The teacher subsequently teaches a lesson, which the supervisor records with an appropriate observational instrument. In the feedback conference, the teacher and supervisor together examine the observational data to determine the consequences of using—or not using—particular techniques. As a result of this examination, the teacher might revise his or her espoused and in-use theories and decide on new instructional experiments to determine their effects on student learning.

There is more to the theory of reflective practice than we have presented here. However, we have described principal features of the theory, particularly those of relevance to clinical supervision.

Why is the theory of reflective practice important for teacher educators? To answer this question, we start by noting that the theory was developed and validated by observing how professionals in various fields actually perform their work. Their observations are corroborated by our own experience as teachers and teacher educators and, we trust, by your experience as well.

Assuming the theory's validity, let us consider how it matches up with conventional teacher education. The prevalent model is for preservice teachers to take a series of university courses in which they learn content-area knowledge (e.g., mathematics, history, biology), research knowledge, and generalized pedagogical knowledge. The expectation is that preservice teachers will acquire this knowledge and apply it in practicums and student teaching. University supervisors are expected to facilitate this transfer process.

This conventional model of professional education is quite different than what the theory of reflective practice suggests is needed. As we see it, the theory suggests that field experiences and clinical supervision should be at the center of teacher education. Preservice teachers should be exposed early to the "messiness" and problematic nature of classroom instruction, and develop skills in problem-posing, problem-solving, experimentation, and use of observational data to refine teaching skills. Formal knowledge (typically codified in textbooks) should be brought in "just-in-time" to inform the preservice teachers' reflections and evolving professional skills.

Inservice education has similar problems, although perhaps not to the same extent. Workshops, conference presentations, and university courses may feature more practical knowledge, but there is still the assumption that teachers will acquire the knowledge and then somehow transfer it to their classroom. The theory of reflective practice suggests that this model of professional education is fundamentally flawed. It does not recognize sufficiently the problematic nature of teaching and the fact that each teacher's instruction is based on his or her individual theory-in-use, which might differ substantially from the "espoused theories" that they learn in workshops, lectures, and courses.

In summary, we believe that the theory of reflective practice provides strong support for clinical supervision as a critical process in teacher education. Furthermore, it provides support for many of the specific conferencing and observational techniques presented in this book. Most importantly, the theory of reflective practice suggests that clinical supervision should play a larger, and different role, than is found in typical teacher education programs.

NOTES

1. Goldhammer, R. (1969). *Clinical supervision: Special methods for the supervision of teachers.* (p. 368). New York: Holt, Rinehart & Winston.

2. Blumberg, A. (1974). *Supervisors and teachers: A private cold war.* Berkeley, CA: McCutchan.

3. Blankenship, G., Jr., & Irvine, J. J. (1985). Georgia teachers' perceptions of prescriptive and descriptive observations of teaching by instructional supervisors. *Georgia Educational Leadership, 1* (1), 7–10; Graybeal, N. D. (1984). Characteristics of contemporary classroom supervisory process. *Dissertation Abstracts International, 45,* 07A. (University Microfilms No. AAG84-22846)

4. Koehler, V. R. (1984). *The instructional supervision of student teachers.* (ERIC Document Reproduction Service No. ED 271 430).

5. Fullan, M. G., & Miles, M. B. (1992). Getting reform right: What works and what doesn't. *Phi Delta Kappan, 73*(10), 744–752.

6. Anthony, P. (1988). Teachers in the economic system. In K. Alexander & D. Monk (Eds.), *Attracting and compensating America's teachers* (pp. 1–68). Cambridge, MA: Ballinger.

7. For other ideas about how educators might use time in the workplace differently, see: Gándara, P. (Ed.) (2000). *The dimensions of time and the challenge of school reform.* Albany, New York: State University of New York Press.

8. Their work is described in several books: Goldhammer, R. (1969). *Clinical supervision: Special methods for the supervision of teachers.* New York: Holt, Rinehart & Winston; Goldhammer, R., Anderson, R. H., & Krajewski, R. J. (1980). *Clinical supervision: Special methods for the supervision of teachers* (2nd ed.). New York: Holt, Rinehart & Winston; Mosher, R. L., & Purpel, D. E. (1972). *Supervision: The reluctant profession.* Boston: Houghton Mifflin; Cogan, M. L. (1973). *Clinical supervision.* Boston: Houghton Mifflin.

9. Goldhammer, *op. cit.,* p. 54.

10. Rogers, C. R. (1951). *Client-centered therapy.* Boston: Houghton Mifflin.

11. Bruner, J. S. (1964). Some theorems on instruction illustrated with reference to mathematics. In E. R. Hilgard (Ed.), *Theories of learning and instruction* (pp. 306–335). Chicago: National Society for the Study of Education.

12. Pajak, E. (1993). *Approaches to clinical supervision: Alternatives for improving instruction.* Norwood, MA: Christopher-Gordon.

13. *Ibid,* pp. 150–151.

14. By "cooperating teacher," we mean a classroom teacher who supervises a preservice intern or practice teacher.

15. Joyce, B. R., Howey, K. R., Yarger, S. J., & Teacher Corps Recruitment and Technical Resource Center Directors (1976). *Inservice teacher education report 1: Issues to face.* Palo Alto, CA: Stanford Center for Research and Development in Teaching. Although this is an old study, it seems likely that the numbers cited in the report would have increased, not decreased, from then to now.

16. Johnson, J., & Yates, J. (1982). *A national survey of student teaching programs.* (ERIC Document Reproduction Service No. ED 232 963)

17. Twa, J. (1984). *Teacher associate perceptions of the effectiveness of the clinical supervision workshop.* (ERIC Document Reproduction Service No. ED 269 855)

18. Glickman, C. D., & Bey, T. M. (1990). Supervision. In W. R. Houston, M. Haberman, & J. Sikula (Eds.), *Handbook of research on teacher education* (pp. 549–566). New York: Macmillan.

19. Nolan, J., Hawkes, B., & Francis, P. (1993). Case studies: Windows onto clinical supervision. *Educational Leadership, 51*(2), 52–56.

20. *Ibid,* p. 54.

21. Shinn, J. L. (1976). Teacher perceptions of ideal and actual supervisory procedures used by California elementary principals: The effects of supervisory training programs sponsored by the Association of California School Administrators. *Dissertation Abstracts International, 37,* 06A. (University Microfilms No. AAG76-27679)

22. Holifield, M., & Cline, D. (1997). Clinical supervision and its outcomes: Teachers and principals report. *NASSP Bulletin, 81* (590), 109–113; Adwani, S. H. (1981). The relationship between teacher and supervisor as perceived by teachers, supervisors and principals in secondary schools in Saudi Arabia. *Dissertation Abstracts International, 42,* 11A. (University Microfilms No. AAG82-09648); al-Tuwaijri, S. H. (1985). The relationship between ideal and actual supervisory practice as perceived by supervisors in Saudi Arabia. *Dissertation Abstracts International, 46,* 11A. (University Microfilms No. AAG85-29492); Yoon, K. O. (1983). Effects of training in clinical supervision on supervising teachers in Korean middle schools. *Dissertation Abstracts International, 37,* 06A. (University Microfilms No. AAG84-08201)

23. Martin, G. S. (1975). Teacher and administrator attitudes toward evaluation and systematic classroom observation. *Dissertation Abstracts International, 37,* 06A. (University Microfilms No. AAG76-05189)

24. Schön, D. A. (1987). *Educating the reflective practitioner.* San Francisco: Jossey-Bass; Schön, D. A. (2000). *The reflective practitioner: How professionals think in action.* New York: Basic Books; Argyris, C., & Schön, D. A. (1974). *Theory in practice: Increasing professional effectiveness.* San Francisco: Jossey-Bass.

25. Ross, D. D. (1990). Programmatic structures for the preparation of reflective teachers. In Clift, R. T., Houston, W. R., & Pugach, M. C. (Eds.), *Encouraging reflective practice in education: An analysis of issues and programs* (pp. 97–118). New York: Teachers College Press, p. 98.

26. Argyris & Schön, p. 7.

27. *Ibid,* p. 30.

28. *Ibid,* p. 14.

29. Ross, p. 98.

30. Goldhammer, *op. cit.*

31. Mosher & Purpel, *op. cit.*

32. Cogan, *op. cit.*

33. Blumberg, A. (1980). *Supervisors & teachers: A private cold war* (2nd ed.). Berkeley, CA: McCutchan.

34. Eisner, E. W. (1985). *The educational imagination: On the design and evaluation of educational programs* (2nd ed.). New York: Macmillan.

35. Hunter, M. (1984). Knowing, teaching, and supervising. In P. L. Hosford (Ed.), *Using what we know about teaching* (pp. 169–193). Alexandria, VA: Association for Supervision and Curriculum Development.

36. Joyce, B., & Showers, B. (1988). *Student achievement through staff development.* New York: Longmans.

37. Glickman, C. D. (1985). *Supervision of instruction: A developmental approach.* Boston: Allyn and Bacon.

38. Costa, A. L., & Garmston, R. (1985). Supervision for intelligent teaching. *Educational Leadership, 42*(5), 70–80.

39. Schön, D. A. (1987). *Educating the reflective practitioner: Toward a new design for teaching and learning in the professions.* San Francisco: Jossey-Bass.

40. Zeichner, K. M., & Liston, D. P. (1987). Teaching student teachers to reflect. *Harvard Educational Review, 57,* 23–48.

41. Garman, N. B. (1986). Reflection, the heart of clinical supervision: A modern rationale for practice. *Journal of Curriculum and Supervision, 2,* 1–24.

42. Smyth, W. J. (1985). Developing a critical practice of clinical supervision. *Journal of Curriculum Studies, 17,* 1–15.

43. Retallick, J. A. (1990, April). *Clinical supervision and the structure of communication.* Paper presented at the annual meeting of the American Educational Research Association, Boston.

44. Bowers, C. A., & Flinders, D. J. (1991). *Culturally responsive teaching and supervision: A handbook for staff development.* New York: Teachers College Press.

Unit Two

The Contexts
and Uses of Clinical
Supervision

OVERVIEW

As the main goal of clinical supervision is teacher development, Chapter 2 presents the models, programs, and responsibilities involved in teacher development. Chapter 3 presents criteria of effective teaching that have been verified through research. Chapter 4 discusses the use of clinical supervision in teacher evaluation. Chapter 5 introduces the process of peer supervision.

OBJECTIVES

The purpose of this unit is to help you develop an understanding of:

Different models of teacher development and different types of teacher development programs

The roles that share responsibility for teacher development

The types of organizational models and their effect on teacher development

Different perspectives from which to define effective teaching and the research that supports them

What is meant by effective teaching

The relationship between clinical supervision and teacher evaluation

The nature of peer consultation in theory and practice

Chapter 2

Using Clinical Supervision to Promote Teacher Development

Author's Note

This chapter celebrates teachers as professionals. Yet I feel an undermining of this celebration by recent accounts of teachers' discontent with their status as professionals. One of these accounts appeared in a 2001 issue of the electronic journal *Educational Policy Analysis Archives*. (The article is available from the Web at http://epaa.asu.edu/epaa/ v9n28.html.) Researchers surveyed over 3000 teachers in four countries and found that, "while more is expected and demanded of schools, and schools and teachers are scrutinized as never before, educational resources have become scarcer, and the status and image of teaching as a profession has declined."

I see two forces at work—those that seek to raise teachers' professional status and help them develop as professionals (that's what this chapter is about) and those that question teachers' expertise and ability to help students learn.

What is the explanation for these two opposing forces? This chapter does not answer the question, but perhaps it provides a few clues to help you with your own explanation. For example, we note that a teacher's classroom instruction is rarely observed, even by other teachers. Perhaps it's human nature to distrust what we can't see. If so, teachers might have much to gain by using the techniques of clinical supervision to observe each other's work, reflect on it, improve it, and make the whole process visible to various stakeholders (including politicians who wish to hold teachers accountable for results).

Another clue to the problem of teachers' professional status might be that traditional supervision has emphasized teacher evaluation rather than teacher development. Also, the teacher development programs that do exist tend to be fragmented.

In this chapter, we focus on teacher expertise as the key goal of professional development. We describe theory and research demonstrating that expertise in teaching does exist, that it tends to increase over the course of a teacher's career, and that it can be increased by various types of professional development activities, particularly those that include elements of clinical supervision.

We also describe two important initiatives to recognize teachers' expertise. One of them is the National Board for Professional Teaching Standards, which assesses and certifies teacher expertise. The other is the creation of positions for teachers as instructional leaders, especially in "professional development schools," where they work alongside university teacher educators to prepare new teachers. We invite you to consider whether these initiatives are the right response—and a sufficiently strong response—to counter teachers' current dissatisfaction with their status as professionals and to satisfy those who distrust teachers' ability to help students learn.

MDG

Even during those periods of intense interest in improving education that seem to occur about once a generation, neither federal or state governments nor colleges or school systems seem inclined to spend much money on the education of teachers. . . . On the assumption that what teachers know (or do not know) matters little to their teaching or to their students' learning, teachers are often treated as conduits for policies rather than important actors in determining what goes on in classrooms.

—Linda Darling-Hammond[1]

INTRODUCTION

Clinical supervision does not exist within a vacuum. It affects—and is affected by—various processes of teacher development and evaluation that extend from initial teacher licensure to the end of a teacher's career. Therefore, to understand clinical supervision, you need to see how it relates to this larger picture. That is the purpose of this chapter.

HELPING TEACHERS DEVELOP AS PROFESSIONALS

Teachers wish to be seen as professionals and accorded the same status enjoyed by other professionals, such as doctors, lawyers, and engineers. Therefore, clinical supervisors need to focus on teachers' classroom instruction, but within the larger context of acknowledging teachers as emerging or experienced professionals.

To provide that acknowledgment, we need to understand what it means to be a member of a profession. Sociologists have extensively studied the characteristics of professions in the United States and elsewhere.[2] Although their definitions of the term *profession* differ, a suitable definition for our purposes was proposed by E. Hoyle: A profession is an occupation whose practitioners possess a high level of skill and perform functions that are central to society.[3] More specifically, a profession has these characteristics:

1. A profession is an occupation which performs a crucial social function.
2. The exercise of this function requires a considerable degree of skill.
3. This skill is exercised in situations which are not wholly routine, but in which new problems have to be handled.
4. Thus, although knowledge gained through experience is important, this recipe-type knowledge is insufficient to meet professional demands and the practitioner has to draw on a body of systematic knowledge.
5. The acquisition of this body of knowledge and the development of specific skills requires a lengthy period of higher education.
6. This period of education and training also involves the process of socialization into professional values.

7. These values tend to center on the preeminence of clients' interests, and to some degree they are made explicit in a code of ethics.

8. Because knowledge-based skills are exercised in nonroutine situations, it is essential for the professionals to have the freedom to make their own judgments with regard to appropriate practice.

9. Because professional practice is so specialized, the organizing profession should have a strong voice in the shaping of relevant social policy, a large degree of control over the exercise of professional responsibilities, and a high degree of autonomy in relation to the state.

10. Lengthy training, responsibility, and client-centeredness are necessarily rewarded by high prestige and a high level of remuneration.[4]

Clinical supervision is best suited to help teachers develop those aspects of professionalism that concern nonroutine problems and the skills, systematic knowledge, and ethical judgement needed to solve them effectively. In fact, these concerns are at the heart of clinical supervision. As we explained in Chapter 1, clinical supervision is grounded in the theory of reflective practice, which provides a framework for focusing on the problematic nature of classroom practice and developing skills for handling it through experimentation, systematic observation, and reflection.

Hoyle's list of the defining characteristics of a profession also emphasizes "expert knowledge" and the "pre-eminence of clients' interests." In the context of education, we interpret clients' interests to be the learning of students in teachers' classrooms. As we demonstrate in Chapter 3, there is a body of expert knowledge about effective teaching methods. Although these methods should not—and can not—be applied in a rote manner, they nonetheless can inform and enhance classroom practice. For this reason, clinical supervisors have the responsibility to draw on this body of expert knowledge (and other bodies of expert knowledge as well) in helping teachers earn recognition as true professionals.

MODELS OF TEACHER DEVELOPMENT

In times of severe teacher shortages, college graduates are recruited into the classroom with the barest of preparation. In some developing countries, a high school diploma will suffice. While these individuals might survive in the classroom, it would be hard to argue that they are professionals by the criteria that we listed in the preceding section. Becoming a full-fledged professional teacher—what we call a "master teacher"—requires extensive development of one's expertise.

What are the features of this developmental process, and what role does clinical supervision play in it? To answer this question, we review several models of teacher development in the next sections.

Leithwood's Multidimensional Model

Kenneth Leithwood reviewed various strands of theory and research and concluded that teachers' development has three central dimensions: (1) development of professional expertise; (2) psychological development; and (3) career-cycle development.[5] Leithwood's analysis of each dimension yields a comprehensive model of how teachers develop throughout their careers. The model has significant implications for the work of clinical supervisors, as we explain below.

Development of Professional Expertise

According to Leithwood's model of teacher development, teachers progress through six stages of professional expertise. Each stage reflects a higher level of proficiency in the classroom and other settings.

The six stages are described in Table 2.1. It is apparent that teachers have different needs at each stage of expertise development. Therefore, clinical supervisors need extensive knowledge about teaching strategies—from the most basic to the most sophisticated. In Chapter 3, we provide an overview about what is known about effective teaching. Most likely, it will serve as a review of what you already know and a launching point for more advanced study of certain topics.

Table 2.1   The Six Stages of Teachers' Development of Professional Expertise

Stages	Characteristics of Expertise
1. Developing survival skills	• Partially developed classroom-management skills • Knowledge about and limited skill in use of several teaching models • No conscious reflection on choice of model • Student assessment is primarily summative and carried out, using limited techniques, in response to external demands (e.g., reporting to parents); may be poor link between the focus of assessment and instructional goal
2. Becoming competent in the basic skills of instruction	• Well-developed classroom-management skills • Well-developed skill in use of several teaching models • Habitual application through trial and error, of certain teaching models for particular parts of curriculum • Student assessment begins to reflect formative purposes, although techniques are not well suited to such purposes; focus of assessment linked to instructional goals easiest to measure
3. Expanding one's instructional flexibility	• Automatized classroom-management skills • Growing awareness of need for and existence of other teaching models and initial efforts to expand repertoire and experiment with application of new models • Choice of teaching model from expanded repertoire influenced most by interest in providing variety to maintain student interest • Student assessment carried out for both formative and summative purposes; repertoire of techniques is beginning to match purposes; focus of assessment covers significant range of instructional goals

(continued)

Table 2.1 (*continued*)

4. Acquiring instructional expertise	• Classroom management integrated with program; little attention required to classroom management as an independent issue • Skill in application of a broad repertoire of teaching models
5. Contributing to the growth of colleagues' instructional expertise	• Has high levels of expertise in classroom instructional performance • Reflective about own competence and choices and the fundamental beliefs and values on which they are based • Able to assist other teachers in acquiring instructional expertise through either planned learning experiences, such as mentoring, or more formal experiences, such as inservice education and coaching programs
6. Participating in a broad array of educational decisions at all levels of the education system	• Is committed to the goal of school improvement • Accepts responsibility for fostering that goal through any legitimate opportunity • Able to exercise leadership, both formal and informal, with groups of adults inside and outside the school • Has a broad framework from which to understand the relationship among decisions at many different levels in the education system • Is well informed about policies at many different levels in the education system

Source: Leithwood, K. A. (1992). The principal's role in teacher development. In M. Fullan & A. Hargreaves (Eds.), *Teacher development and educational change* (pp. 86–103). London: Falmer Press, p. 89.

Leithwood's model of stages of professional expertise emphasizes teachers' growing capacity for reflection—from "no conscious reflection on choice of model" in Stage 1 to "reflective about own competence and choices and fundamental beliefs and values on which they are based" in Stage 5. Consistent with this view, we ground clinical supervision in the theory of reflective practice (see Chapter 1). The work of clinical supervision is to help teachers reflect on their instruction to identify problems and opportunities for improvement; to determine what kinds of observational data will help them; and to reflect on the resulting data how their instructional actions affect student behavior and learning.

Table 2.1 shows that when teachers reach the fifth stage of professional expertise, they are ready and eager to promote other teachers' development. One path toward that goal is for themselves to become clinical supervisors. Later in the chapter, we consider how experienced teachers can support other teachers' development in various roles that involve clinical supervision—as a mentor, university supervisor, cooperating teacher, or peer consultant.

Teachers who reach the sixth and final stage of expertise in Table 2.1 contribute not only to other teachers' development, but also to their school, school system, and the teaching profession. In effect, they become instructional leaders.

Clinical supervisors have an important role to play at this stage. Because they work directly with teachers, they are in an excellent position to identify teachers who have the talent to become instructional leaders. They can encourage these teachers to apply for leadership positions or programs of study (e.g., administrative licensure programs) that prepare them for these positions. In addition, clinical supervisors can recommend these teachers to others by word of mouth or by writing reference letters. Because of their first-hand knowledge about a teacher's expertise, their recommendations carry special weight for those who make decisions about leadership positions or admission to programs of study.

Career Development

Leithwood posits that the careers of teachers typically pass through five stages. The stages are derived from studies of teachers conducted by various researchers.[6] Table 2.2 provides a description of each stage.

Leithwood's analysis of teachers' career development reveals that each stage marks a new challenge for teachers. Many of them respond to the challenge by growing professionally. However, some stagnate, become bitter, or decline in effectiveness. Obviously, clinical supervision and other forms of professional development will need to accommodate these individual differences.

Table 2.2   The Five Stages of Teachers' Career Cycle

Stages	Characteristic conditions
1. Launching the career	• Easy beginnings: developing positive relationships with students and feeling a sense of instructional mastery and enthusiasm • Painful beginnings: experiencing role overload, anxiety, difficult students, close monitoring, and professional isolation
2. Stabilizing	• Making a commitment to the profession and the employer making a commitment to the teacher • Feeling confident about one's basic instructional skills • Feeling integrated into a group of peers • Possibly seeking greater responsibilities
3. Facing new challenges	• Some teachers moving into "master teacher" status or seeking promotion to positions of greater responsibility • Other teachers experiencing mediocre instructional success and considering alternative careers
4. Reaching a professional plateau	• Some teachers no longer striving for promotion and become the backbone of the school • Other teachers becoming bitter and cynical and stop seeking opportunities for professional development
5. Preparing for retirement	• Some teachers "contracting" by specializing in what they do best • Other teachers becoming disenchanted, tired, and bitter about past experiences with change

Source: Adapted from: Leithwood, K. A. (1992). The principal's role in teacher development. In M. Fullan & A. Hargreaves (Eds.), *Teacher development and educational change* (pp. 86–103). London: Falmer Press, pp. 92–93.

Consider the case of teachers who are in a positive growth state at a particular career stage. Given how busy educators are, it might be easy to ignore these teachers in order to devote more energy to other demands and crises. Yet these teachers deserve the full attention of clinical supervisors and others, for they are the ones who can provide instructional leadership to a school or school system. Indeed, they are the ones on whom the future of the teaching profession depends.

Teachers who are in a state of stagnation or decline pose a different challenge for clinical supervisors. They require intensive clinical supervision, and possibly counseling as well, in order to avoid having them hinder students' learning and "infect" other teachers with their negativism. In Chapter 4, we discuss how these teachers become identified through a formal process of teacher evaluation and how they might be helped through plans of assistance involving clinical supervision.

Some teachers who are in a state of stagnation or decline realize their condition and need help in considering new career options. Because clinical supervision is intensive and focused on the individual teacher, the supervisor might be the first and most important colleague with whom a teacher can express his or her career frustrations. Of course, for this to happen, there must be trustful and open communication between the teacher and supervisor. We discuss these aspects of communication in several chapters, but particularly in Chapter 6.

Psychological Development

Leithwood claims that teachers progress through four stages of ego, moral, and conceptual development over the course of their careers. The stages are derived from Loevinger's theory of ego development, Kohlberg's theory of moral development, and Hunt's theory of conceptual development.[7]

The four stages are described in Table 2.3. As teachers move from one stage to the next, their reasoning about moral, interpersonal, and academic aspects of classroom instruction becomes more sophisticated. They also become more sophisticated in their view of themselves as members of the teaching profession.

In working with teachers as a clinical supervisor, you will find it helpful to assess their stage of psychological development. Teachers at one of the first two stages might express simplistic concerns about their instruction relative to teachers at the higher stages. Also, they might not be as able to analyze and interpret observational data, or use the data as a basis for generating more effective ways to teach. It might be tempting for you to do the thinking for such teachers. However, the teachers might not be able to make sense of your ideas or become overly dependent on you as an authority figure.

A more effective approach would be to ask questions that stimulate Stage 1 and 2 teachers to think for themselves and to praise them for independent thinking. For example, a teacher might look at observational data that show many students off task for significant amounts of time, and ask you, "What should I do to correct this situation?" The temptation is to answer the question, but this only encourages dependence. Instead, the supervisor could ask, "If you really want students to be on task, what are some things you can do?" or "When you've seen classrooms where students are on task most of the time, what kinds of things is the teacher doing?"

This technique of questioning (discussed further in Chapter 8) encourages teachers to think for themselves and thus progress to Stages 3 and 4 in Leithwood's model of

Table 2.3   The Four Stages of Teachers' Psychological Development

Stages	Characteristics of teachers
Stage 1 (Simplistic)	• See choices as black and white • Believe strongly in rules and roles • View authority as the highest good • Discourage divergent thinking and rewards conformity and rote learning
Stage 2 (Conformist)	• Wish to be like their peers • Provide instruction with explicit rules that do not accommodate individual differences or special circumstances
Stage 3 (Conscientious)	• Appreciate multiple possibilities for explaining and designing instruction • Appreciate the need for exception to rules, given the circumstances • Provide rationally planned instruction that is achievement-oriented and grounded in good interpersonal communication
Stage 4 (Inner-directed)	• Appreciate the interdependent nature of relationships and therefore establish classroom control collaboratively with students • Appreciate multiple perspectives and synthesize them • Understand the reasoning behind rules and therefore can apply them wisely • Can provide instruction that balances interpersonal and academic-achievement orientations • Encourages students to engage in complex cognitive functions

Source: Adapted from: Leithwood, K. A. (1992). The principal's role in teacher development. In M. Fullan & A. Hargreaves (Eds.), *Teacher development and educational change* (pp. 86–103). London: Falmer Press, pp. 90–91.

psychological development. The long-term benefit of this approach to supervision is that, as teachers become more independent and creative in their thinking, they will facilitate the same kind of thinking in their students.

Berliner's Model of Instructional Expertise

In recent decades, researchers have become interested in the nature of expertise. They have addressed such questions as how experts and novices differ in their approach to their work and how expertise develops over time. Experts in such diverse fields as radiology and chess-playing have been studied. Experts in classroom instruction have been studied, too. David Berliner has synthesized this research into a model of teacher development of instructional expertise.[8] To an extent, the model overlaps Leithwood's developmental model of professional expertise (see above), but it has a more specific focus. Leithwood considers the full range of teachers' work—some of which occurs outside the classroom—whereas Berliner' model only involves classroom instruction.

Berliner's model specifies five stages in the development of instructional expertise.

- ***Stage 1: Novice Level.*** At this stage, teachers are learning the basic vocabulary and rules of instruction. They are also gaining classroom experience, which they are likely to view as more important than "book knowledge" about teaching. Students and many first-year teachers are at this novice stage of expertise.

- *Stage 2: Advanced Beginner Level.* Many second- and third-year teachers are at this stage of instructional expertise. They are able to link their book knowledge with their growing body of experience. Thus, when they confront new tasks and problems in their classroom, they are able to link them to previous instances in their experience and recall how they handled them. They also know the limit of instructional principles. For example, they might value the principle of waiting 3 seconds after asking question in order to give students time to think, but realize that there are occasions when longer or shorter wait times might be effective.

- *Stage 3: Competent Level.* Many third- and fourth-year teachers achieve a level of expertise characterized as competence, but according to research evidence reviewed by Berliner, some do not. Competent teachers have a sense of personal agency: They set rational instructional goals and means for achieving those goals. Also, they can size up an instructional situation and decide what is worth attending to and what can be ignored. Because they feel in control of instruction, they take more responsibility for their successes and failures than teachers at lower stages of expertise development.

- *Stage 4: Proficient Level.* Teachers who reach this stage of expertise have achieved a certain amount of automaticity in their instruction. They are like experienced drivers who handle a car skillfully without having to consciously think about each procedure or decision. Also, they have acquired a wealth of teaching experience that allows them to see patterns in new teaching situations that less experienced teachers cannot. For example, when they get a new group of students to teach or observe another teacher's class, they can "size up" the class quickly. They know which of their customary teaching strategies will work and what modifications are necessary.

- *Stage 5: Expert Level.* According to Berliner, teachers who are at the expert level of instruction act "effortlessly and fluidly."[9] They feel at one with their students and the curriculum, so it is not necessary to consciously plan and execute each instructional move. When things do not go as planned, expert teachers can bring their highly developed skills of analysis to improvise solutions. Although Berliner does not make this point explicitly, it seems that expert teachers are more likely than teachers at lower levels of expertise to produce genuinely creative ideas to improve classroom instruction.

As a clinical supervisor, you should find it helpful to keep Berliner's model of instructional expertise in mind as you work with teachers. By the end of the first supervisory cycle (planning conference, classroom observation, feedback conference), you should have a good sense of the teacher's level of expertise. Novice or advanced-beginner teachers will need guidance to help them distinguish between more significant and less significant problems in their instruction. For example, they might feel that deficiencies in their classroom management are the central issue, whereas it might be clear to you that the their inability to motivate students to learn is the core issue.

Novice and advanced-beginner teachers might need more guidance in seeing cause-and-effect patterns in the observational data that are reviewed in the feedback conference. This is because the ability to see patterns—rather than isolated details—requires a substantial experience base, which they lack (through no fault of their own). Also, these teachers are more easily threatened, because flaws in their instruction (perhaps glaring flaws) will be revealed by the supervisory process. As a clinical supervisor, you will need to build trust with novices and advanced beginners so that their feelings of threat and anxiety do not block the learning process.

In working with teachers at the proficient or expert levels, you might find that your supervision is much more collegial in nature. By this, we mean that you and the teacher will coinvestigate his or her classroom instruction. You will find much to admire in it, and problems of practice will be opportunities to work together to generate creative solutions. You might find it appropriate to share your own experiences and instructional strategies, because you know that the teacher will not feel threatened by them or feel compelled to adopt them in order to please you.

Fuller's Model of Teacher Concerns

Frances Fuller's model of teacher development is based on changes in teachers' concerns.[10] She found that teachers progress through three major stages:

- *Covert Concerns about Self.* Early in their initial preparation, teachers tend to be concerned about the scope of their responsibilities. For example, they ask themselves questions about their responsibilities relative to the cooperating teacher during field experiences and whether they or other persons have responsibility for student misbehavior in class.

- *Overt Concerns about Self.* Once beginning teachers resolve their concerns about scope of responsibilities, they become concerned about their professional adequacy. For example, they start wondering whether they are good enough to survive annual evaluations and receive contract renewals.

- *Concern about Students.* As teachers become more experienced, the focus of concern moves from self to the students. Among other matters, they are concerned about students who fail to learn or students whom they feel they are not reaching.

Obviously, these concerns do not occur in strict progression. Experienced teachers might have occasion to question their scope of responsibility, and student teachers might have mature, insightful concerns about their students. Fuller's stages of concern are broad generalizations.

As a supervisor, it is helpful for you to know about Fuller's model as a check on whether you are addressing teachers' felt concerns—not just the concerns that you might have about their instruction. For example, if a student teacher is concerned about the extent to which she is free to bring her own curriculum ideas into the cooperating teacher's classroom, it might be difficult for you to turn her attention to issues involving her classroom instruction. The teacher's felt concern needs to be addressed first. Once the concern is addressed and resolved, you will be more likely to work with the teacher on concerns having to do with teaching methods and student learning.

In Chapter 7, we revisit Fuller's model in our discussion of how to address teachers' concerns as part of the planning process.

TYPES OF TEACHER DEVELOPMENT PROGRAMS

"When all you've got is a hammer, the whole world becomes a nail." In the case of teacher development, this truism implies that if an individual is only skilled in clinical supervision, he or she will try to solve all teacher-development problems with it. Clinical supervision is a highly useful tool, but other methods of teacher development are useful as well. Clinical supervision works best when it is deliberately selected as the best tool in the toolbox rather than because it is the only thing lying around.

What is the full range of methods available for teacher development? Roseanne Vojtek and one of us (Gall) reviewed the literature on teacher development (also called *professional development* or *staff development*) to answer this question.[11] They identified six major methods (they referred to them as *models*) of teacher development. Table 2.4 describes the key features of each method and the teacher-development objectives for which each is best suited.

The expert-presenter method is widely used in teacher education.[12] Preservice teachers take courses in which the instructor typically lectures about various topics. Inservice teachers attend workshops and conferences where presenters give talks, often about current trends in education. From the perspective of reflective-practice theory (explained in Chapter 1), the lectures and talks can help teachers improve their instruction, but only under certain conditions: if the teacher sees the presenter's content as relevant to a problem that he or she is facing in the classroom, and if the content is not too great a challenge to the teacher's espoused theories or theories-in-use. In practice, it is unlikely that any one lecture or talk can address the diversity of teachers' classroom situations and understanding of instruction. Some teachers might benefit from the presentation, but many others might not.

The skill-training method has been found to be effective in helping teachers improve their instruction.[13] Undoubtedly this is because the method includes efforts to help teachers in their own classroom context and because the theoretical basis for instructional skills is specifically addressed. However, the skills covered in the training program typically are prespecified. Therefore, teachers possibly might be expected to learn skills that they have mastered already or that they do not see as relevant to their problems. Also, if the skills conflict with a teacher's espoused theories or theories-in-use, the teacher might comply with the training program's requirements, but not internalize the skills and use them on a regular basis.

Action research is compatible to a large extent with the precepts of clinical supervision. A teacher (sometimes a group of teachers) develops ideas about how to improve instruction in his or her classroom, tries them out while collecting relevant data, and then reflects on the data. Depending on the reflections, the teacher might change his or her instruction, or develop new—and presumably better—ideas for subsequent action-research projects.[14] It seems reasonable that a supervisor, mentor, or other guide could facilitate this process.

The focus of organization development (OD) is on the formal and informal procedures, norms, and structures of a school (or other system) rather than an individual teacher. OD

Table 2.4   Six Methods for Promoting Teacher Development

Teacher development method	Key features of method	Objectives for which the method is best suited
1. Expert presenter	Teachers assemble to listen to an expert talk about a topic	• Developing teachers' knowledge and understanding • Changing teachers' attitudes
2. Skill training	Trainer presents theory underlying the skills; explains and models the skills. Teacher practices the skills and receives feedback; is coached to promote transfer of training to own classroom	• Developing teachers' instructional skills and strategies • Developing teachers' ability to improve students' academic achievement • Developing teachers' ability to develop and implement curriculum • Developing teachers' ability to reflect and make sound decisions
3. Action research	Teachers do research in their own work setting to answer their questions or test new ideas	• Changing teachers' attitudes • Developing teachers' ability to engage in school restructuring
4. Organization development	OD specialist helps teachers and other staff diagnose strengths and weaknesses of their school or system, develop a plan of action, implement the plan, and evaluate its success	• Changing teachers' attitudes • Developing teachers' ability to develop and implement curriculum
5. Change process	Staff developers help teachers make a decision to a adopt a system-wide innovation, put the innovation into action, and institutionalize it	• Developing teachers' ability to engage in school restructuring
6. Clinical supervision	Supervisor identifies a teacher's concerns and goals, collects classroom observation data, and reviews data with the teacher	• Developing teachers' instructional skills and strategies • Developing teachers' ability to reflect and make sound instructional decisions

Source: Adapted from: Gall, M. D., & Vojtek, R. O. (1994). *Planning for effective staff development: Six research-based models.* Eugene, OR: ERIC Clearinghouse of Educational Management, pp. 26–27. (ERIC Document Reproduction Service No. ED372464)

consultants attempt to improve these procedures, norms, and structures using principles from the social sciences.[15] Because school organization strongly affects teachers' work, any substantial change in the organization provides opportunities for teacher development. For example, an OD intervention might be used to help a school make the transition from a traditional class schedule to a block schedule. As teachers participate in the transition process with facilitation by OD consultants, teachers might develop new espoused theories and theories-in-use that fundamentally change their instructional practices.

In using the term change-process method, we are referring specifically to the model developed by Michael Fullan, based on his review of the research literature and educational practice.[16] The method focuses on processes that lead to the successful adoption of innovations (curriculum, teaching strategies, assessment strategies, etc.). The processes occur in three major stages: initiation, implementation, and institutionalization. Some of the processes of the change-process method are similar to those in OD, but the focus of the former is solving an organizational problem whereas the focus of the latter is adopting an innovation. The change-process method is relevant to teacher development, because adopting an innovation often results in substantial growth in teachers' capacity to provide effective instruction.

We see, then, that all of the five staff-development methods described above and in Table 2.4 can contribute to teacher development, each in a somewhat different way. The sixth method shown in Table 2.4 is clinical supervision, which is the subject of this book. Relative to the other methods, the unique contribution of clinical supervision is that it is tailored to the particular needs of the individual teacher. The focus of clinical supervision is not a particular body of knowledge, set of skills, organizational problem, or curriculum adoption, but rather the teacher and the specific context of his or her instructional practice.

Of the other methods shown in Table 2.4, clinical supervision is most similar to action research, which also focuses on the individual teacher's problems of practice. (Group action-research projects are also possible.) The main difference is that an intrinsic feature of clinical supervision is a strong interpersonal relationship between the teacher and a supervisor skilled in conferencing and collecting of objective observational data. By contrast, action research is either done by the teacher alone or with the facilitation of an educator who is skilled in quantitative or qualitative research methodology, or both. Of course, facilitators can employ the various techniques described in this book; to the extent that they do, their work will represent some mix of clinical supervision and action research. In fact, we predict that action research projects will produce greater gains in teacher development if the facilitator has been trained in techniques of clinical supervision. We also believe the converse is true: You will be a better clinical supervisor if you have been educated in the theory and practice of action research.

STANDARDS-BASED TEACHER DEVELOPMENT

Various organizations and commissions are currently developing standards for teacher education and performance. Among them are the Interstate New Teacher Assessment and Support Consortium (INTASC—a project of the Council of Chief School Officers), the National Council for Accreditation of Teacher Education (NCATE), the Council for Exceptional Children (CEC), and the International Society for Technology in Education (ISTE).[17] These evolving standards constitute sets of goals that teachers and teacher educators can use in designing development programs.

One of the most important and visible of the organizations involved in the effort to develop standards is the National Board for Professional Teaching Standards (hereafter, "National Board").[18] Just as medical specialists seek board certification to document their expertise for colleagues and patients, so now can teachers document their "master teacher" status for other educators, parents, and the community.

Teachers need to develop their skills and build a record of accomplishments over a period of years in order to pass the assessments that are required in order to earn a certificate. As we explain below, clinical supervision is helpful—perhaps essential—in facilitating the specific types of teacher development necessary to earn National Board certification.

Philosophy of the National Board for Professional Teaching Standards

The National Board has three purposes:

- to establish high standards that define what a master teacher should know and be able to do.
- to operate a system to assess and certify teachers who meet these standards.
- to support reforms that improve student learning.

This statement of purposes emphasizes the fact that the characteristics of effective teaching need to be made explicit and public. Undoubtedly, the particular standards specified by the National Board will change as research knowledge about effective teaching improves.

Our review of research on effective teaching in Chapter 3 gives you a reference point for judging the adequacy and scope of the National Board's current list of standards. Also, one purpose of the conferencing techniques that we present in Unit 3 is to help teachers make explicit their instructional concerns and strategies. As they practice making them explicit, they will become more attuned to the National Board's emphasis on explicit definitions of instructional concepts and observable referents for them.

The National Board builds the standards for each certificate around five propositions:

1. Teachers are committed to students and their learning.
2. Teachers know the subjects they teach and how to teach those subjects to students.
3. Teachers are responsible for managing and monitoring student learning.
4. Teachers think systematically about their practice and learn from experience.
5. Teachers are members of learning communities.

The first three propositions refer to curriculum, instruction, and assessment. Unit 4 of this book presents observation instruments relating to each of these three cornerstones of classroom instruction, including their alignment.

The fourth proposition involves the reflective process. The model of clinical supervision that we present in this book is built on the theory of reflective practice (discussed in Chapter 1). As a clinical supervisor, you will help teachers develop their ability to reflect about their classroom instruction, which is consistent with this proposition.

The final proposition has to do with teachers learning together to improve their instruction. Peer consultation, which we discuss in Chapter 5, supports this proposition because it calls for teachers to collect observational data in each other's classrooms and to hold collegial conferences to reflect on the data's implications for the improvement of instruction.

National Board Certificates and Assessments

The National Board has created—or is in the process of creating—a set of certificates. Each certificate has a subject area and developmental level associated with it, and also a set of standards. For example, teachers can earn a certificate in language arts at the adolescence/young adulthood level. Table 2.5 shows the standards associated with this certifi-

人工

Table 2.5 National Board Standards for the Language-Arts Certificate at Adolescence Young Adulthood Level

The requirements for the Adolescence and Young Adulthood/English Language Arts (AYA/ELA) certificate are organized into the following fifteen standards.

Preparing the Way for Productive Student Learning

I. Knowledge of students
Accomplished AYA/ELA teachers systematically acquire a sense of their students as individual language learners.
II. Knowledge of English language arts
Accomplished AYA/ELA teachers know their field and draw on this knowledge to set attainable and worthwhile learning goals for students.
III. Engagement
Accomplished AYA/ELA teachers actively involve each of their students in language learning.
IV. Fairness
Accomplished AYA/ELA teachers demonstrate through their practices toward all students their commitment to the principles of equity, strength through diversity, and fairness.
V. Learning environment
Accomplished AYA/ELA teachers create an inclusive, caring, and challenging classroom environment in which students actively learn.
VI. Instructional resources
Accomplished AYA/ELA teachers select, adapt, and create curricular resources that support active student exploration of language processes and of a wide range of literature.

Advancing Student Learning in the Classroom

VII. Integrated instruction
Accomplished AYA/ELA teachers frequently integrate reading, writing, speaking, and listening opportunities in English studies and across the other disciplines.
VIII. Reading
Accomplished AYA/ELA teachers engage their students in reading and responding to literature, as well as interpreting and thinking deeply about literature and other sources.
IX. Writing
Accomplished AYA/ELA teachers immerse their students in the art of writing for a variety of purposes.
X. Discourse
Accomplished AYA/ELA teachers foster thoughtful classroom discourse that provides opportunities for students to listen and speak in many ways and for many purposes.
XI. Language study
Accomplished AYA/ELA teachers strengthen student sensitivity to and proficiency in the appropriate uses of language.
XII. Assessment
Accomplished AYA/ELA teachers use a range of formal and informal assessment methods to monitor student progress, encourage student self-assessment, plan instruction, and report to various audiences.

(*continued*)

Table 2.5   (*continued*)

XIII. Self-reflection

Accomplished AYA/ELA teachers constantly analyze and strengthen the effectiveness and quality of their teaching.

XIV. Professional community

Accomplished AYA/ELA teachers contribute to the improvement of instructional programs, advancement of knowledge, and practice of colleagues in the field.

XV. Family outreach

Accomplished AYA/ELA teachers work with families to serve the best interests of their children.

cate. The approach to clinical supervision that we take in this book is consistent with the view of teaching and teacher professionalism expressed in these standards.

The National Board assessments for each certificate consist of two major parts—portfolios and assessment-center exercises.

Portfolios

Candidates for a National Board certificate are required to submit a set of portfolio entries according to specifications. Of these entries, four are classroom-based: two ask teachers to videotape and analyze classroom instruction; and two ask teachers to collect and analyze student work. For example, the following is one of the required entries for the Early Childhood/Generalist certificate:

> *Teachers are asked to feature a learning experience that engages children in the investigation of a science concept. Central to teachers' written responses is a detailed examination of a learning experience they videotape. They are also asked to describe how this learning experience is embedded within an ongoing series of activities designed to promote children's understanding of science concepts and processes. Teachers submit a videotape and a written commentary.*[19]

Clinical supervision develops teachers' ability to prepare this and other related portfolio entries for National Board certification. The conferencing techniques in Unit 3 focus on the process of analyzing and reflecting on teaching/learning processes in the teacher's classroom. Chapter 11 describes how video recordings and portfolios can be used to collect data about classroom instruction and other aspects of teachers' professional work.

Assessment-Center Exercises

In addition to portfolios, candidates for a National Board certificate are required to complete a full day of assessment exercises that focus on pedagogical content knowledge. The exercises present simulations of situations to which teachers must respond or questions about pedagogical content topics and issues. For example, the following is an example of an assessment exercise for the National Board certificate for mathematics at the early-adolescence level:

> *Using student artifacts from an instructional strand involving number/operation sense and algebra/functions, teachers will be asked a content knowledge question that focuses*

on this content strand(s) to be followed by pedagogical content knowledge questions that require teachers to demonstrate their ability to identify individual and group misconceptions from student work, design instruction to fix misconceptions, and plan to deepen/ extend student understanding of the topic under study.[20]

Clinical supervision does not purport to teach this type of specialized pedagogical content knowledge. However, clinical supervisors need to have a broad understanding of effective content-specific and general teaching strategies. An overview of these strategies is presented in Chapter 3. In addition, clinical supervisors need to know a range of teacher development programs that teachers can access in order to acquire more pedagogical knowledge. Earlier in this chapter, we provided a model that specified various types of such programs, some of which are more appropriate for this purpose than others.

Benefits of National Board Certification

The number of teachers holding a National Board certificate was approximately 10,000 at the end of the year 2000. These teachers are a resource that can be accessed for school improvement and teacher development in ways described in the next section. In addition, they strengthen the status of teaching as a profession.

Dolores Bohen conducted a research study of thirteen National-Board-certified teachers to determine the benefits they received from the certification process.[21] She found these benefits:

- *Greater Professional Confidence.* Teachers reported that the certification process strengthened their skills and professional judgment in improving student learning.

- *Improved Analysis of Instruction.* Teachers improved their ability to justify why they took particular instructional actions both to themselves and to their colleagues.

- *Clearer Focus on Student Outcomes.* Teachers found that their instruction changed as they focused more sharply on student learning. They eliminated unimportant classroom activities and increased the use of assessment as a learning tool.

- *Greater Commitment to Professional Growth.* Teachers found that the earned certificate was not a culmination of their professional development, but rather a catalyst to keep learning both on their own and in collaboration with colleagues.

These are highly desirable goals for teacher development. National Board certification is not the only way to pursue them, but it is an excellent resource for doing so. As we demonstrated above, the techniques of clinical supervision are consistent with these goals and can help teachers achieve them.

SHARING RESPONSIBILITY FOR TEACHER DEVELOPMENT

Supervisors of preservice and inservice teachers often have other responsibilities. University professors need to teach courses, manage programs, and engage in research and scholarship. School administrators have responsibility for public relations, curriculum development, budget, student discipline, health, safety, and nutrition, among other duties. As one of our administrator colleagues pointed out, when confronted with the fact that school administrators seem more concerned with budgets than supervision, "If you want to get fired, making a mistake in the budget is much quicker than making an omission in supervision."

Amid the busy work life of teacher educators and administrators, political leaders and their constituents are calling for improvements in students' test performance and a system of accountability for schools and teachers. The organizations that represent teachers also must heed this call. They are saying, "Let's evaluate teachers regularly. If they need help, let's provide it. If they are still unable (or unwilling) to improve, let's dismiss them and replace them."

To carry out the ultimate purpose of clinical supervision (the improvement of instruction), we need some new roles. One might be for someone other than the principal to do public relations, nutrition, inoculation, budgets, and discipline so the principal has more time for instructional leadership activities such as clinical supervision. For the principal of a small school, who also teaches, coaches, and does almost everything else to provide excellence to the patrons of a rural, or isolated, school, sharing the role of classroom observer with teachers may create a new role for the teachers and modify one for the principal. On the other hand, a department head in a large school might simply expand an existing role by taking a more active part in observing and providing feedback to teachers.

What are the appropriate titles for these roles and who can fill them? It seems to depend on the situation. In some provinces of Canada, principals belong to the same professional association as the teachers they supervise. In some parts of the world, the person might be called *inspector*. In others, it might be *mentor* or *peer consultant* or *instructional leader*.

If these instructional leaders are principals or other administrators, they must have the time, and use it, to be in classrooms making objective and relevant observations. If the instructional leaders are teachers, they need the time and the skills to carry out the planning, recording, and feedback phases of the clinical-supervision cycle. Two cycles per year are not enough to generate and sustain substantial changes in teaching behavior. Six or eight cycles would be more realistic.

The immediate reaction to such a plan is concern for its cost. If every teacher were willing to devote 1 hour per month either to observing or conferring with others, most schools could accommodate this within their schedules. In return for this "donated" time, each teacher would receive the benefit of several observations and conferences with a qualified colleague who would be serving as a constructively critical friend. Additional time, in the form of paid substitutes, can be provided by the school board.

School Principals

The courts, arbitrators, and hearing panels regard the principal as the person most responsible for making judgments in respect to the evaluation of teachers. In some jurisdictions, the superintendent is responsible by law or regulation, but may delegate the responsibility to others—usually principals. Given this responsibility, the principal has the difficult task of also being a clinical supervisor in the collegial, constructively critical mode we have advocated.

We know some principals who are able to do formal evaluations *and* clinical supervision, while also maintaining a high level of trust and mutual respect with their teachers. Their competence in the techniques of clinical supervision is a major source of this respect and trust. Despite the encouragement that such principals provide, the majority of teachers do not feel that they are getting the kind of supervision they want and need.

Our response to the existing situation is twofold. First, we need more principals who are trained and experienced in systematic observation and feedback techniques. When they have become skilled, their evaluation activities can provide useful information for the improvement of instruction. These evaluation activities can be a part of instructional leadership rather than empty ritual. Second, the principal needs to share the instructional leadership of the school with teachers and others who are taking on new roles in the instructional program.

There will be a new role for the principal to play in managing the logistics to make collegial observation and analysis possible. Another role may be to provide inservice training or staff development activities that enable teachers to develop the skills necessary to become effective colleagues in a program that uses peer observation and analysis. Another role for the principal will be to work with probationary teachers (those who have not attained tenure) or with teachers who would prefer not to work with peers.

According to Kenneth Leithwood, the most important role of the principal is to work with teachers to develop a vision for the school—a set of goals and the means for accomplishing them.[22] He reviewed research findings indicating that effective principals use this vision to generate "subtle, sometimes opportunistic teacher development strategies."[23] These strategies include those we mentioned above, but also such activities as helping teachers gain access to outside resources, informing teachers of professional opportunities, and relating teachers' reflections about their classroom instruction to the larger school vision.

One role we do not advocate for a principal is as a member of the committee administering a program of assistance for a teacher who is on notice if that teacher was put on notice by the principal in question. There is often a question of bias or personal conflict in such cases, and it is best to have a "neutral" administrator on the committee, as we suggest in Chapter 4.

Other Administrators

Vice principals can perform any of the supervisory functions we describe above for principals. Also, administrators in the central office of larger school districts often have skills for observing and conferencing with teachers and could benefit from spending time in the schools. This would do much to overcome their tendency to become isolated and deskbound by their traditional duties.

Subject-matter specialists for larger school districts are another source of instructional leadership to encourage clinical supervision. They can model effective supervisory practices, train teachers in observation and conferencing techniques, and administer peer consultation programs (see Chapter 5). These activities would do much to facilitate the adoption of new curriculum content and new curriculum-specific teaching strategies for which subject-matter specialists are responsible.

Teachers

Education as a profession has tended to move from an "inspector" model of employee monitoring to a more democratic, collaborative one. The participation of the teacher in setting goals for self-improvement, choosing sources of feedback, and making decisions about desirable changes has received increased attention over the years. The responses to surveys of teachers and supervisors in several countries have indicated that this is the kind of supervision teachers are seeking (see Chapter 1).

The most available source of expertise is teachers themselves. They have the ability to analyze their own teaching on the basis of objective data, to observe in others' class-rooms and record data teachers cannot record themselves, and to help one another analyze these data and make decisions about alternative strategies. Teachers can do these things without formal report writing or other procedures associated with official evaluation.

Many of the meetings teachers attend deal with procedural and bureaucratic matters. As a contrast, consider department meetings in a secondary school or unit meetings in an elementary school where faculty members regularly view excerpts from videotapes made in their classrooms on a revolving basis so that they can analyze and discuss the content, methodology, and techniques of their teaching as a substantial part of the meeting. If this were to become a widespread practice, we should see some striking improvements, as-suming that the participants have the interpersonal communication skills mentioned above rather than to "cut each other down."

The new roles have several advantages in addition to the likelihood that teachers will respond more positively to a new kind of leadership. They can provide a career ladder for teachers who do not wish to become administrators, yet do wish to advance in the profes-sion. They can provide a means for teacher organizations to play a positive role in the im-provement of competence within the profession.

If successfully implemented, such a program could be cost-beneficial. Two examples may illustrate the point. In a case that one of us consulted on (Acheson), litigation brought by a teacher cost nearly a quarter of a million dollars in attorney fees alone. In another, a reinstated teacher became a nonproductive liability that, over the years, probably cost a half million dollars in salary, administrative time, legal fees, and the like. If these cases had been worked out cooperatively by the school districts and teacher organizations rather than as labor–management confrontations, those same funds could have bought a lot of released time for collegial supervision.

Experiments with team teaching might not have proved that it increased achievement by students, but they did show that teachers can benefit from working closely with colleagues. In a team, teachers vicariously pick up teaching techniques from one another and are ex-posed to an expanded repertoire of strategies. If teachers were trained in systematic obser-vation procedures, they would be the ideal persons to provide feedback to one another. They and their professional organizations are opposed to becoming evaluators of other teachers, but they are usually enthusiastic when given responsibilities for staff development.

To make use of the talents and skills of teachers, some adjustments need to be made to allow and encourage them to observe in one another's classrooms and to have time to meet and discuss what they have observed. Effective collegial supervision also requires training: teachers must be given the opportunity to develop the skills of systematic obser-vation and helpful feedback.

Creating instructional leadership roles for teachers requires some imagination. For one thing, teachers in this role will need a label or title. We also need to define the func-tions. For example, we might call them master teachers and place them in charge of stu-dent teachers and teacher aides in addition to setting a minimum number of classroom observations and conferences with experienced teachers. Another area of special concern could be assisting new teachers in the classroom and acculturating them about the ways of the school and the profession. Some states have designated teachers to be "mentors" to perform these functions.

These ideas about teachers as instructional leaders might seem impossibly idealistic. Yet they are in place in some school systems. In Chapter 5, you will read about schools in which teachers observe and confer with each other in a process called *peer consultation.* Similar processes are widespread in Japan, where school-based professional development (called *kounaikenshuu)* is considered part of teachers' regular work.[24] One component of kounaikenshuu is lesson study, which involves a group of teachers who collaborate to design, teach, reflect on, and improve a lesson. The lesson is taught by one teacher, but every teacher in the group assists in its preparation and observes its implementation while also videotaping it or taking notes. Collaborative reflections in a conference after the lesson provide a strong basis for personal and collective professional development.

Department Heads

Department heads in secondary schools have the advantage of being subject-matter specialists in their field. Thus they avoid the skepticism principals often receive, as reflected in comments like, "How can a former math teacher supervise and evaluate a foreign language teacher?" Department heads are also concerned about, and in immediate contact with, the curriculum in their department. However, they have often shied away from assuming responsibilities for supervising teachers or making major decisions about the curriculum. Also, the departments in traditional secondary schools often exist as administrative conveniences rather than as centers of instructional leadership.[25] A redefinition of the role and provision for relevant training are needed to make department heads true instructional leaders.

What might a department head hope to accomplish by taking on a new role as instructional leader? To answer the question, let's imagine a possible case. Pat is head of a high school mathematics department and receives a stipend plus a free period each day for carrying out the tasks of the assignment. Pat has had training and experience in using the skills of observing and analyzing teaching and giving feedback to the seven department members. Some of them have similar skills, so sometimes Pat takes their classes while they observe a colleague. At least ten observations are made each month so each teacher (including Pat) has six to eight per year. These are regarded as formative by the teachers, and they choose goals to work on that are consistent with their growth needs and concerns.

In addition to the personal growth that these teachers achieve, there are some spin-offs. Because they observe one another's classes, there is a coherence to the program. They know what others are doing and can articulate sequences of courses and activities. They have a mutual sense of psychological and professional support. They share teaching ideas, and when curriculum is being modified, they analyze the effects at a concrete level. They have overcome their apprehension about videotaping their own teaching for self-analysis. The students are also accustomed to having observers and recorders in the room. One can see the effects of Pat's leadership (and the cooperation of colleagues) in morale, school climate, student achievement, and job satisfaction.

If department heads are to assume greater responsibility as instructional leaders, several other changes may need to occur. There should be prerequisite training in supervision skills and curriculum matters. Most incumbents will need more time for classroom visits than they now have. There also should be a proportionate increase in authority to accompany any increase in responsibility. For example, the department head might have the authority to change teaching assignments, allocate materials, modify curriculum, and establish teaching programs. Writing formal evaluations of their fellow teachers would place the same strain on the trust relationship that has been mentioned earlier; hence we would not recommend it.

Training for New Roles

In order to have the skills ("techniques," we have called them) necessary to carry out the functions of these new roles, principals, department heads, and teachers need training and practice. We have found that 20 to 30 hours of instruction plus an equal amount of practice (six to ten observations using different techniques, including three to five full cycles with planning before and feedback after) should be adequate.

It is desirable to have both teachers and administrators in such a class. If the training is undertaken within a school system, teachers' apprehensions are allayed when they learn what the purposes are and what the effects can be. Administrators with only moderate motivation to become better supervisors can benefit from the competition and modeling by teachers who are enthusiastic and resourceful in completing their assignments.

The first three to five observations (which can be 20 to 30 minutes in duration) should be strictly to gain experience with several different observation techniques, such as at-task, selective verbatim, interaction patterns, and classroom movement. Teachers are usually willing to let a colleague practice his or her newly acquired skills in their classrooms. They are likely to be interested in seeing the data, even though a feedback conference is not part of the assignment.

When the observers feel confident, planning and feedback conferences should be added as part of the assignment. Observers who are practicing these new skills are often rewarded by the response they get from teachers who find the systematic observational records to be interesting and relevant.

Students

Students can supply useful data for the feedback process. Questionnaires can be used to tap their perceptions, and interviews with them can provide a rich source of information. Students can also operate videotape cameras for the teachers who are undertaking self-analysis.

Self-analysis

This technique has not had the amount of use that it deserves. Theodore Parsons, in the 1960s, developed guides that can be used to analyze one's own videotapes.[26] Minicourses, which were self-instructional units for teachers who wanted to develop new skills, used self-analysis of videotapes guided by a teacher's handbook as the feedback phase of a demonstration-practice strategy.[27] They were successful in helping teachers to change their classroom behavior. Recent emphasis on "reflective teaching" revives the need for thoughtful self-analysis.

ORGANIZATIONAL STRUCTURES AND TEACHER DEVELOPMENT

The way a school—or any organization—is structured influences the types of teacher development and clinical supervision that will be possible within it. Table 2.6 shows various factors that characterize different organizations.

Starting with the "autocratic command" column and moving to the left, one can see historical progression from despotic to democratic forms of governance. Communication patterns move from "down only" to "up and down" and then "across." How we deal with these organizational differences can vary from not recognizing them to treating them as data for designing teacher-development programs.

In the organizational structure labeled "Think Tank," all the staff are "transcendent" in the sense that they are at the level of self-actualization. The organization depends on the individual contributions they make to clients, each other, and society. Let's assume they are all Nobel Laureates, the leaders in their respective fields. Would it make sense to have them punch a time clock, or be closely supervised to make certain they are "working"?

Rather than to "boss," the role of administrators is to provide support and resources to further the endeavors that the staff choose. The role of each staff member is to be a unique specialist "doing his or her own thing," using the creative zeal and insight that led to being selected for this role. The communication patterns are bound to be "across." The notion of talking down to a colleague or taking a problem "up" to the boss seems alien. The goal of staff development is to facilitate the improvement goals that each individual has personally set.

The motivational organization is well illustrated by many of the service clubs that do good things for communities and develop leadership for worthwhile projects. This supportive form of organization emphasizes cooperation, congeniality, and shared leadership. Differences are negotiated through democratic procedures—debating and voting. Staff development activities might emphasize organizational goals, and group participation might be required.

The collegial-collaborative organizations, at least in education, exist on paper more often than they do in school buildings. One is more likely to see mere congeniality than genuine collegiality or collaboration. There is clearly a trend toward the latter, but one is much more apt to find feudal institutions out there than the kind outlined in Table 2.6. The strength of the trend can be assessed by determining whether the organization's teacher-development programs are individualistic or collaborative in nature.

Some Examples of Organizational Forms

The kinds of organizations represented in Table 2.6 exist in many forms. For an example of an autocratic command system, one could study the Ford Motor Company when Henry, Sr., was at the helm or analyze the Family Saud in present-day Saudi Arabia.

The custodial or maintenance system that functioned throughout the Middle Ages was based on land ownership. In present-day China, the word for "feudal" is used to describe the more conservative citizens. The supportive, motivational organization can be

Table 2.6 Characteristics of Seven Kinds of Organizations

	Liberate	Delegate	Participate	Sell	Tell	Yell	Hell
	Transcendent (think tank)	Specialist division of labor	Collegial collaboration	Supportive (motivational)	Custodial (maintenance)	Autocratic command system	Competitive cold war
Depends on	Individual contribution to society	Specialized competence-	Cooperation	Leadership	Economic resources	Power	Winning
Management based on	Providing resources and support	Integration	Togetherness	Support	Material rewards	Authority	Glory
Employee status	Autonomous	Expert	Responsibility	Performance	Security	Obedience	Contestant
Employee psychological result	Self-actualizing and altruistic	Doing your thing	Self-discipline	Participation	Organizational dependency	Personal dependency	Free-floating hostility
Employee needs met	Seeing the effects	Achievement	Self-realization	Higher-order	Maintenance	Subsistence	Victories
Morale measure	Continuing to work doing own thing	Production	Commitment to task and team	Motivation	Satisfaction	Compliance	Ethnocentrism
Basic roles	Unique specialist	Nominal peers Specialty-related	Colleagues Task-related	Partners	Benevolent owner grateful subject	Boss and subordinate	Competitors

(continued)

Table 2.6 (*continued*)

Basic skills	Creativity, surgence, insight	Specialty and complementary	Specialty plus interdisciplinary and collaboration	Serving as a model or good example for others	Majestic wisdom and judgment obedience and compliance	Boss: managing, directing, evaluating Sub: listening, doing, reporting	One-upmanship, debating, blaming, and compromising
Nature of relationship	Mutual respect	Polite and respectful	Open, trusting developing informal, personal	A covenant	Noblesse oblige paternalistic allegiance	Status-determined formal impersonal	Impersonal distant mistrustful
Power distribution	Shared	Nominal half-and-half all power is in own area	Nominal half-and-half flexible according to task need	Shared delegated	Controlled bestowed	Fixed: boss has it all	Nominal half-and-half used to counter and cancel each other
Communication	Across	Task focused restrained	Mutual	Across friendly	Up and down	One way	Across Hostile Distorted
How differences are handled	Writing an article or book	Avoidance compartmentalized into discipline areas	In the open used as information for problem solving	Negotiated	Mediated by the liege	Not recognized	To spar and wage war indirectly through task

Source: This table is derived from a variety of sources. The framework is from Abraham Maslow, *The Farther Reaches of Human Nature* (New York: Viking Press, 1971), pp. 284–286, which in turn draws on Keith Davis, *Human Relations at Work*, 3rd ed. (New York: McGraw-Hill, 1967), p. 480. The notion of a competitive cold war within an organzation was suggested in a speech by Sherman Grinnell in Atlanta, c. 1976. The term "free-floating hostility" is from Meyer Friedman and Ray H. Rosenman, *Type A Behavior and Your Heart* (New York: Knopf, 1974). An earlier version of this table appeared in Keith A. Acheson, *Techniques in the Evaluation of Teachers* (Salem: Confederation of Oregon School Administrators, 1982); the above version is from Keith A. Acheson, "Instructional Leaders for the 1990s: Improving the Analysis of Teaching," *Oregon School Study Council Bulletin* 33, No. 6 (February 1990).

examined on given days of the week at the luncheon meetings of service clubs. Many student organizations operate along similar lines.

Two examples leap to mind to illustrate the specialist division of labor: a medical clinic and a university. A number of modern-day electronic firms combine the compartmentalization of specialists with the autocratic tendencies of the two owners who invented their widget in a garage a few years ago.

The competitive cold war takes over in specialist organizations when there is a budget crunch followed by a scramble for scarce resources. Some universities have had an uncommon amount of experience with this state of affairs.

Collegial collaboration is the form of organization preferred by most educators who have been studying school organizations in recent years. It also represents what they see as the evolving nature of the relationships teachers are seeking with their peers and colleagues (as opposed to traditional supervision and evaluation arrangements). In a number of our graduate courses and workshops, practicing teachers and administrators have been asked if they know of schools that are operated as either autocratic, custodial, supportive, specialist, competitive, or collegial institutions. The answer, in general, appears to be "all of the above."

Effect of Organizational Structure on the Role of Supervisor

The effect of organizational structure on the role of the supervisor is profound. In teacher-development programs based on collegial, collaborative precepts, school principals must modify their role as "boss supervisor" to that of "team-leader supervisor." Communication patterns must change from "top down" to "across." Controversy and conflict among teachers or departments must not be suppressed (the boss has all the answers), but treated as data to be discussed.

The transcendent or collegial-collaborative organizational structure appears to be the kind that many teachers would like. The function of the administration is not to manage what people will do, but to provide assistance to the laureates who are doing the work of the organization, that is, teaching. Going a step beyond autonomy, of course, one can find anarchy.

Discussion of differences implies disagreement. Being able to disagree is not the same as being disagreeable. In the collegial, collaborative organization, disagreeable people may be as disruptive as they are in any other organization. One trait of being disagreeable is always to look for what is wrong without recognizing what is good, what is working well, what is commendable.

Professional Development Schools

Many of the trends in teacher development described in this chapter are exemplified in a new form of organizational structure known as *professional development schools* (PDS).[28] A PDS blends two organizational structures—schools and a local university—for the purpose of teacher development. The teachers fall along the total continuum of development: primarily preservice teachers, but also beginning teachers and veteran teachers with varying amounts of experience.

The primary instructors in a PDS are university instructors and supervisors and school teachers, all working together as a collaborative faculty. Depending on the PDS setting, even preservice teachers can play an instructional role: raising questions for inquiry, applying their knowledge to school reform initiatives, and consulting with peers to improve each other's instruction. In other words, each individual in a PDS—preservice teacher, university teacher educator, school teacher educator—is both a teacher and a learner about the nature of effective instruction.

Applying the chart of organizational structures shown in Table 2.6, we would characterize PDSs as an organizational structure based on collegial collaboration.

The PDS movement grew out of the work of several groups, most notably, the Holmes Group[29] and the National Board for Professional Teaching Standards (described above). These groups realized that school improvement and teacher development needed to be linked if either one was to advance. Additionally, school practice and university-based research needed to be linked.

PDSs provide these linkages because they bring school and university instructors together for a shared purpose, namely, teacher development. As prospective and experienced teachers become more skilled, they are better able to engage in the work of school improvement. Also, as university researchers and school teachers work together to improve the knowledge base of teaching, there is more opportunity to generate knowledge that addresses problems of practice and also to put that new knowledge into practice.

Schools and universities are experimenting with different types of PDS models.[30] One of their commonalities is clinical supervision, although it might be called by other names, such as mentoring or coaching. For example, Lynne Miller and David Silvernail described a PDS involving a partnership between the University of Southern Maine and a local school (Wells Junior High School).[31] The teacher education program is jointly directed by the two institutions.

All students in the program (called *interns*) do a 1-year internship at the school. Supervision is provided by both university and school-based site coordinators. In addition, they receive systematic coaching from their cooperating teachers, which include pre- and postconferences around a teaching episode.

An interesting feature of this particular PDS is a supervisory process called the *videotaped observation conference*. It has the following steps:

1. The intern teaches a lesson which is videotaped.
2. The intern, the cooperating teacher, and the supervisor view the videotape of the lesson; only the intern comments and is encouraged to analyze his/her teaching.
3. The cooperating teacher and the intern have a conference, which is videotaped by the supervisor.
4. The intern leaves and the cooperating teacher and the supervisor view the tape of the conference; only the cooperating teacher comments and is encouraged to analyze his/her coaching.
5. The cooperating teacher and the supervisor discuss the conference.[32]

This supervisory process exemplifies the collegial collaboration that characterizes the organizational structure of a PDS. School and university staff members work together to promote interns' learning. Also, supervision is an opportunity for the school and university staff members to develop their own professional skills.

Research on the effectiveness of professional development schools is scant, but the available evidence is demonstrating positive effects.[33] Efforts are underway to ensure that teacher education programs that incorporate this innovative organizational structure meet high-quality standards.[34]

NOTES

1. Darling-Hammond, L. (1994). Developing professional development schools: Early lessons, challenge, and promise. In L. Darling-Hammond (Ed.), *Professional development schools: Schools for developing a profession* (pp. 1–27). New York: Teachers College Press, p. 4.

2. Freidson, E. (1986). *Professional powers: A study of the institutionalization of formal knowledge.* Chicago: University of Chicago Press.

3. Hoyle, E. (1980). Professionalization and deprofessionalization in education. In E. Hoyle & J. Megarry (Eds.), *World yearbook of education, 1980: The professional development of teachers.* London: Kegan Page.

4. Hoyle, E. (1995). In L. W. Anderson (Ed.), *International encyclopedia of teaching and teacher education* (2nd ed., pp. 11–15). Oxford, England: Pergamon, p. 12.

5. Leithwood, K. A. (1992). The principal's role in teacher development. In M. Fullan & A. Hargreaves (Eds.), *Teacher development and educational change* (pp. 86–103). London: Falmer.

6. Ball, S., & Goodson, I. (Eds.). (1985). *Teachers' lives and careers.* Lewes, England: Falmer; Huberman, M. (1988). Teachers' careers and school improvement. *Journal of Curriculum Studies, 20*(2), 119–132; Sikes, P. J., Measor, L., & Woods, P. (1985). *Teacher careers: Crises and continuities.* Lewes, England: Falmer.

7. Hunt, D. (1966). A conceptual systems change model and its application to education. In O. J. Harvey (Ed.), *Experience, structure and adaptability* (pp. 277–302). New York: Springer-Verlag; Kohlberg, L. (1970). *Moral development.* New York: Holt, Rinehart & Winston; Loevinger, J. (1966). The meaning and measurement of ego development. *American Psychologist, 21,* 195–206.

8. Berliner, D. C. (1995). Teacher expertise. In L. W. Anderson (Ed.), *International Encyclopedia of Teaching and Teacher Education* (2nd ed., pp. 46–52). Oxford, England: Pergamon.

9. *Ibid,* p. 48.

10. Fuller, F. F. (1969). Concerns of teachers: A developmental conceptualization. *American Educational Research Journal, 6,* 207–226.

11. Gall, M. D., & Vojtek, R. O. (1994). *Planning for effective staff development: Six research-based models.* Eugene, OR: ERIC Clearinghouse on Educational Management. (ERIC Document Reproduction Service No. ED372464). For another synthesis of literature and practice, see: Sparks, D., & Loucks-Horsley, S. (1989). Five models of staff development for teachers. *Journal of Staff Development, 10*(4), 40–57.

12. Davidson, N., Henkelman, J., & Stasinowsky, H. (1993). Findings from a NSDC status survey of staff development and staff developers. *Journal of Staff Development, 14*(4), 58–63.

13. Showers, B., Joyce, B., & Bennett, B. (1987). Synthesis of research on staff development: A framework for future study and a state-of-the-art analysis. *Educational Leadership, 45*(3), 77–87.

14. For a more detailed description of action research, see: Mills, G. E. (2000). *Action research: A guide for the teacher researcher.* Upper Saddle River, NJ: Merrill.

15. Schmuck, R. A., & Runkel, P. J. (1994). *The handbook of organization development in schools and colleges* (4th ed.). Prospect Heights, IL: Waveland Press.

16. Fullan, M. G. (2001). *The new meaning of educational change.* (3rd ed.). New York: Teachers College Press.

17. Because the work of these organizations is ongoing, we recommend that you contact their websites in order to get the most up-to-date information about their efforts to develop standards for teaching and teacher education.

18. The Web home page for the National Board for Professional Teaching Standards is http://www.nbpts.org/. From this home page, you can access many types of information about the National Board's philosophy and operations.

19. http://www.nbpts.org/seeking/sample.html

20. http://www.nbpts.org/seeking/ov-eam.html

21. Bohen, D. B. (2001). Strengthening teaching through national certification. *Educational Leadership, 58*(8), 50–53.

22. Leithwood, *op. cit.*

23. Leithwood, *op. cit.,* p. 99.

24. Stigler, J. W., & Hiebert, J. (1999). *The teaching gap.* New York: The Free Press. See, in particular, Chapter 7.

25. Little, J. W. (1990). Conditions of professional development in secondary schools. In M. W. McLaughlin, J. E. Talbert, & N. Bascia (Eds.) *The contexts of teaching in secondary schools: Teachers' realities* (pp. 187–223). New York: Teachers College Press.

26. Parsons, T. (1968). Guided self-analysis system for professional development education series. Berkeley: University of California Press.

27. Borg, W. R., Kelley, M. L., Langer, P., & Gall, M. D. (1970). *The Minicourse: A microteaching approach to teacher education.* Beverly Hills, CA: Macmillan Educational Services.

28. Book, C. (1996). Professional development schools. In J. P. Sikula, T. J. Buttery, & E. Guyton (Eds.), *Handbook of research on teacher education* (2nd ed., pp. 194–210). New York: Macmillan.

29. Holmes Group. (1990). *Tomorrow's schools.* East Lansing, MI: Author.

30. For example, see: Byrd, D. M., & McIntyre, D. J. (1999). *Research on professional development schools: Teacher education yearbook VII.* Thousand Oaks, CA: Corwin.

31. Miller, L., & Silvernail, D. L. (1994). Wells Junior High School: Evolution of a professional development school. In L. Darling-Hammond (Ed.), *Professional development schools: Schools for developing a profession* (pp. 28–49). New York: Teachers College Press.

32. *Ibid,* p. 39.

33. Teitel, L. (2001). How professional development schools make a difference: A review of research. *ATE Newsletter, 34*(1), 1, 6–7.

34. Levine, M. (Ed.). (1998). Designing standards that work for professional development schools. Washington, DC: National Council for Accreditation of Teacher Education.

Chapter 3

Using Clinical Supervision to Promote Effective Teaching

Author's Note

What does it takes to be a good teacher? It's an important question, so I don't mind that I've spent much of my career trying to answer it.

Among other approaches, I've tried addressing the question from the perspective of a student—a role I was in recently. My goal was to learn how to create a website, so it would be easy for people to access my vita and working papers. I defined a good teacher as anyone who could help me toward that goal.

I started by attending a workshop. The instructor tried to be helpful, but he had too many students. His presentation was too abstract and general for my purposes. When I got confused, there was no opportunity to ask questions.

Subsequently, I approached several colleagues who specialize in educational technology. One of them, Irene Smith, was especially helpful. She gave me a simple software program (Claris Home Page), and suggested I work through its tutorial and come to her whenever I had questions. Sure enough, I had questions—many of them. And Irene had the answers—clear answers. In addition, she was supportive and encouraging and delighted when I showed signs of learning.

In short, Irene was effective because she was knowledgeable, supportive, clear, approachable, and sensitive to my individual learning needs. I suspect that other intrinsically motivated learners would want their teachers to have the same qualities.

The qualities of a good elementary or secondary teacher are harder to define. Curriculum goals are often ambiguous, and students show up for class not necessarily because they want to, but because they must. Also, school-age students can't rely on their own assessment of learning progress (as I did), but must take tests designed by the teacher—or by the teacher's district or state.

For many decades, researchers have sought to define what it means to be a good teacher under these difficult conditions—ambiguous curriculum goals, unmotivated students, imposed testing. In this chapter, we review what the researchers have learned. I think you'll find that most of the qualities of good teaching they've identified are consistent with those you'd want from a teacher as you pursue your own learning goals.

In my opinion, the one thing supervisors cannot do is duck the question of what it means to be a good teacher by saying that it's impossible to answer, because all teachers are unique. At some level, this might be true, but in fact teachers are expected to follow certain norms that imply certain notions of good teaching.

You undoubtedly have some conception of the qualities you expect to see in a good teacher. We invite you to make explicit what these qualities are, and then compare them with the qualities identified in the research literature that we review in this chapter.

MDG

In various research studies I have been a part of over the past fifty years, I have found that many popular, respected practices were not supported by research. Indeed, <u>practice often went in a direction opposite from the existing research evidence</u>. Thus, while educational practice kept moving in the direction of the progressive, student-centered approaches, the research evidence kept growing in support of traditional, teacher-centered learning.

—Jeanne Chall[1]

INTRODUCTION

We reviewed various models of clinical supervision in Chapter 1. One of their common elements is the goal of helping teachers become more effective. But what does "effective" mean?

The same question arises in connection with the standards for the teaching profession being developed by various agencies and commissions. These standards, which we discussed in Chapter 2, represent a consensus of beliefs about what constitutes an effective teacher. However, the basis for these beliefs—and therefore the underlying meaning of teacher effectiveness—is not always clear.

One basis for deciding what it means to be an effective teacher is the empirical knowledge that is generated by researchers who study teachers and the learning process. However, some educators reject this approach by arguing that the criteria of effective teaching differ for every instructional situation and every teacher, and therefore no empirical generalizations are possible. We are sympathetic to this argument, but our experience and examination of the research literature suggests otherwise.

As a demonstration of this point, we suggest that you list five characteristics of a good elementary, secondary, or college teacher. (You can elaborate on this task by listing five characteristics of an *ineffective* teacher.) Most educators find this task relatively easy. Moreover, they usually agree with one another's lists. Rarely do we find a controversial characteristic—one that some educators think represents good teaching and other educators think represents bad teaching. Disagreement, if it occurs, usually concerns the relative importance of characteristics.

Richard and Patricia Schmuck interviewed more than two hundred teenage students to find out, among other things, what they considered to be the characteristics of good and bad teaching.[2] Here are the most frequently occurring answers. To what extent do these characteristics agree with your list?

Characteristics of Good Teaching

- Gives students respect, is patient, and easy to get along with.
- Makes the subject interesting and fun by involving students in activities and demonstrations.
- Tells jokes and smiles a lot—good sense of humor.
- Listens to students' questions and makes changes in class to help students learn.

Characteristics of Bad Teaching

- Low respect for students, lacks patience, and treats you like you are stupid.
- Seldom smiles, very serious and stern, and issues either too harsh or too permissive discipline.
- Doesn't care about or pay attention to individuals; not helpful.
- Doesn't explain well, lazy, hands out worksheets and tests; you have to learn everything on your own.
- Has favorites; favors the smart students or one sex over the other.

Before you finalize your list of characteristics of good teaching, we recommend that you read the research findings in this chapter. To understand the research, however, you need to know something about how it is conducted. Often, researchers compare the teaching practices of more effective teachers and less effective teachers. This type of inquiry is commonly called causal-comparative or correlational research. Another research paradigm is to have a group of teachers (the experimental group) try a particular teaching practice. A different group of teachers (the control group) is asked to follow their usual practices or try a different teaching practice. If the experimental teaching method produces superior results, it is considered effective. This type of inquiry is commonly called experimental research.

In correlational research, it is necessary to identify a criterion by which to define the more effective and less effective teachers whose teaching practices are to be compared. Similarly, in experimental research, it is necessary to identify a criterion to determine the relative effectiveness of the experimental and control groups.

Researchers have used various criteria in their studies. These criteria reflect different perspectives about what is important in schooling. If you do not agree with the criteria used by the researchers, you probably will disagree with their conclusions about what constitutes effective teaching. Because the criteria are so important to understanding this research, we have organized the following review into sections that correspond to different criteria of teaching effectiveness.

EFFECTIVE TEACHING OF ACADEMIC KNOWLEDGE AND SKILLS

Much of the general public and many educators believe that the major purpose of school is to help students acquire the knowledge and skills associated with reading, mathematics, history, geography, music, art, foreign languages, and other academic disciplines studied in the K–12 curriculum. From this perspective, a teacher is more or less effective depending on how much of the academic curriculum is mastered by his or her students.

The usual research procedure to determine how much is learned by the students of a particular teacher is to give the entire class a standardized achievement test before and after a period of instruction (usually at the start and end of a school year). Teachers whose students make substantial gains in their test scores are considered more effective, whereas teachers whose students make small gains are considered less effective.

The meaning of teacher effectiveness in this type of research obviously depends on the achievement test that is used. If a teacher's students make large gains on a reading test, the teacher can be judged to be effective in teaching reading, but that does not mean he is necessarily effective in teaching mathematics. It would be necessary to give the students a mathematics achievement test to make this determination.

In short, the achievement test used by a researcher places limits on the generalizability of the teaching methods that are found to be effective. Teachers who are effective in teaching reading might rely on method A more extensively than teachers who are less effective in teaching this subject. However, this does not mean necessarily that method A is effective for teaching another academic subject, such as mathematics. In the following research review, we emphasize teaching methods that were found to be effective across at least several school subjects.

Nine Teacher Characteristics Associated with Gains in Student Academic Achievement

Barak Rosenshine and Norma Furst synthesized the research that was done on teacher effectiveness up until approximately 1970.[3] They identified nine characteristics of teachers whose students make greater gains in academic achievement than students of other teachers. Those characteristics are:

1. clarity.
2. variety in use of materials and methods.
3. enthusiasm.
4. task-oriented, businesslike approach to instruction.
5. avoidance of harsh criticism.
6. indirect teaching style.
7. emphasis on teaching content covered on the criterion achievement test.
8. use of structuring statements that provide an overview for what is about to happen or has happened.
9. use of questions at multiple cognitive levels.

Research studies reported after 1970 have continued to demonstrate the effectiveness of these teacher characteristics in promoting student learning. Procedures for observing each characteristic are described in Unit 4.

Direct and Indirect Teaching

Ned Flanders initiated an important line of research on effective teaching in the 1960s.[4] He identified two contrasting styles of teaching—direct and indirect. Direct teaching is characterized by teacher reliance on:

1. lecture.
2. criticism.
3. justification of authority.
4. giving directions.

Indirect teaching is characterized by teacher reliance on:

1. asking questions.
2. accepting students' feelings.
3. acknowledging students' ideas.
4. giving praise and encouragement.

Many research studies have found that students of "indirect" teachers learn more and have better attitudes toward learning than students of "direct" teachers.[5] However, Flanders believes that both direct and indirect behaviors are necessary in good teaching. For example, teachers can effectively use a direct teaching strategy, such as lecture and demonstration, to clarify a difficult curriculum topic. Even in this situation, however, the teacher can make the lecture and demonstration more indirect by asking questions occasionally to determine whether students are following the presentation. Effective teaching behavior, then, involves appropriate use of indirect teaching techniques, not total reliance on them.

The Explicit Teaching Model

Researchers have made a concerted effort to identify teacher behaviors that facilitate student learning in specific curriculum areas. Much of this research has focused on reading and mathematics instruction at the primary and elementary school levels, because mastery of these subjects is critical to subsequent academic achievement.

Barak Rosenshine synthesized the findings of this body of research into an organized model of teaching, which he calls "explicit teaching."[6] The teaching is "explicit" because the teaching goals and steps are predictable and can be clearly analyzed and described. The six parts of the explicit teaching model are described in Table 3.1. You will note that the first five parts of the model correspond approximately to a daily lesson plan. The sixth part—review—is incorporated into the lesson plan at periodic intervals. There is a striking correspondence between the explicit teaching model and Madeline Hunter's model of effective teaching.[7] Her model, sometimes called Instructional Theory into Practice (ITIP), has had a major influence on American education. The seven components of the model and their counterpart in the explicit teaching model (in parentheses) are as follows:

1. anticipatory set (review).
2. stating of objectives (presentation).
3. information input (presentation).
4. modeling (presentation).
5. checking for understanding (presentation; correction and feedback).

Table 3.1   The Six Elements of the Explicit Teaching Model

1. *Review.* Each day, start the lesson by correcting the previous night's homework and reviewing what students have recently been taught.

2. *Presentation.* Tell students the goals of today's lesson. Then present new information a little at a time, modeling procedures, giving clear examples, and checking often to make sure students understand.

3. *Guided practice.* Allow students to practice using the new information under the teacher's direction; ask many questions that give students abundant opportunities to correctly repeat or explain the procedure or concept that has just been taught. Student participation should be active until all students are able to respond correctly.

4. *Correction and feedback.* During guided practice, give students a great deal of feedback. When students answer incorrectly, reteach the lesson if necessary. When students answer correctly, explain why the answer was right. It is important that feedback be immediate and thorough.

5. *Independent practice.* Next, allow students to practice using the new information on their own. The teacher should be available to give short answers to students' questions, and students should be permitted to help each other.

6. *Weekly and monthly reviews.* At the beginning of each week, the teacher should review the previous week's lesson. At the end of the month, the teacher should review what students have learned during the last four weeks. It is important that students not be allowed to forget past lessons once they have moved on to new material.

Source: Adapted from: Rosenshine, B. V. (1986). Synthesis of research on explicit teaching. *Educational Leadership, 43*(7), 60–68.

6. guided and independent practice (guided practice; independent practice).

7. closure (weekly and monthly review).

Hunter based her model on a different, older base of research knowledge than did Rosenshine, yet they drew similar conclusions about the elements of effective teaching.

Rosenshine claims that the explicit teaching model is applicable to any "well-structured" school subject, such as "mathematical procedures and computations, reading decoding, explicit reading procedures such as distinguishing fact from opinion, science facts and concepts, social studies facts and concepts, map skills, grammatical concepts and rules, and foreign language vocabulary and grammar."[8] These examples represent what is generally known as lower-cognitive objectives. Effective teaching of higher-cognitive objectives requires different methods, which are discussed in the next section. Rosenshine further delimited the situations for which the explicit teaching model is effective:

> It would be a mistake to say that this small-step approach applies to all students or all situations. It is most important for young learners, slow learners, and for all learners when the material is new, difficult, or hierarchical. In these situations, relatively short presentations are followed by student practice. However, when teaching older, brighter students, or when teaching in the middle of a unit, the steps are larger, that is, the presentations are longer, less time is spent in checking for understanding or in guided practice, and more independent practice can be done as homework because the students do not need as much help and supervision.[9]

These qualifications about the use of the explicit teaching model have an important implication for the supervision of teachers. Specifically, they imply that a supervisor should not use the explicit teaching model, or any other teaching model, as an absolute set of criteria for evaluating a teacher or for setting improvement goals. Rather, the supervisor needs first to determine the teacher's instructional context through a planning conference (see Chapter 7). Then the supervisor and teacher can discuss appropriate teaching methods to use in that context. This discussion, in turn, provides a basis for determining which aspects of the teacher's behavior to record during the observation phase of the supervision cycle.

Effective Teaching of Thinking Skills

A distinction between lower-cognitive and higher-cognitive learning outcomes is often made. In Bloom's taxonomy, for example, six cognitive levels of learning are distinguished.[10] The knowledge, comprehension, and application levels are generally considered to be lower-cognitive learning outcomes, whereas the analysis, synthesis, and evaluation levels are higher-cognitive learning outcomes. (These outcomes sometimes are called "thinking skills.") Many educators are concerned about the development of students' thinking skills in addition to their mastery of the basic school curriculum. Nancy Cole observed that lower-cognitive and higher-cognitive objectives in the curriculum reflect different theories about learning and different measurement approaches.[11] With respect to lower-cognitive learning, Cole observed:

> By the 1960s, behavioral psychology dominated conceptions of learning in psychology and in education. The learning theory with which a generation of educators grew up came directly from this field. It was heavily based on studies of animal learning and was closely connected with the learning of specific, discrete skills described as precise, well-delimited behaviors. . . .
>
> The theories that supported behavioral psychology were well suited to the political times of increasing public concern that children were not learning to read, write, nor perform basic arithmetic operations. There was also public concern that students were not learning basic factual information. The result of this merging of theoretical and political orientation was a decade (the seventies) in which the strongly dominant conception of educational achievement in public discussion was in terms of specific, separate, basic skills and facts.[12]

Much of the research that led to the development of the explicit teaching model described above involved this conception of learning.

Cole observed that another conception of learning recently has come into prominence:

> Alongside the conception of achievement as mastery of basic skills and facts, and often competing with it, stands a dramatically different conception of educational achievement. This conception focuses on a more complex level of achievement—the achievement of higher order skills (using such terms as critical thinking or problem solving) and of advanced knowledge of subjects (using words such as understanding or expertise).[13]

Measurement experts are currently working to develop tests that assess students' learning of thinking skills. These tests are strikingly different from the multiple-choice response tests traditionally used to assess student achievement.[14]

If you and the teacher value the teaching of thinking skills, you will need to decide which teaching practices and assessment techniques are effective for this purpose. Research on this problem is still fragmentary, but it does provide general guidance.

Discussion Method

The discussion method is, at this time, the best validated approach for promoting higher cognitive learning.[15] Most of this research, however, has involved college students and other adult learners. There is no reason why younger students would not benefit from discussion teaching, but it might be more difficult to create the necessary classroom conditions. For example, M. D. Gall and Joyce Gall stated that the essential elements of a discussion are small group size (six to eight students) and students talking to each other rather than to the teacher.[16] The teacher can set the problem for discussion, but then serves primarily as moderator and facilitator of student-to-student interaction. We, and others, have found it possible to train even young students in discussion skills and to organize them into small groups.

Higher-Cognitive Questions

Another teaching practice to promote the development of thinking skills is asking higher-cognitive questions. These questions can be asked in a variety of instructional contexts: in discussions, in inquiry teaching, in reviewing what students have read (i.e., the traditional recitation), and even interspersed in a lecture or demonstration.

Researchers have not yet determined for certain the effectiveness of higher-cognitive questions. Philip Winne reviewed the research and concluded that it made no difference to student learning whether the teacher emphasized higher-cognitive or lower-cognitive questions.[17] Doris Redfield and Elaine Rousseau reviewed essentially the same research, but concluded that teacher emphasis on higher-cognitive questions led to more learning.[18] Complicating the picture is Barak Rosenshine's review of three major classroom studies, from which he concluded that lower-cognitive questions were more effective.[19] Also complicating the picture is that most of the studies included in the reviews did not differentiate the effects of higher-cognitive questions on thinking skills and on lower-cognitive learning outcomes.

Our view of the situation is that higher-cognitive questions are probably necessary, but not sufficient, for the development of students' ability to think. Higher-cognitive questions cue students that thinking is expected and important. However, these questions might be ineffective if the student is unable to respond appropriately. For example, the three studies reviewed by Rosenshine were done in primary-grade classrooms in low-achieving urban schools. Higher-cognitive questions, in the absence of any other intervention, might very well have no effect on—or even frustrate—these students. By contrast, Christiaan Hamaker found in his review of research that higher-cognitive questions inserted in reading passages had a consistently positive effect on students' thinking skills.[20] Most of this research involved college students, which is a population that would be able to handle the response demands of questions at the higher-cognitive levels.

For younger students, we think teachers should ask higher-cognitive questions routinely, but also provide appropriate instruction and conditions for answering them. This means, for example, modeling the appropriate thinking processes, which can be done by "thinking aloud" for students. Also in contrast to explicit teaching, the teacher needs to give students opportunities for self-expression (rather than carefully defined tasks), substantial projects and tasks (rather than drill-type worksheets), and elaborated, open-ended feedback (rather than correct–incorrect feedback).

Constructivist Teaching

In recent years, researchers and practitioners have come to conceptualize the teaching of thinking skills as a process of helping the learner construct deep understandings of a particular academic discipline. This type of teaching is sometimes called constructivist teaching, as Jacqueline and Martin Brooks explain:

> *Traditionally, learning has been thought to be a 'mimetic' activity, a process that involves students repeating, or miming, newly presented information . . . in reports or on quizzes and tests. Constructivist teaching practices, on the other hand, help learners to internalize and reshape, or transform new information. Transformation occurs through the creation of new understandings . . . that result from the emergence of new cognitive structures . . . . For example, . . . many high school students read Hamlet, but not all of them transform their prior notions of power, relationships, or greed. Deep understanding occurs when the presence of new information prompts the emergence or enhancement of cognitive structures that enable us to rethink our prior ideas.[21]*

Although constructivist teaching methods appear to have merit, little is known about how effective they actually are in helping students develop deep understanding of academic concepts and principles. There is concern, though, that these methods might be difficult to implement in conventional classroom settings.[22] In particular, Lee Shulman and Kathleen Quinlan have reviewed research indicating that the quality of teaching for understanding is dependent on the teacher's own understanding of the subject matter and ability to transform that understanding into accurate representations (e.g., examples, models, and explanations of concepts such as ecology in biology, the preterite tense in Spanish, and acceleration in mathematics).[23] In addition to accuracy, the representations should connect with students' prior understandings.

We suspect that many teachers have not had the opportunity to study their academic discipline in sufficient depth to create powerful representations of key disciplinary concepts and use other constructivist teaching methods effectively. In fact, a substantial percentage of teachers are "misassigned," meaning that they teach subjects for which they hold no teaching license or endorsement during some or all of a school day.[24]

Although research on constructivist teaching is fragmentary, it appears to have promise for developing students' ability to think. For certain teachers, it might be a worthwhile professional goal to learn about this model and experiment with its use.[25]

Effective Use of Time in Teaching

Classroom instructional time is a limited resource. Researchers have found that teachers' use of this resource affects how well students master the curriculum.

One aspect of time is *allocated time,* which is the amount of time that the teacher provides for instruction on each subject or topic. David Berliner and his colleagues found that some elementary teachers spend as little as 16 minutes per average day on mathematics instruction, whereas other teachers spend as much as 50 minutes per average day.[26] The range of allocated time was even greater in reading instruction: from a low of 45 minutes per average day to a high of more than 2 hours per average day. Walter Borg concluded from his review of research on allocated time that the more time a teacher allocates to instruction in a particular content area, the more students learn about that content area.[27]

If allocated time is the focus of supervision, the supervisor and teacher can review how the teacher plans the amount of time to be spent on each subject during a typical school day. In secondary school instruction, this type of planning is not relevant because the length of class periods and course subjects are fixed. However, most secondary teachers have discretion about allocation of time for particular topics—for example, in a U.S. history class, how much time to spend on the Civil War versus the Reconstruction period following the war. Similarly, the teacher might have discretion about how much time to allocate to historical facts versus historical concepts. The teacher and supervisor can discuss alternative time allocation patterns and their respective merits.

Students are seldom attentive during the total time allocated for each subject. The percentage of allocated time that students are attentive is sometimes called *engaged time* or *at-task time*. Walter Borg concluded from the review of research mentioned above that classes with a high percentage of at-task time have better academic achievement than classes with a low percentage of at-task time. For this reason, at-task time is a frequent focus of clinical supervision. Chapters 10 and 12 present procedures for collecting observational data on this important instructional variable.

If students' at-task time is found to be low, the supervisor and teacher should consider methods for improving it. One possibility is for teachers to increase substantive interaction with students. (Substantive interaction involves explaining content to students, asking them questions, giving feedback, and providing assistance during seat work.) We make this suggestion because Charles Fisher and colleagues found that teachers who had more substantive interaction with their students had a higher percentage of student at-task time.[28] Their research involved elementary teaching, but it seems reasonable that a similar relationship would be found in secondary school teaching.

A high rate of substantive interaction might not be necessary if students are motivated and have good independent learning skills. Students who are lacking in these characteristics, however, can easily get off task if left to work on their own for long periods of time. For these students, substantive interaction with the teacher is likely to be effective.

Homework extends the amount of possible time that students can be engaged in mastering the curriculum. Harris Cooper found in his extensive review of the research on homework that it has relatively little effect on elementary school students' achievement, but a substantial effect on the achievement of older students.[29] The supervisor and teacher can review the teacher's homework policy to determine whether homework is desirable for his or her students; and if so, the amount and type of homework that should be assigned, and how it should be reviewed in class and graded.

Generic Guidelines for Good Teaching

Jere Brophy recently synthesized the literature on teaching to derive a set of principles that teachers can use to design and deliver effective instruction.[30] The principles draw, in part, from the research that we reviewed above. In addition, they draw from theory and

Table 3.2 Generic Guidelines of Good Teaching

1. *Supportive classroom climate.* Students learn best within cohesive and caring learning environments.
2. *Opportunity to learn.* Students learn more when most of the available time is allocated to curriculum-related activities and the classroom management system emphasizes maintaining students' engagement in those activities.
3. *Curricular alignment.* All components of the curriculum are aligned to create a cohesive program for accomplishing instructional purposes and goals.
4. *Establishing learning orientations.* Teachers can prepare students for learning by providing an initial structure to clarify intended outcomes and cue desired learning strategies.
5. *Coherent content.* To facilitate meaningful learning and retention, content is explained clearly and developed with emphasis on its structure and connections.
6. *Thoughtful discourse.* Questions are planned to engage students in sustained discourse structured around powerful ideas.
7. *Practice and application activities.* Students need sufficient opportunities to practice and apply what they are learning, and to receive improvement-oriented feedback.
8. *Scaffolding students' task engagement.* The teacher provides whatever assistance students need to enable them to engage in learning activities productively.
9. *Strategy teaching.* The teacher models and instructs students in learning and self-regulation strategies.
10. *Cooperative learning.* Students often benefit from working in pairs or small groups to construct understandings or help one another master skills.
11. *Goal-oriented assessment.* The teacher uses a variety of formal and informal assessment methods to monitor progress toward learning goals.
12. *Achievement expectations.* The teacher establishes and follows through on appropriate expectations for learning outcomes.

Source: Brophy, J. (2001). Introduction. In J. Brophy (Ed.), *Advances in research on teaching* (Vol. 8, pp. 1–23). Oxford: JAI Elsevier.

research on curriculum-instruction-assessment alignment, social-constructivist instruction, and standards-based curriculum. The principles do not define a single model of teaching (e.g., explicit teaching), but instead are at a level of generality that can accommodate various teaching methods, school subjects, and grade levels.

The principles are stated succinctly in Table 3.2. To fully understand their meaning and research findings on which they are based, you and the teachers whom you supervise will find it helpful to read one of the sources in which they are presented.[31] This reading should renew your appreciation for the complexity and subtlety of the instructional process. Also, it should stimulate teachers to generate additional ideas for improving their instruction.

EFFECTIVE DEVELOPMENT OF STUDENT ATTITUDES AND MOTIVATION TO LEARN

Attitudes and learning motivation involve the affective domain of education. They are not easy terms to define, but their manifestations are easy to recognize. We usually can tell through observation whether students are eagerly involved in a learning task, bored by it, or repelled by it. Also, most students, if asked, will tell you which subjects they like and dislike.

Researchers generally distinguish three components of attitudes: beliefs, feelings, and actions. For example, a student who has a positive attitude toward mathematics might believe that math plays an important role in the world of work, might experience positive feelings when working on a challenging math problem, and might act by choosing to learn something new about mathematics rather than engaging in some other activity. Of the three components of attitudes, the most observable—and probably the most important—is action.

By observing how students act in situations that allow choice, we can tell fairly well whether they have a positive or negative attitude toward an "object" (a person, event, book, place, etc.). A positive attitude is manifested by choosing to approach the object, whereas a negative attitude is manifested by choosing to avoid the object. School attitudes can be internalized at different levels of personality. At a superficial level of internalization, the student is motivated to learn, but only with proper stimulation by the teacher. At the deepest level of internalization, the attitude has become an integral part of the student's personality. We can say that the attitude has become a value because it motivates much of the student's life without external prompting. David Krathwohl and colleagues developed a taxonomy that differentiated the various levels at which attitudes can be internalized.[32]

Each of us has many different attitudes. In other words, we have opinions and feelings about virtually everything with which we come into contact. With respect to education, students usually have an attitude toward each subject they study, toward their teachers, toward their school, and even toward themselves (sometimes called academic self-concept or academic self-esteem).

The development of positive academic attitudes is an important outcome of instruction. One of the most famous of educators, John Dewey, made this point compellingly:

> *Perhaps the greatest of all pedagogical fallacies is the notion that a person learns only the particular thing he is studying at the time. Collateral learning in the way of formation of enduring attitudes of likes and dislikes, may be and often is much more important than the spelling lesson or lesson in geography or history that is learned. For these attitudes are fundamentally what counts in the future.[33]*

In the public school curriculum, academic knowledge and skills are given more emphasis than attitudes, yet some instructional outcomes involving attitudes can be found. Teachers of social studies typically want students to develop informed beliefs about important social issues and to act as responsible citizens. Teachers of foreign languages typically want students to appreciate the cultures that speak the language they are teaching. And teachers of scientific disciplines want students to value scientific inquiry and to develop an appreciation of the natural world.

Which teaching methods are effective for helping students develop these and other attitudes? Research has been done to answer this question, but the findings are not yet definitive. Therefore, they should be presented as tentative when used in clinical supervision.

Researchers have investigated the effects of teacher enthusiasm on student attitudes. A. Guy Larkins and colleagues reviewed this research and concluded that teaching with enthusiasm generally promotes positive student attitudes.[34] Procedures for observing a teacher's level of enthusiasm are described in Chapter 11.

Another teaching technique whose effect on student attitudes has been investigated is use of praise. N. L. Gage reviewed this research and concluded that teacher praise has a positive effect on student attitudes.[35] More recent research suggests that the effectiveness of teacher praise depends on its content and context.[36] Guidelines for effective use of praise are presented in Chapter 9.

Wilbert McKeachie and James Kulik reviewed research at the college level comparing the effectiveness of the lecture method and the discussion method in changing attitudes.[37] They concluded that discussion is the more effective method. In a review of research involving younger students, Joyce and M. D. Gall similarly concluded that the discussion method has positive effects on the attitudes of elementary and high school students. The Galls claim that the distinguishing characteristic of discussion is its emphasis on student-to-student interaction, which is lacking in lecture and other common methods such as recitation and seatwork.[38]

Although discussion is effective in developing student attitudes, it has the potential to be misused. For example, discussion can change students' attitudes by exposing them to new information that changes their belief system (a component of attitudes). Therefore, the teacher must be careful that students do not learn inaccurate information. Another pitfall is that a discussion can reinforce existing negative attitudes, such as racial prejudice, if all the students in the group feel the same way about the topic being discussed.[39] This problem usually can be avoided by forming heterogeneous discussion groups.

Cooperative learning has become a popular teaching method in recent years. It is similar to the discussion method in that students contribute to each other's learning by working together in small groups. It differs from the discussion method, however, because it usually requires the completion of a specific academic task—such as a list of ideas, a visual display, or the solution to a problem—that can be evaluated and graded. By contrast, discussion does not usually have a tangible goal that can be evaluated, and students are not required to cooperate with each other, except by listening carefully to each other and avoiding personal attacks.

Research on cooperative learning has found that it is effective both for improving students' academic achievement and for developing important social attitudes. Robert Slavin, who reviewed this body of research, stated that these attitudinal outcomes include: increased liking and respect among students of different racial or ethnic backgrounds, improved social acceptance of mainstreamed students by their classmates, more friendships among students, gains in self-esteem, and liking of school and of the subject being discussed.[40]

Student motivation to learn is not quite the same thing as an attitude, but it is similar. We can think of motivation to learn as how the student feels about becoming engaged in instruction, whereas an attitude is how the student feels following instruction.

Jere Brophy identified various teaching methods that can increase student motivation to learn. The methods stem from two basic principles:

> *In order to motivate their students to learn, teachers need both to help their students appreciate the value of academic activities and to make sure that the students can succeed in these activities if they apply reasonable effort.[41]*

For example, if students believe that they are likely to fail their general science course even if they apply effort, they will lack motivation and develop a negative attitude toward the course and toward science generally. Also, if students do not see the relevance of science to their lives or do not value the consequences of doing well in the course (e.g., a good grade, teacher and parent approval), they will not be motivated to learn. Teaching methods that allow students to be successful or that show them the importance of the topic being studied are likely to be effective in improving students' motivation to learn.

To summarize, various teaching methods can improve students' attitudes and motivation to learn. The implications for clinical supervision are clear. If the teacher is concerned about his or her students' attitude to instruction, the supervisor and teacher can plan to collect observation data on the teacher's use of the practices described above—enthusiastic teaching style, praise, discussion and cooperative learning, the opportunity for students to experience academic success, and helping students see the relevance and value of learning. What all these teaching practices have in common is the development of a positive classroom climate involving all participants: teacher with students and students with each other.

TEACHER EFFECTIVENESS IN RESPONDING TO STUDENT DIVERSITY

The typical criterion in research on teacher effectiveness is how much the teacher's class as a *whole* learns over a particular period of time. Thus, we would conclude that a teacher is effective if the mean score of the class on an achievement test increases from its first administration to the second. However, you need to realize that the gain might result from a small number of students benefiting substantially from instruction, while other students learn relatively little or nothing at all.

Some researchers deal with this problem by investigating whether teachers behave differently toward different groups of students. Other research concerns whether different teaching practices are effective for different groups of students. For example, teaching method A might be effective for male students, whereas teaching method B is effective for female students.

In this section, we briefly review major findings on effective teaching of different types of students present in a typical classroom.

Effective Teaching of Students Who Differ in Achievement Level

Thomas Good reviewed the research literature on differential teacher treatment of high-achieving and low-achieving students.[42] He identified seventeen teaching practices that are used with different frequencies with these two groups of students. The teaching practices are listed in Table 3.3. They define a pattern of diminished expectations for low-achieving students' ability to learn, and perhaps a lower regard for their personal worth as learners.

Academic achievement is highly correlated with social class, meaning that low-achieving students are more likely to come from disadvantaged home backgrounds, whereas high-achieving students are likely to come from advantaged home backgrounds. Therefore, the differential teaching practices listed in Table 3.3 suggest a pattern of discrimination based on students' social class as well as their achievement level.

Table 3.3   Differences in Teacher Behavior toward High-Achieving and Low-Achieving Students

1. Wait less time for "lows" to answer questions.
2. Give "lows" the answer or call on someone else rather than try to improve their responses by giving clues or using other teaching techniques.
3. Reward inappropriate behavior or incorrect answers by "lows."
4. Criticize "lows" more often for failure.
5. Praise "lows" less frequently than "highs" for success.
6. Fail to give feedback to the public responses of "lows."
7. Pay less attention to "lows" or interact with them less frequently.
8. Call on "lows" less often to respond to questions, or ask them only easier, nonanalytical questions.
9. Seat "lows" farther away from the teacher.
10. Demand less from "lows."
11. Interact with "lows" more privately than publicly and monitor and structure their activities more closely.
12. Grade tests or assignments in a differential manner, so that "highs" but not "lows" are given the benefit of the doubt in borderline cases.
13. Have less friendly interaction with "lows," including less smiling and less warm or more anxious voice tones.
14. Provide briefer and less informative feedback to the questions of "lows."
15. Provide less eye contact and other nonverbal communication of attention and responsiveness in interacting with "lows."
16. Make less use of effective but time-consuming instructional methods with "lows" when time is limited.
17. Evidence less acceptance and use of ideas given by "lows."

Source: Good, T. L. (1987). Two decades of research on teacher expectations: Findings and future directions. *Journal of Teacher Education, 38,* 32–47.

If observational data reveal that a teacher treats high-achieving and low-achieving students differently, the clinical supervisor can help the teacher recognize this pattern of behavior and adopt more equitable, effective patterns. For example, suppose a teacher discovers that he waits less time for low-achieving students to respond than he waits for high-achieving students. This teacher might set the goal of giving low-achieving students at least as much time to respond, and perhaps more time if they need it. Similar goals for equitable treatment of low-achieving or socially disadvantaged students could be set for the other sixteen teacher behaviors listed.

Effective Teaching of Ethnically and Racially Different Students

There is research evidence that some teachers act differently toward students depending on their ethnic background or race. An important study of this phenomenon was done by Gregg Jackson and Cecilia Cosca.[43] Their study was sponsored by the U.S. Commission on Civil Rights to determine whether teachers in the Southwest distribute their verbal behavior differentially among Anglo and Chicano students. Observers recorded verbal behaviors in fourth-, eighth-, tenth-, and twelfth-grade classes in fifty-two schools. A modified form of the Flanders Interaction Analysis System (see Chapter 12) was used to classify each verbal interaction and whether it was directed to, or initiated by, an Anglo student or a Chicano student.

Jackson and Cosca found that teachers directed significantly more of their verbal behaviors toward Anglo students than toward Chicano students. The most striking results were that teachers "praised or encouraged Anglos 35% more than they did Chicanos, accepted or used Anglos' ideas 40% more than they did those of Chicanos, and directed 21% more questions to Anglos than to Chicanos."[44] The researchers also found that Anglo students initiated more verbal behaviors than did Chicano students. In a review of related research, M. D. and Joyce Gall found that black students tend to participate less in discussions than white students.[45]

The research discussed above consists of older studies, so they might not accurately represent current practices. However, because of the importance of student ethnicity and race, clinical supervisors should be sensitive to whether teachers provide equal opportunities for students of all ethnic backgrounds and races to learn, and also whether teachers include multicultural dimensions of the curriculum in their instruction.

Educators differ in what they consider effective teaching practices for these purposes. The differences reflect different philosophies of multicultural education. James Banks distinguished between three such philosophies.[46] They are as follows:

1. *Cultural pluralism:* the goal of the curriculum is to help students function more effectively in their own ethnic culture and to help liberate them from ethnic oppression.

2. *Assimilationism:* the goal is to help students develop a commitment to the common culture and its values.

3. *Multiethnicism:* the goal is to help students learn how to function effectively within the common culture, their own ethnic culture, and other ethnic cultures.

It is important for teachers to be clear about which of these philosophies, or other philosophy, guides their instruction. Otherwise, they run the risk of ignoring multicultural aspects of teaching, or, worse, succumbing to their prejudices and thereby depriving some students of equal opportunity for learning.

Geneva Gay reviewed the literature on effective multicultural teaching practices and teacher characteristics to create a model of instruction that she labels *culturally responsive teaching*.[47] The key characteristics of culturally responsive teaching are listed in Table 3.4. (The characteristics are consistent with other syntheses of the literature on effective multicultural pedagogy.[48]) These probably are effective teaching practices and qualities, irrespective of the teacher's philosophy of multicultural education. The picture that emerges from the list is of a teacher who respects all students, takes responsibility for knowing about their cultural backgrounds, and uses this knowledge in his or her teaching.

Effective Teaching of Male and Female Students

There is strong evidence that some teachers treat boys and girls differently during classroom instruction. For example, Jere Brophy found that teachers interact more frequently with boys, give them more feedback and help, and criticize and praise them more frequently.[49] These differences perhaps are more pronounced in traditionally male-

Table 3.4 Effective Practices in Culturally Responsive Teaching

1. Acknowledging the legitimacy of the cultural heritages of different ethnic groups, both as legacies that affect students' dispositions, attitudes, and approaches to learning and as worthy content to be taught in the formal curriculum.
2. Building bridges of meaningfulness between home and school experiences as well as between academic abstractions and lived sociocultural realities.
3. Using a wide variety of instructional strategies that are connected to different learning styles.
4. Teaching students to know and praise their own and each others' cultural heritages.
5. Incorporating multicultural information, resources, and materials in all the subjects and skills routinely taught in schools.

Source: Gay, G. (2000). *Culturally responsive teaching: Theory, research, & practice.* (p. 29). New York: Teachers College Press.

stereotyped subjects, such as mathematics. For example, in research on fourth-grade mathematics classes, Elizabeth Fennema and Penelope Peterson found that teachers

1. initiated more interactions with boys for the purpose of socializing and classroom management.
2. received and accepted more "call out" responses from boys.
3. more frequently called on boys for both the answers and the explanations of how the answers were obtained when working on word problems.[50]

These findings indicate that teachers tend to treat boys more favorably than girls. If a teacher is observed to do this, the clinical supervisor can help the teacher reallocate interaction patterns so that girls are treated more equitably. In the case of traditionally male-stereotyped subjects, more radical changes might be necessary. Fennema and Peterson found that competitive games tended to help boys learn basic math skills, but tended to harm girls' learning of these skills. A different pattern was found for cooperative learning activities: they tended to help girls, but not boys, learn math problem-solving skills. These findings suggest that teachers need to learn how to maintain a delicate balance of competitive and cooperative activities, so that both boys and girls have equal opportunity to use learning styles that are effective for them.

Fennema and Peterson also make this recommendation:

Perhaps the most important thing that a teacher can do is to expect girls to work independently. Teachers should encourage girls to engage in independent learning behavior and praise them for participating in and performing well on high-level cognitive mathematics tasks.[51]

This type of encouragement may not be necessary for the typical male student, for whom independence and problem solving have been internalized as part of his role identity.

Although Fennema and Peterson's recommendations focus on mathematics instruction, they seem appropriate to other male-stereotyped subjects, such as the sciences and mechanical trades.

Effective Teaching in Response to Individual Students' Interests and Needs

The preceding discussion focused on effective methods for teaching particular groups of students, such as males and females or students who share a certain ethnicity. However, each student is also a unique individual. Teachers must attempt to understand and accommodate this uniqueness if they are to be truly effective. This is a difficult task, because we humans are so complex. It seems impossible for a teacher to know even a few students in depth and respond accordingly.

Research knowledge about how teachers can effectively respond to individual diversity among students is scant. There has been some theoretical work, in particular, the theory of multiple intelligences developed by Howard Gardner.[52] However, there is little empirical research testing the theory's validity and its educational implications. At the present time, then, we must look to "best practices," that is, the practices recommended and used by expert teachers and other educators.[53]

In general, best practices for accommodating student diversity involve:

- using the theory of multiple intelligences to identify and develop each student's strengths and weaknesses.
- acknowledging students' different interests by giving them choices with respect to curriculum, class assignments, and homework.
- representing facts, concepts, and skills in different forms (e.g., examples, analogies, videos, demonstrations) to accommodate individual differences in students' preferences for cognitive processing.
- providing extra time to complete assignments and tests for students who need it.
- providing extra instruction (e.g., by peer tutoring and cooperative learning) for students who need it.

Carol Ann Tomlinson has compiled a list of these and other best practices for accommodating student diversity.[54] The list is presented in Chapter 12.

EFFECTIVE CLASSROOM MANAGEMENT

Daniel Duke defines classroom management as "the provisions and procedures necessary to establish and maintain an environment in which instruction and learning can occur."[55] This definition implies that classroom management is not the same thing as teaching, but is a necessary precondition for teaching.

As one would expect, researchers have found that students' academic achievement is higher in well-managed classrooms.[56] This is probably because students are more on task in such classrooms, and their learning processes are better organized.

Many teachers, both preservice and inservice, have difficulty managing their classroom. This difficulty typically is manifested in two ways: (1) the progression of classroom events is disorganized and frequently interrupted, and (2) many of the students are off task. The occurrence of these problems is usually distressing for the teacher, as well as for the clinical supervisor. Therefore, supervisors should know effective classroom management practices that can help the teacher bring the class under control.

Carolyn Evertson reviewed the research that she and others have done to identify practices used by teachers who are effective classroom managers.[57] The practices are listed in Table 3.5. These effective management practices were identified by research in elementary and junior high school classes, but they seem equally applicable to high school classes.

As shown in Table 3.5, carefully formulated rules and procedures are at the heart of a good classroom management system. The teacher needs to analyze instruction in a classroom setting in all its complexity, and formulate a rule or procedure to cover each situation. Walter Doyle's comprehensive analysis of classroom management suggests that rules and procedures are needed for all the tasks and situations shown in Table 3.6.[58] The list of tasks and situations demonstrates that managing a classroom is a complex process. It also suggests how a class can easily get out of control if students do not have clear rules and procedures to follow.

Another important aspect of classroom management is the teacher's procedures for handling student misbehavior. Common types of misbehavior are: tardiness, cutting class, failure to bring supplies and books to class, inattentiveness, noisiness, call-outs, and verbal or physical aggression. Even effective teachers experience student misbehavior, but they manage it differently than less effective teachers. One of their primary techniques is to deal with the misbehavior early before it has a chance to escalate. Another technique is to use an intervention that stops the misbehavior with the least disruption to the ongoing

Table 3.5   Practices of Teachers Who Are Effective Classroom Managers

Rules and Procedures

1. *Analysis.* The teacher carefully analyzes the rules and procedures that need to be in place so that students can learn effectively in the classroom setting.
2. *Description.* The teacher states the rules and procedures in simple, clear language so that students can understand them easily.
3. *Teaching.* The teacher systematically teaches the rules and procedures at the start of the school year, or when beginning a new course with new students.
4. *Monitoring.* The teacher continuously monitors students' compliance with the rules and procedures, and also careful record keeping of students' academic work.

Physical Arrangement of Classroom and Supplies

1. *Visibility.* Students should be able to see the instructional displays. The teacher should have a clear view of instruction areas, students' work areas, and learning centers to facilitate monitoring of students.
2. *Accessibility.* High-traffic areas (areas for group work, pencil sharpener, door to the hall) should be kept clear and separated from each other.
3. *Distractibility.* Arrangements that can compete with the teacher for students' attention (seating students facing the windows to the playground, door to the hall, face to face with each other but away from the teacher) should be minimized.
4. *Supplies.* The teacher takes care to secure an adequate supply of textbooks and materials for all the students in the classroom.

Source: Evertson, C. M. (1987). Managing classrooms: A framework for teachers. In Berliner, D. C., & Rosenshine, B. V. (Eds.). *Talks to teachers* (pp. 52–74). New York: Random House.

Table 3.6   Classroom Tasks and Situations for Which a Teacher Needs Rules and Procedures

1. Seat assignment in the classroom
2. Start and end of class (e.g., "Be in your seat and ready to work when the bell rings.")
3. Handing in of assignments, materials, etc.
4. Permissible activities if a student completes seatwork early
5. Leaving the room while class is in session
6. Standards for the form and neatness of one's desk, notebooks, assignments, etc.
7. Supplies and materials to be brought to class
8. Signals for seeking help or indicating a willingness to answer a teacher question addressed to the class as a whole
9. Acceptable noise level in the room
10. Acceptability of verbal and physical aggression
11. Moving around the room to sharpen pencils, get materials, etc.
12. Storage of materials, hats, boots, etc., in the classroom
13. Consumption of food and gum
14. Selection of classroom helpers
15. Late assignments and make-up work

Source: Doyle, W. (1986). Classroom organization and management. In M. C. Wittrock (Ed.), *Handbook of research on teaching* (3d ed., pp. 392–431). New York: Macmillan.

instruction. Eye contact, physical proximity to the misbehaving student, or "the look" are examples of such interventions. In the words of Walter Doyle, "successful interventions tend to have a private and fleeting quality that does not interrupt the flow of events."[59]

Other techniques are also effective in managing student misbehavior. Discussion of these techniques, as well as comprehensive models of classroom discipline, is available in various sources.[60]

EFFECTIVE PLANNING AND DECISION MAKING

Madeline Hunter defined teaching as "the process of making and implementing decisions, before, during, and after instruction, to increase the probability of learning."[61] If this is true, it is important for the clinical supervisor to help teachers make the most effective decisions possible.

Teacher decisions that are made before and after instruction are commonly referred to as teacher planning. This planning is important for the obvious reason that it affects the instruction that students receive in the classroom. For example, Christopher Clark and Penelope Peterson found in their review of research that teachers' plans influence the content of instruction, the sequence in which topics get taught, and the allocation of time to different topics and subjects.[62]

Christopher Clark and Robert Yinger did a research study in which they found that teachers engage in as many as eight different types of planning during the course of a school year.[63] Two of the types—unit planning and lesson planning—involve the content of instruction. The other six types involve planning for different time spans of instruction: daily, weekly, short-range, long-range, term, and yearly. Clark and Yinger also found that planning is not a linear process and that it does not occur at a single point in time. Rather, teachers develop their plans incrementally, starting from a general idea and then gradually elaborating it. The development of their plans is influenced by their reflections on previous plans and experience in the classroom. Clark and Yinger's study involved elementary school teachers, but the findings seem equally applicable to teachers of other grade levels.

Clinical supervisors find that some teachers have difficulty with instruction because they do not plan effectively. One approach to helping these teachers is to ask them to make written lesson plans. However, the research reviewed above suggests that this approach is not sufficient, because it does not acknowledge the incremental, cyclical nature of lesson planning or the fact that other types of planning (e.g., unit, weekly) might be more important to a particular teacher. The writing of structured lesson plans might be a useful starting point for the development of planning skills, but it probably should not be the only focus of clinical supervision.

Researchers have not determined whether particular types of planning are more effective than other types in promoting student learning. It seems likely, though, that more effective teachers engage in careful, reflective planning, whereas less effective teachers engage in sporadic or no planning. A clinical supervisor who agrees with this supposition would work with teachers to increase the amount of time they spend planning and help them develop detailed, reflective plans of the various types described above.

We turn now to the decisions that teachers make during the act of instruction. These decisions—sometimes called interactive decisions—involve a deliberate choice to act in a specific way while teaching. Clark and Peterson, in their review of research, found that "on the average, teachers make one interactive decision every 2 minutes."[64] This research finding supports Madeline Hunter's characterization of teaching as a process of decision making.

Researchers have discovered several principles of effective interactive decision making.[65] One of their findings involves teachers' decision making when they judge students' classroom behavior to be unacceptable. Teachers who are prone to consider alternative teaching strategies to handle the problem, but who decide not to implement them, have lower-achieving classes.

Teachers who do not act on alternatives perhaps have a rigid teaching style. Supervisors need to help them learn how to make on-the-spot changes in teaching strategy to accommodate the idiosyncratic, circumstantial nature of student behavior in the classroom.

Another finding is that the decisions of effective teachers are more conceptually based, rapid, and simpler than the decisions of less effective teachers. This finding suggests that clinical supervisors should recommend to teachers that they learn a conceptual model, or models, of teaching. A starting point might be to have teachers study the models presented in this chapter. In addition, the supervisor can recommend that teachers learn other models through workshops, courses, or independent study. It makes sense that these models would facilitate decision making. They simplify the teacher's thinking by focusing attention on salient aspects of instruction. This simplification, in turn, enables quick decisions and changes in actions without disturbing the flow of instruction.

EFFECTIVE IMPLEMENTATION OF CURRICULUM CHANGE

The school curriculum is constantly changing. The following are just a few examples of curriculum innovations that are currently being introduced into many schools: standards-based instruction; instruction in mathematical problem solving; study skills instruction;

interdisciplinary curriculum; performance assessment; thinking skills instruction; project-based learning; technology-enhanced curriculum. Even the traditional curriculum changes with each new textbook adoption. Some textbook topics are added or given more emphasis, while others are dropped or given less emphasis. The curriculum also is revised to reflect changing perspectives about ethnicity, gender, and other aspects of society.

The manner in which a teacher implements a curriculum change affects students' learning. For example, suppose a school district changes its mathematics curriculum to put more emphasis on problem solving. Teachers who implement the new curriculum fully will give their students more opportunity to learn mathematical problem-solving skills than teachers who implement it halfheartedly or not at all. As would be expected, researchers have found that students' opportunity to learn a curriculum affects how much of the curriculum they actually learn.[66]

The preceding analysis demonstrates that one aspect of effective teaching is implementation of curriculum change. Clinical supervisors should be sensitive to this aspect of teachers' work and help teachers who experience difficulty with it. To do this, supervisors need to be knowledgeable about the process of curriculum implementation and factors that affect it. The following discussion focuses on teacher characteristics that affect curriculum implementation. Research on other factors is reviewed in other sources.[67]

One of the supervisor's first tasks is to assess the teacher's level of implementation of the curriculum change. Gene Hall and Shirley Hord conducted research that is relevant to this task.[68] They found that there are eight levels at which teachers can implement curriculum change or any other kind of change. The levels are shown in Table 3.7. Hall and Hord have developed several interview procedures that supervisors can use to assess the level at which the teacher is implementing a curriculum change.[69]

As a supervisor, you will want to know not only teachers' level of implementation, but also their concerns about using the new curriculum. Hall and Hord found that these concerns follow a predictable progression of stages. The stages are shown in Table 3.8.

Table 3.7   Levels at Which Teachers Implement Educational Change

- *Level 0—nonuse.* The teacher has no knowledge of or involvement with the new curriculum.
- *Level I—orientation.* The teacher is acquiring information about the new curriculum.
- *Level II—preparation.* The teacher is preparing for first use of the new curriculum.
- *Level III—mechanical use.* The teacher is trying to master the basics of the new curriculum.
- *Level IVA—routine.* The teacher's use of the new curriculum is stabilized.
- *Level IVB—refinement.* The teacher varies use of the new curriculum to increase its impact on students.
- *Level V—integration.* The teacher combines his or her own efforts with those of colleagues to maximize the benefits of the new curriculum for students.
- *Level VI—renewal.* The teacher reevaluates his or her quality of use of the curriculum, modifies the new curriculum in a major way to improve its effectiveness, studies new developments relating to the curriculum, searches for new alternatives, and explores new goals for self-improvement or improvement of aspects of the school system that relate to the curriculum.

Source: Hall, G. E., & Hord, S. M. (2001). *Implementing change: Patterns, principles, and potholes.* (p. 82). Boston: Allyn and Bacon.

Table 3.8   Stages of Concern About Implementing a Curriculum Change

Stages of concern	Typical expressions of concern
	Self concerns
0. Awareness	I am not concerned about it (the curriculum change).
1. Informational	I would like to know more about it.
2. Personal	How will using it affect me?
	Task concerns
3. Management	I seem to be spending all my time getting material ready.
	Impact concerns
4. Consequences	How is my use affecting kids?
5. Collaboration	I am concerned about relating what I am doing with what other instructors are doing.
6. Refocusing	I have some ideas about something that would work even better.

Source: Adapted from Hall, G. E., & Hord, S. M. (2001). *Implementing change: Patterns, principles, and potholes.* (p. 61). Boston: Allyn and Bacon.

The first three concerns focus on the self, and are typical of teachers whose use of the new curriculum is at level 0 (nonuse) or I (orientation). Management concerns typify teachers at level II (preparation) or III (mechanical use). Finally, impact concerns typify teachers at level IVB (refinement), V (integration), or VI (renewal).

The supervisor can assess the teacher's concerns in the conference phase of the clinical supervision cycle. Another approach is to administer the Stages of Concern Questionnaire (SoCQ), a simple paper-and-pencil instrument consisting of thirty-five rating items.[70]

Walter Doyle and Gerald Ponder identified additional teacher concerns that affect teachers' implementation of a curriculum change.[71] They found that teachers follow a "practicality ethic" in deciding how much commitment to make to a curriculum change. This means that teachers judge the curriculum change to be practical to the extent that it is (1) stated clearly and specifically, (2) congruent with teachers' existing beliefs and practices, and (3) cost-effective in terms of benefits to students relative to teachers' expenditure of energy. Research by Georgea Mohlman, Theodore Coladarci, and N. L. Gage confirmed the importance of the practicality ethic in determining the extent to which teachers implement a curriculum change.[72]

To summarize, one indicator of effective teaching is how well the teacher implements a curriculum change. Effective teachers achieve a high level of implementation (levels IVB, V, and VI in Hall's model), whereas ineffective teachers are fixated at lower levels. Their fixation might be caused by unresolved concerns or perceptions that the new curriculum is impractical. Supervisors can help these teachers by addressing their concerns and perceptions through a clinical supervision process.

A DEFINITION OF EFFECTIVE TEACHING

We invite you to develop your own definition of effective teaching by drawing on the body of research knowledge reviewed above. We undertook this exercise for ourselves and developed the following definition:

Effective teaching involves the ability to:

- provide instruction that helps students develop the knowledge, skills, and understandings intended by curriculum objectives.
- create an instructional climate that causes students to develop positive attitudes toward school and self.
- adjust instruction so that all students learn, irrespective of their ability, ethnicity, or other characteristic.
- manage the classroom so that students are engaged in learning all or most of the time.
- make sound decisions and plans that maximize students' opportunity to learn.
- respond to initiatives for curriculum change so that the new curriculum's intents are fully realized.

The research reviewed in this chapter demonstrates that there is a growing body of knowledge about teaching practices that can improve teachers' instruction. Because research is an ongoing enterprise, supervisors and teachers should stay informed about new developments. However, this does not mean that teachers should abandon the way they currently teach and unconditionally adopt research-validated practices. Rather, practices that are supported by research evidence should be viewed as possible alternatives to a teacher's current practices. We make this recommendation based on our view of clinical supervision as a process of helping teachers reflect on data (clinical observations, research findings, etc.) and use these reflections to experiment with their instruction for the purpose of continuous professional development.

NOTES

1. Chall, J. S. (2000). *The academic achievement challenge: What really works in the classroom?* New York: Guilford Press, p. 180.

2. Schmuck, R. A., & Schmuck, P. A. (2001). *Group processes in the classroom* (8th ed., pp. 292–293). Boston: McGraw-Hill.

3. Rosenshine, B., & Furst, N. (1973). The use of direct observation to study teaching In R. M. W. Travers (Ed.), *Handbook of research on teaching* (2nd ed., pp. 122–183). Chicago: Rand McNally.

4. Flanders, N. A. (1970). *Analyzing teaching behavior.* Reading, MA: Addison-Wesley.

5. These studies are reviewed in: Gage, N. L. (1978). *The scientific basis of the art of teaching.* New York: Teachers College Press.

6. Rosenshine, B. V. (1986). Synthesis of research on explicit teaching. *Educational Leadership, 43*(7), 60–68.

7. Hunter, M. (1984). Knowing, teaching, and supervising. In P. L. Hosford (Ed.), *Using what we know about teaching* (pp. 169–192). Alexandria, VA: Association for Supervision and Curriculum Development.

8. Rosenshine, "Synthesis," p. 60.

9. *Ibid.,* p. 62.

10. Bloom, B. S. (Ed.). *Taxonomy of educational objectives: The classification of educational goals. Handbook 1: Cognitive domain.* New York: Longman.

11. Cole, N. S. (1990). Conceptions of educational achievement. *Educational Researcher, 19*(3), 2–7.

12. *Ibid.,* p. 2.

13. *Ibid.,* p. 3.

14. See, for example: Shavelson, R. J., Carey, N. B., & Webb, N. M. (1990). Indicators of science achievement: Options for a powerful policy instrument. *Phi Delta Kappan, 71,* 692–697. See also the discussion of performance assessment in Chapter 11.

15. Gall, J. P., & Gall, M. D. (1990). Outcomes of the discussion method. In W. W. Wilen (Ed.), *Teaching and learning through discussion* (pp. 25–44). Springfield, IL: Charles C. Thomas.

16. Gall, M. D., & Gall, J. P. (1976). The discussion method. In N. L. Gage (Ed.), *The psychology of teaching methods: The seventy-fifth yearbook of the National Society for the Study of Education* (pp. 166–216). Chicago: University of Chicago Press.

17. Winne, P. H. (1979). Experiments relating teachers' use of higher cognitive questions to student achievement. *Review of Educational Research, 49,* 13–49.

18. Redfield, D. L., & Rousseau, E. W. (1981). A meta-analysis of experimental research on teacher questioning behavior. *Review of Educational Research, 51,* 237–245.

19. Rosenshine, B. V. (1976). Classroom instruction. In N. L. Gage (Ed.), *The psychology of teaching methods: The seventy-fifth yearbook of the National Society for the Study of Education* (pp. 334–371). Chicago: University of Chicago Press.

20. Hamaker, C. (1986). The effects of adjunct questions on prose learning. *Review of Educational Research, 56,* 212–242.

21. Brooks, J. G., & Brooks, M. G. (1993). *The case for constructivist classrooms.* Alexandria, VA: Association for Supervision and Curriculum Development, p. 15.

22. Windschitl, M. (1999). The challenges of sustaining a constructivist classroom culture. *Phi Delta Kappan, 80,* 751–755.

23. Shulman, L. S., & Quinlan, K. M. (1996). The comparative psychology of school subjects. In D. C. Berliner & R. C. Calfee (Eds.), *Handbook of educational psychology* (pp. 399–422). New York: Macmillan.

24. Ingersoll, R. (1999). The problem of underqualified teachers in American secondary schools. *Educational Researcher, 28*(2), 26–37.

25. Constructivist teaching methods are also discussed in Chapters 9 and 12.

26. Berliner, D. C. (1987). Knowledge is power: A talk to teachers about a revolution in the teaching profession. In D. C. Berliner & B. V. Rosenshine (Eds.), *Talks to teachers* (pp. 3–33). New York: Random House.

27. Borg, W. R. (1980). Time and school learning. In C. Denham & A. Lieberman (Eds.), *Time to learn* (pp. 33–72). Washington, DC: U.S. Department of Education.

28. Fisher, C. W., Berliner, D. C., Filby, N. N., Marliave, R., Cahen, L. S., & Dishaw, M. M. (1980). Teaching behaviors, academic learning time, and student achievement: An overview. In C. Denham & A. Lieberman (Eds.), *Time to learn* (pp. 7–32). Washington, DC: U.S. Department of Education.

29. Cooper, H. (1989). *Homework.* New York: Longman.

30. Brophy, J. (2001). Introduction. In J. Brophy (Ed.), *Advances in research on teaching* (Vol. 8, pp. 1–23). Oxford: JAI Elsevier; Brophy, J. (1999). *Teaching* (Educational Practices Series No. 1). Geneva: International Bureau of Education.

31. *Ibid.*

32. Krathwohl, D. R., Bloom, B. S., & Masia, B. B. (1964). *Taxonomy of educational objectives. Handbook II: Affective domain.* New York: McKay.

33. Dewey, J. (1938). *Experience and education.* New York: Collier, p. 48.

34. Larkins, A. G., McKinney, C. W., Oldham-Buss, S., & Gilmore, A. C. (1985). *Teacher enthusiasm: A critical review.* Hattiesburg, MS: University of Southern Mississippi.

35. Gage, N. L., *The scientific basis of the art of teaching, op. cit.*

36. Brophy, J. (1981). Teacher praise: A functional analysis. *Review of Educational Research, 51,* 5–32.

37. McKeachie, W. J., & Kulik, J. A. (1975). Effective college teaching. In F. N. Kerlinger (Ed.), *Review of research in education* (Vol. 3, pp. 165–209). Itasca, IL: Peabody.

38. J. P. Gall and M. D. Gall, *op. cit.*

39. This phenomenon was observed in the following study: Mitnick, L. L., & McGinnies, E. (1958). Influencing ethnocentrism in small discussion groups through a film communication. *Journal of Abnormal and Social Psychology, 56,* 82–90.

40. Slavin, R. E. (1989/1990). Research on cooperative learning: Consensus and controversy. *Educational Leadership, 47*(4), 52–54.

41. Brophy, J. (1987). On motivating students. In D. C. Berliner & B. V. Rosenshine (Eds.), *Talks to teachers* (pp. 201–245). New York: Random House; *Ibid.,* p. 207.

42. Good, T. L. (1987). Two decades of research on teacher expectations: Findings and future directions. *Journal of Teacher Education, 38,* 32–47.

43. Jackson, G., & Cosca, C. (1974). The inequality of educational opportunity in the Southwest: An observational study of ethnically mixed classrooms. *American Educational Research Journal, 11,* 219–229. The report of the Jackson and Cosca study used the term Anglo to refer to white persons not of Spanish-speaking background. The term Chicano was used to refer to Mexican Americans.

44. *Ibid,* p. 227.

45. Gall & Gall, "Outcomes of the Discussion Method."

46. Banks, J. A. (1999). *An introduction to multicultural education.* Boston: Allyn and Bacon.

47. Gay, G. (2000). *Culturally responsive teaching: Theory, research, & practice.* New York: Teachers College Press.

48. Foster, M. (1995). African American teachers and culturally relevant pedagogy. In J. A. Banks & C. A. M. Banks (Eds.),

Handbook of research on multicultural education (pp. 570–581). New York: Macmillan; see also the set of multicultural competencies identified as important for psychologists serving clients: Hansen, N. D., Pepitone-Arreola-Rockwell, F., & Greene, A. F. (2000). Multicultural competence: Criteria and case examples. *Professional Psychology, 31,* 652–660.

49. Brophy, J. E. (1985). Interactions of male and female students with male and female teachers. In L. C. Wilkinson & C. B. Marrett (Eds.), *Gender influences in classroom interaction* (pp. 115–142). Orlando, FL: Academic Press.

50. Fennema, E., & Peterson, P. L. (1987). Effective teaching for boys and girls: The same or different? In D. C. Berliner & B. V. Rosenshine (Eds.), *Talks to teachers* (pp. 111–125). New York: Random House.

51. *Ibid.,* p. 124.

52. Gardner, H, (1983). *Frames of mind: The theory of multiple intelligences.* New York: Basic Books.

53. For example: Campbell, L., & Campbell, B. (1999). *Multiple intelligences and student achievement: Success stories from six schools.* Alexandria, VA: Association for Supervision and Curriculum Development.

54. Tomlinson, C. A. (1999). *The differentiated classroom: Responding to the needs of all learners.* Alexandria, VA: Association for Supervision and Curriculum Development.

55. Duke, D. L. (1979). Editor's preface. In D. L. Duke (Ed.), *Classroom management: The seventy-eighth yearbook of the National Society for the Study of Education* (Part 2, pp. xi–xv). Chicago: University of Chicago Press.

56. This research is reviewed in: Good, T. (1979). Teacher effectiveness in the elementary school: What we know about it now. *Journal of Teacher Education, 30,* 52–64.

57. Evertson, C. M. (1987). Managing classrooms: A framework for teachers. In D. C. Berliner & B. V. Rosenshine (Eds.), *Talks to teachers* (pp. 52–74). New York: Random House.

58. Doyle, W. (1986). Classroom organization and management. In M. C. Wittrock (Ed.), *Handbook of research on teaching* (3d ed., pp. 392–431). New York: Macmillan.

59. *Ibid,* p. 421.

60. Examples of such sources are: Cummings, C. (1983). *Managing to teach.* Edmonds, WA: Teaching Inc.; Charles, C. M. (2001). *Building classroom discipline* (7th ed.). Boston: Addison-Wesley Longman.

61. Hunter, M. (1979). Teaching is decision making. *Educational Leadership, 37*(1), 62–67.

62. Clark, C. M., & Peterson, P. L. (1986). Teachers' thought processes. In M. C. Wittrock (Ed.), *Handbook of research on teaching* (3d ed., pp. 255–296). New York: Macmillan.

63. Clark, C. M., & Yinger, R. J. (1979). *Three studies of teacher planning* (Research Series No. 55). East Lansing: Michigan State University.

64. Clark & Peterson, "Teachers' Thought Processes," p. 274.

65. Doyle, W. (1977). Learning the classroom environment: An ecological analysis. *Journal of Teacher Education, 28,* 51–55; Morine. G., & Vallance, E. (1975). *Special study B: A study of teacher and pupil perceptions of classroom interaction* (Technical Report No. 75-11-6). San Francisco: Far West Laboratory for Educational Research and Development; Peterson, P. L., & Clark, C. M. (1978). Teachers' reports of their cognitive processes during teaching. *American Educational Research Journal, 15,* 555–565.

66. Rosenshine & Furst, "The Use of Direct Observation to Study Teaching."

67. Fullan, M. (2001). *The new meaning of educational change* (3rd ed.). New York: Teachers College Press.

68. Hall, G. E., & Hord, S. M. (2001). *Implementing change: Patterns, principles, and potholes.* Boston: Allyn and Bacon.

69. *Ibid,* Chapter 5.

70. The SoCQ and scoring procedures are described in chapter 4 and several appendices of *Ibid.*

71. Doyle, W., & Ponder, G. (1977). The practicality ethic and teacher decision-making. *Interchange, 8*(3), 1–12.

72. Mohlman, G. G., Coladarci, T., & Gage, N. L. (1982). Comprehension and attitude as predictors of implementation of teacher training. *Journal of Teacher Education, 32,* 31–36.

Chapter 4

Using Clinical Supervision in Teacher Evaluation

Author's Note

The first edition of this book did not have a chapter on the evaluation of teachers. Our concern was that evaluation often has the effect of "de"valuing teachers rather than making them feel valued. However, because clinical supervisors are often required to evaluate as well as foster professional growth, we began this chapter with the second edition.

It has been interesting to view the process of teacher evaluation from a variety of perspectives. As teacher educators we see it as evidence of increasing competence. Being called as an expert witness in hearings, arbitration, and litigation casts a different light on one's perspective. The current emphasis on standards colors the picture in a different hue (and cry). Advisors to graduate students doing research in the area of teacher evaluation get a different look at some of the inherent problems.

Knowing some of the people who have written books on the subject provides additional insights. Reading the books is also informative. For the present we are staying with the basic scheme that came to light in the second edition.

KAA

The easiest way to identify specific behaviors is by observing them. Final scores, whether in sports or tests, indicate whether you have a winner or loser, but only observation can yield the information necessary to change a loser to a winner. To be useful, observation must be valid, objective, and recorded. A recorded observation enables observer and performer to "play back" the performance so that salient cause-effect relationships can be identified.

—Madeline Hunter

INTRODUCTION

In Chapter 1 there is a reference to the "sting" of evaluation. Two decades after that sentence was first published, in 1980, the evaluation of teachers still stings. During the intervening years, a few developments have affected the relationship between the techniques of clinical supervision, which concentrate on teacher growth and development, and the legal accountability requirements for evaluating teachers.

A 1986 study in Canada by Keith Acheson[1] described programs in each of the four western provinces that incorporated collegial observers as well as evaluative personnel in staff development. Some of these programs separate summative evaluation from formative or developmental activities. This separation is warranted; however, in most situations, those who are charged with responsibilities that call for clinical supervision techniques are also required to make summative evaluations of some kind. Therefore, both concerns will be addressed simultaneously in this chapter.

Other changes with respect to the preservice preparation, inservice development, and periodic evaluation of teachers were brought home by a colleague from Germany, who has followed the development of microteaching at Stanford University in the early 1960s, the experimentation with minicourses at the Far West Laboratory in the late 1960s, emphasis on competency-based education for teachers and students in the 1970s, the shift from quantitative to qualitative research in the 1980s, and the move toward collaborative school organizations in the 1990s. In all these trends, an objective observer can provide perceptions that are informative and useful for instructors and leaders who are caught up in their own subjective interpretations of day-to-day activities, just as an objective observer from another country can see the forest more clearly than those who are busy with the trees. What we see (with the help of our friend) is an encouraging impetus toward liberating teachers from the isolation and powerlessness they have often felt. Enlightened professional development techniques and activities have given teachers the opportunity to analyze and improve what they do.

If these kinds of insights can be provided by observers who also evaluate, that is, retain, promote, renew, dismiss, reprimand, grant tenure, reward, and punish, then let us proceed. If they are better supplied by peers, colleagues, and collaborators, then let us continue to experiment, test, and improve those kinds of arrangements. In the meantime we shall continue to include the cycle of planning, observing, and giving feedback from clinical supervision within the cycle of summative evaluation. We shall also extend our view of that cycle to include the larger concerns of setting, situation, structure, and style. We will consider some variations on the evaluator-supervisor mode of analyzing teaching and will also look at some alternative roles that observer/analysts may play.

THE TENSION BETWEEN ACCOUNTABILITY AND PROFESSIONAL GROWTH

In everyday language, evaluation, supervision, and other functions that use analysis of teaching sound pretty much the same. There are important differences, however, in considering who will do it and why. An evaluator can either value or devalue something. A supervisor can either oversee, inspect, and look for what is wrong, or have "super vision" to perceive what will make things better or even better. Whatever the case, analysis of what teachers do is essential to supervision. It is also essential to teacher evaluation, peer coaching, collegial observation, and peer consultation.

There are several roles developing in education that fit the general title of instructional leader. Those who traditionally have been called supervisors, especially clinical supervisors as we have defined them, certainly qualify. Those who evaluate teachers also deserve the title. As mentioned, however, evaluation introduces a sting to supervision. Stated more colorfully, it is the fly in the ointment. Nonetheless, the need for accountability coexists with the need for professional growth in teaching.

This chapter will look at how clinical supervision relates to these other roles, and will advocate using the techniques that are described in other chapters in performing the roles. Goal setting, planning for observation, observation, and feedback are functions of all these roles.

Our solution has been to place the planning, observation, and feedback in an expanded schema that includes district standards or criteria of effective teaching; job descriptions or consideration of the unique situation; goal setting; formal evaluation or report writing; programs of assistance for teachers with serious deficiencies; and dismissal—which requires consideration of contracts, grievances, arbitration, hearings, and litigation. Before describing this schema, two issues need to be discussed that arise from combining the accountability requirements of teacher evaluation with the professional growth goals of clinical supervision.

The Threat of Evaluation

There are a number of ways of dealing with the sting of evaluation. One is to emphasize it. Those of us old enough to remember the use of iodine as first aid for cuts also recall parents who believed that medicines that did not sting, taste bitter, or cause gagging could not be effective. One can take the iodine approach to evaluating teaching. Many evaluators believe that fear is an effective motivator for teachers.

Another way to deal with the sting is to remove it. We have worked with groups of teachers who observe in one another's classrooms and give only positive feedback. Unconditional positive regard is something we have all been seeking since our mothers pushed us out. Knowing that someone has such regard for us can also be a powerful motivator.

An alternative is to use both of the above sources of motivation in an intermittent reinforcement menu. This approach appeals to gamblers in casinos. Teachers in classrooms also receive both kinds of reinforcement from their students and others. That phenomenon is not a gamble but a sure bet.

There is abundant evidence from our research and that of our colleagues, students, and others that the threat of evaluation can destroy the potential of clinical supervision techniques to foster teacher self-analysis, reflection, and growth. Nevertheless, we shall no doubt have to cope with both aspects of the plan–observe–feedback cycle simultaneously in the foreseeable future.

Our best solution, for the present, is to have the observations of the evaluator-supervisor of preservice or inservice teachers augmented by those of peers (other teachers whose data will not be used for judgmental, threatening purposes). The techniques both kinds of observers can use are those described in the following chapters. The difference lies in their intended outcomes and the degree of trust the observed teacher is willing to bestow.

Consistency of Evaluation with Components of Clinical Supervision

Clinical supervision has three major components that should be repeated several times in a given year. A trained observer (1) meets with the teacher and plans for the next observation; (2) observes a lesson systematically and nonjudgmentally and records information related to the objectives set during the planning conference; and (3) meets with the teacher to (a) analyze together the data recorded by the observer, (b) interpret the meaning of the information from the teacher's perspective, and (c) reach decisions about the next steps.

Laws concerned with teacher evaluation often require a goal-setting conference, "multiple" observations (which means "two" to many evaluators), and a postevaluation interview or conference.

Some authorities, believing it is sufficient for observers merely to observe and then confer with teachers, advocate elimination of the planning conference. Our view of what can be accomplished by expert observation of teaching implies a need for planning the observation with the teacher. The logic goes like this: The goal of observation is feedback—information that is useful, relevant, objective, accurate, understandable. The goal of feedback is analysis, interpretation, and decision making by the teacher, with the assistance of the observer. If these goals are to be reached, the teacher and the observer need to plan the observation together.

The planning, when it is in conjunction with formal evaluation, needs to be consistent with official standards or criteria, and for inservice teachers it should be compatible with the job description. The observation, recording of data, and feedback need to be in concert with the planning. If this is the case, and there are several observations, the evaluator should be able to write a reasonable and fair summative report at the conclusion of several clinical supervision cycles.

CLINICAL SUPERVISION AND TEACHER EVALUATION

Although the primary purpose of clinical supervision is to help teachers develop and improve through cooperative planning, observation, and feedback, it is often part of a larger process that has as its purpose decisions about tenure, promotion, retention, and dismissal. The additional components needed to build a system of teacher evaluation that is consistent with the tenets of clinical supervision are: district standards, job descriptions, performance goals, formal evaluations, plans of assistance, postevaluation conferences, and postdismissal activities. Figure 4.1 is a graphic representation of how these are related.

District Standards

The teacher needs to be aware of the criteria that will be used to evaluate performance. These include specific criteria for a given teacher in a particular situation and also general criteria or standards that are applied to all teachers in a district. These general criteria are best developed by a committee of teachers, administrators, and others before being adopted by the school board as official policy before copies are placed in the hands of all teachers.

The total number of standards needs to be kept under control. One way to accomplish this is to identify fifteen to twenty general standards, each with three to five "indicators" stated in more explicit, behavioral terms.

An Example

One example of district standards that was developed by this process (over a period of several years) is included in Table 4.1.[2] Note that the committee organized their standards around a model of what a competent teacher should do before teaching, during teaching, and after teaching. The logic of the sequence is appealing: knowing about students, setting objectives relative to that knowledge, planning instruction based on those objectives, and conducting instruction that reflects the plans. Knowledge of subject matter and classroom management are components of teaching that will be important to any group of educators. Evaluation of students and communication with peers and parents are some of the competencies that are demonstrated after teaching or outside the classroom setting.

District standards serve several purposes. They serve as the reference for contract renewal, promotion, and tenure decisions. They also figure prominently in fair dismissal hearings, arbitration, and litigation about teacher evaluation.

Over the years, the notions of educators have changed in regard to what the criteria of good teaching should be. In the 1950s we looked at the characteristics of a good teacher—personality variables, qualities of character, and the like. In the 1960s attention shifted to what teachers do, or should do, as part of the teaching process. These behaviors were often called "competencies." Since the 1970s we have tended to talk about "teacher effec-

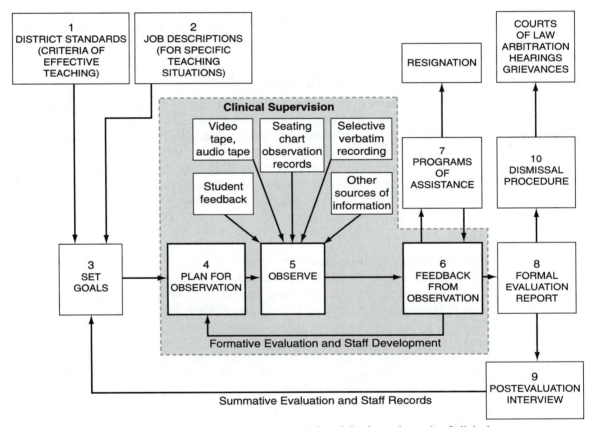

Figure 4.1 The teacher evaluation process. Note that boxes 4, 5, and 6 refer to the cycle of clinical supervision.

Source: Adapted from Keith A. Acheson, *Techniques in the Evaluation of Teachers.* Salem, OR: Confederation of Oregon School Administrators, 1982.

Table 4.1   District Standards of Competent Performance

District standards of competent performance

A standard is composed of three parts: a statement which establishes a general behavior, a list of indicators which specify how that behavior will be identified, and a principal's judgment as to the level of competent performance. The statement and indicators are listed for each standard. The level of expected performance of these standards will be determined by the professional judgment of the principal. The judgment is influenced by the teacher's assignment, class size, experience, and available resources. To determine if the requirements of the standard have been met, the statement of general teacher behavior, all of the indicators, and the performance level must be considered.

Section I—Instructional development

Area: Diagnosing

Standard 1 The competent teacher establishes procedures for gathering data by

a. completing the diagnosis for each student

b. using the diagnostic tools which are pertinent to the teacher's goals

c. using a variety of diagnostic instruments and techniques

d. requesting assistance from others, when needed, for more comprehensive diagnosis

Standard 2 The competent teacher interprets diagnostic data to identify the needs and concerns of both the individual and the group by

a. identifying the achievement level of each student

b. explaining the significance of the achievement level diagnosed

Area: Prescribing

Standard 3 The competent teacher utilizes diagnostic data to establish instructional objectives and relates these to individual needs by

a. writing instructional objectives

b. preparing objectives that show the data gathered in diagnosis are utilized

c. preparing objectives in terms of student performance

d. preparing objectives that are measurable

e. preparing both short- and long-term objectives for any assigned class

Standard 4 The competent teacher plans lessons to meet individual and group needs by

a. planning lessons that are consistent with the objectives

b. planning lessons that include appropriate activities which meet individual and group needs

c. planning to use appropriate resource materials related to instructional objectives

d. planning alternatives to meet the needs of individual students

e. accepting and using student feedback in planning instruction

Area: Facilitating

Standard 5 The competent teacher utilizes knowledge of subject matter by

a. using words and content appropriate to the subject area and students' abilities

b. using available media effectively and efficiently

c. requesting and using materials and facilities based on instructional objectives

d. knowing and utilizing community agencies, groups, and individuals to further the educational program

Standard 6 The competent teacher uses effective classroom management techniques by

a. showing respect for students

b. providing an atmosphere in which students remain at task

c. exhibiting consistency when dealing with behavior problems

(continued)

Table 4.1   District Standards of Competent Performance (*continued*)

d. exhibiting positive verbal and nonverbal influence on students

Standard 7 The competent teacher applies learning theory by

a. utilizing and building upon students' interests and prior knowledge

b. providing feedback as students progress toward goals

c. allowing for a balance between intake of information and the expression of student ideas

d. providing the individual with activities to develop attitudes, appreciations, and values

Standard 8 The competent teacher uses a variety of instructional techniques appropriate to the students' needs by

a. giving directions in a clear, concise manner

b. phrasing questions so students may respond appropriately

c. using strategies which involve students in higher levels of thinking

d. pacing the activities within a lesson according to the needs of students

Area: Student Performance Evaluation

Standard 9 The competent teacher establishes procedures for assessing student performance by

a. selecting means of evaluation which are appropriate to the objectives

b. planning measurement procedures for specific purposes

c. utilizing procedures whereby students receive feedback on their individual performance

d. presenting information that indicates evaluation has taken place for each student

Standard 10 The competent teacher interprets the results of student performance assessment by

a.identifying the reasons why students have or have not met the performance objectives

Standard 11 The competent teacher utilizes the results of student performance assessment by

a. using objective data to arrive at a grade or indicator of student progress to be reported to parents and student

b. providing feedback that facilitates the student accomplishment of goals.

c. planning changes in teaching strategies based on the results of the evaluation.

Section II—Professional development

Area: Communication

Standard 12 The competent teacher communicates effectively with students by

a. listening to and considering student comments and suggestions

b. being open to suggestions about ways in which to present material

c. conveying an attitude that promotes participation in activities

Standard 13 The competent teacher communicates effectively with colleagues and staff by

a. participating in the group decision-making process

b. listening to and considering suggestions from the staff

c. sharing ideas and resources with others

Standard 14 The competent teacher communicates responsibly to the public the significance of the school program by

a. answering parents' inquiries promptly, honestly, and discretely

b. initiating when necessary communication with parents

c. having available or locating information to relate district philosophy to the community at large

Area: School Relationships

Standard 15 The competent teacher has a consistent and professional attitude toward accomplishment of own school goals by

(*continued*)

Table 4.1 District Standards of Competent Performance (*continued*)

a. contributing to the decision-making process and abiding by group decisions

b. accepting shared responsibilities in and out of the classroom during the school day

c. maintaining consistency in record keeping as defined by building or district administrative regulations and procedures

d. using adopted courses of study or adjusting teaching objectives to include such adoptions

e. carrying out reasonable requests given by proper authority

Standard 16 The competent teacher has a consistent and professional attitude toward the accomplishment of district and state goals by

a. adhering to and enforcing school law, state board regulations, school board policy, and established administrative procedures.

b. adhering to the Employee Conduct and Responsibility requirements as stated in the Board Policy Handbook.[2]

Source: Adapted from Beaverton, Oregon Schools Personnel Handbook.

tiveness" in terms of what students are able to do before and after working with a particular teacher.

Teacher evaluation in the past has sometimes made use of several sources of information. Observation by supervisors is one. Another is student ratings of teachers. Systematic observation instruments used by others besides supervisors form another possibility. So does self-evaluation. Gains shown by students, as measured by test scores or other criteria, are another possible source. Scores on standardized teaching tests might be used.

Unfortunately, the most common source of information has been the evaluator's subjective feelings, which are influenced by the teacher's personality, style, philosophy (in relation to the evaluator's), staff relations, social patterns, and other factors, all of which may be important but are not central to teaching effectiveness.

Job Descriptions

Related to district standards are job descriptions. They should contain some of the same language and be consistent with the standards. In addition, they explicate the duties and responsibilities of the teacher. The district standards would be the basis for judging incompetent performance, whereas the job description would be the basis for judging neglect of duty.

Once a district has a set of standards like those that have been illustrated, there are several possibilities for how they can be used in the process of evaluating teachers. The characteristics can be emphasized: *is neat, orderly, cooperative* or *is creative, enthusiastic, energetic.* Using personal traits as the basis for summative evaluations has a long tradition but has not been very effective in either encouraging teachers to change or dismissing those who don't.

Another possibility is to use the processes as absolute standards: *reinforces positive behavior immediately and explicitly* or *does not plan lessons to meet individual needs.* Beginning teachers and teachers who are insecure may welcome the reassurance of an explicit set of expectations. It is also possible that the most spectacular teachers any of us ever knew don't give a hoot about such expectations.

A third possible use of official standards is to emphasize student outcomes: *made, on the average, a gain of 1 year in reading comprehension.* Most teachers are apprehensive about too much emphasis being placed on what their pupils accomplish: "But you gave me a bunch of turkeys this year." As the coach of a professional football team said in turning down an attractive college job, "I don't want my career to depend on what a bunch of adolescents do on a Saturday afternoon."

A fourth possibility is to borrow an idea from business and industry and have "job targets" as an aspect of "management by objectives." To do this well, one needs explicit and irrefutable descriptions of the essential elements of a particular job.

A fifth possibility—the one advocated here—is to have a set of standards, which apply to all teachers, and job descriptions that describe unique duties and responsibilities that apply to teachers with specific assignments in specialized areas of the school program. Some examples of teachers with specialized assignments are counselors, special education teachers, and resource center coordinators.

The following job description (Table 4.2) illustrates an assignment in which performance would be assessed on the basis of the primary accountabilities in addition to the general standards for all teachers.[3] The standards and job descriptions provide guidelines for teachers to refer to in setting annual goals for self-improvement, staff development, and professional advancement. The concerns teachers can translate into goals or targets can come from a variety of sources. In the past, leaders who evaluated teaching have used various criteria of teaching performance—traits, competencies, and effectiveness: that is, what kinds of people teachers are, what they can do, and what they accomplish. The situation within which they teach has relevance, as does the organizational nature of the school in particular. Other factors that need to be recognized are the social system within and around the school; the legal, governmental, and political conditions; the economy within which the school exists; and the influential culture(s) of the community referred to as parts of the "setting."

Goals can serve two kinds of needs—growth needs and deficiency needs. Teachers with deficiency needs, previously identified by evaluations with respect to district standards or job descriptions, must attend to these concerns before concentrating on goals that are strictly for personal growth. Although building on strengths is a desirable activity, it should not prevent a teacher from eliminating undesirable practices or cultivating desirable ones that have hitherto been missing.

Performance Goals

To evaluate a teacher on the basis of the complete list of district standards would be a large undertaking if it were to be done objectively. An alternative is to concentrate on a few items that are of concern to the teacher, or the observer, and agree on these as goals for a given year. The formal evaluation then is based on the progress that was made toward accomplishing the goals. If a teacher develops a serious problem in mid-year, the goals should be modified to address the problem.

Teachers have a tendency to look for "safe" goals when they know they will be evaluated on the basis of them. The observer needs some skill at negotiating, or insisting on, goals that are important. Skill is also required in stating goals clearly. Some questions can be asked about a goal statement:

Table 4.2   Position Description

Position description

Position: Teacher

Reports to: Principal (or His/Her Designee)

Position Purpose:

Implements, supervises, and maintains a high quality learning environment for students within the specific curriculum and standards of the district.

Nature and Scope:

The teacher is a professional with the responsibility for implementing a curriculum. Inherent in this responsibility is the requirement of related academic knowledge, technical skills, and professional attitudes and judgments.

The teacher must have the ability to diagnose the needs of learners and to evaluate their performance. The teacher must also be able to prescribe learning activities appropriate to student needs and to constructively evaluate these activities. The teacher effects an optimum learning climate through appropriate and maximum use of all resources available, and through the use of effective instructional and classroom management techniques.

In addition to the requirement of technical competence, the teacher maintains an attitude and conduct which is consistent with the district policy of professional conduct. The teacher follows building and district procedural guidelines and policy.

Primary Accountabilities:

1. Identifies the needs of students through diagnostic procedures and relates instructional objectives to these needs. Plans, prepares, and executes appropriate lessons, utilizing appropriate resource materials and activities.

2. Maintains student records as required by the school.

3. Communicates with parents, students, and other professional staff regarding student progress (behavioral and academic).

4. Follows a curriculum that is prescribed by state, district, or building.

5. Assures students of learning opportunities within a classroom environment that facilitates learning.

6. Meets the district's Standards of Competent Performance at all times.

7. Follows district and school policies, procedures, rules, regulations, and guidelines and the provisions of the contract.

Source: School District 48J, Beaverton, OR.

Is the called-for behavior (a) observable, (b) measurable, (c) describable?

Is it clear what the criterion level will be? (How much is enough?)

Under what conditions will the behavior take place?

Is it related to the district standards or job description?

Is it important?

What resources will be required?

How will the teacher proceed to reach the goal?

Figure 4.2 shows a form used in a school district to record the goals of educators (teachers, administrators, and others) for a given year.

```
                        Eugene Public Schools
                  School District No. 4J, Lane County
                          Eugene, Oregon


                          EDUCATOR GOAL PLAN


        Educator's Name_____

        Assignment _____ Year _____ Building _____


     I.  GOAL STATEMENT


        List the activities/behaviors you have planned to accomplish this goal.




     II.  MONITORING
         List the planned activities and/or procedures for measuring goal accomplishment.



        Approved by _____(Supervisor's Signature) Date _____

    III.  ANALYZING AND ASSESSING
         Educator:  Comment on the degree to which this goal was accomplished and list
         the data used to support your judgment.




        Educator's Signature _____Date _____

        Supervisor:  Comment on the degree to which this goal was accomplished.




        Supervisor's Signature _____ Date _____

     1984 - Form EG-3 (One sheet should be used for each goal developed by/for
            the educator.)
```

Figure 4.2 Educator goal plan.

Source: Eugene Public Schools, School District 4J, Lane County, Eugene, OR, 1984.

Formal Evaluations

Sometimes teachers are not very good at writing clear goal statements, and some adminis-trators are not very good at writing formal evaluations. The written evaluations tend to be euphemistic and not explicit. When a dismissal occurs and the teacher has had 10 years of these vague kinds of evaluation, it is difficult to make the case. If one purpose for the for-mal evaluation is to assist the teacher's growth in instructional effectiveness, then vague generalities in the report are not very helpful. Crisply stated goals and explicit yearly evaluations could be computer-stored and accessed as a database for making decisions about inservice staff development.

Plans of Assistance

"Due process" requires that before a permanent teacher is summarily dismissed for lack of competence, there be an effort to help remedy the deficiencies. One way to do this is through an official plan of assistance. In some states this is explicitly required by law. A point of contention in dismissal hearings is often whether a plan of assistance was properly designed and carried out.

When a plan of assistance is called for, often the principal who put the teacher on notice is then expected to design and conduct the remedial program. If there is tension between the principal and the teacher, and there often is, then it is difficult to conduct a truly helpful program. The formation of a small committee to assume this responsibility is recommended. One member should be a neutral, i.e., objective, administrator; another can be a person chosen by the teacher to serve as advocate for the teacher. The third person can be someone with special knowledge, expertise, or skill in the area(s) of the teacher's deficiency. In Oregon, the Fair Dismissal Appeals Law requires that permanent teachers who are deficient in complying with district standards are entitled to a program of assistance. Probationary teachers are entitled to a hearing.

The committee should reach agreement on what the plan of assistance will consist of, how long it will last, and what will be accepted as satisfactory evidence that the deficiency has been remedied. The committee can call on other people and resources to carry out the planned activities.

Postevaluation Conferences

The teacher and observer should meet to discuss the formal evaluation before it is placed in the permanent personnel file. The teacher should have the opportunity to write a rebuttal that will be filed along with the evaluation if there is irreconcilable disagreement. The postevaluation conference is also a good place to begin outlining the next year's goals for most teachers. For a few teachers, this conference will be held to discuss a dismissal notice.

Postdismissal Activities

When the evaluation process results in a dismissal, there are almost always additional activities. These may take many forms: grievances, arbitration, hearings, or even lawsuits. There are several implications for clinical supervision techniques in connection with these occurrences. Consider an observer on the witness stand being cross-examined by the teacher's attorney.

"On what basis were these judgments made?" Systematic observational data recorded in the classroom can help answer this question.

"Did the teacher receive any feedback from these observations?" A record of postobservation conferences is useful.

"Was any help provided to the teacher?" If a plan of assistance was carried out it needs to be on record.

Several problems develop from these relationships. The use of systematic classroom observational data as evidence in a dismissal may tarnish the image of objective data as helpful to a teacher's growth. The remedial, corrective, or negative nature of a plan of assistance may diminish the luster of those same techniques that were used to promote strengths. When observation is regarded as inspection, when data become evidence, and when feedback equals criticism, the trust relationship so vital to good supervision is difficult to establish or restore. One way of dealing with this dilemma is to separate formative (growth) activities from summative (judgmental) evaluation by using colleagues for the former and evaluators for the latter.

Approximately thirty dismissal cases have been studied in some depth in connection with preparing expert testimony. Several things become obvious in reading the personnel files and listening to the testimony at these hearings. If the school district administrators do a conscientious job of carrying out all the elements previously described, and if they have documented all the events carefully, they will prevail. If, on the other hand, they have been careless, arbitrary, or capricious, the teacher will win.

CONCLUSION

Clinical supervision is the heart of a good teacher evaluation system. The planning, observation, and feedback cycle should occur several times so that the teacher has an opportunity to grow and improve as well as to be evaluated. Where plans of assistance are required, the clinical cycle is again the key tool, but is used more frequently and with greater intensity.

School administrators tell us that when intensive assistance has been called for, approximately half of the teachers recover, a quarter resign voluntarily, and a quarter are dismissed (and usually appeal the decision). In cases where dismissed teachers have been reinstated by an arbitrator or hearing panel, it is usually because the district has failed to provide due process, such as a satisfactory program of assistance. Some of the records for an unsatisfactory program have been:

- setting an unreasonable number of goals for the teacher.
- not providing feedback after observations.
- displaying evidence of prejudice or vindictiveness.
- not providing sufficient time for the program to have an effect.

NOTES

1. Keith A. Acheson, *Teacher evaluation policies and practices in four western provinces and four northwest states,* report of a study supported by the Canadian Embassy, 1986.

2. Adapted from Beaverton, Oregon, Schools Personnel Handbook.

3. School District 48J, Beaverton, OR.

Chapter 5

Peer Consultation*

Author's note

Interest in the roles that peers can play using the techniques of clinical supervision spans 40 years. The invention of the portable videotape recorder in 1961 led to a study of direct and indirect styles of feedback with or without television recordings of actual teacher behavior.[1] The effect of television recordings was significant; the effects of style were not. There have been studies of this type in which the control group outdid the experimental groups.

Twenty-five years later two studies looked at the effects of teachers using these techniques with other teachers.[2, 3] Other studies and projects have shown benefits derived from collegial approaches to using the techniques advocated in this book. Who does it appears to be important along with what it is, and how it is done. Why it is done is usually called "professional development," or "professional growth," with "accountability" given as a second reason. We suspect that the second reason overwhelms the first. Other writers seem to agree. A stronger discomfort results from what hundreds of teachers have told us—that the "what," i.e., any sort of observation and feedback, seldom occurs. Encouraging teachers to gain the skills and take the time to help others grow as professionals in return for receiving similar help strikes many teachers (not all teachers) as a worthwhile activity.

The major obstacle is time. Teachers (and administrators) may use lack of time as a handy excuse for not doing many desirable things. However, it is also a valid excuse for conscientious educators. A half-century in schools, colleges, and universities substantiates, for this observer, that the number of responsibilities laid on educators has grown immense.

If we would put a higher priority on what is described in the chapter that follows we could solve the time problem. Twenty minutes is enough for an observation (twenty is plenty). Planning conferences can take as little as five minutes if both participants know what they are talking about. Data from observations can be given to the teacher immediately. Conferences can take place before and after the school day.

KAA

Nothing new that is really interesting comes without collaboration.

—James Watson, Nobel laureate, co-discoverer of the double helix

---

*We acknowledge the work of Neil Stephenson Smith[2]; Mohammed Shamsher[3]; Smith and Acheson[4]; Acheson, Shamsher, and Smith[5]; and all who have participated in the British Columbia Teachers' Federation Program for Quality Teaching since 1982.

INTRODUCTION

Peer consultation is a school-based process in which teachers work in consort with colleagues in a reciprocal way to provide one another with descriptive feedback and discussion about observed teaching in order to enhance professional growth and organizational development. This definition has also been used to analyze other models of collegial observation in relation to their implementation. The underlying theoretical and philosophical principles differed. They were divided into two broad categories: peer coaching for technical proficiency and peer consultation for critical reflection.

Three questions are important here. *What is peer consultation?* The answer will be discussed through a look at the literature, some comparisons, and a review of research conducted within the Program for Quality Teaching (PQT) of the British Columbia Teachers' Federation in recent years. These studies have been compared with subsequent projects in other settings and differing situations. *Why do teachers get involved in peer consultation?* Individual experiences will be analyzed through interviews. *Where does peer consultation appear to work best?* The levels of participant involvement will be considered and the conditions and factors which influenced the chances for success of various programs will be described.

About two hundred interviews have been conducted with teachers, principals, and other educators who have been associated with peer consultation. The interviews were analyzed according to the aforementioned three key questions. Questionnaires surveyed PQT participants at the end of the first year and fifth year. Notes from observations of teachers doing peer consulting, written feedback from participants at instructional sessions, and follow-up interviews with selected teachers, facilitators, and developers at the end of the fifth year of operation (for PQT) and after 1 to 4 years of operation for other projects were added to the database. Another rich source of information was participation as developers, presenters, or active members in the project(s).

Our research was not designed to evaluate the effectiveness of peer consultation in relation to student achievement, but, rather, to describe how teachers and administrators, with different goals and organizational needs, have interpreted it. Contacts with actively involved educators included elementary schools in inner-city Winnipeg, Manitoba and suburban Portland, Oregon; several school districts in Saskatchewan and Alberta; two high schools and a medical school in Oregon; and a community college in Alberta, in addition to those in British Columbia. These contacts have been followed up by personal visits at varying intervals of months or years.

Peer Coaching toward Technical Proficiency

Here, coaching practice seemed to be aimed at safeguarding adoptions of new models of instruction. Most of them were linked with peer *coaching*, for example, Instructional Theory into Practice (ITIP) and Teacher Effectiveness Training (TET), are grounded in behaviorist learning theory. The coaching practices connected with these models appeared to work from the same theoretical system. Teachers' behaviors with colleagues in the coaching relationships corresponded to those they employed with the students in their classrooms: demonstration-practice-feedback-reinforcement-refinement. A key word was *training*—"to bring a person to a desired state or standard of efficiency by instruction and practice." The responsibility of the peer coach was to ensure that his or her partner deviated as little as possible from the prescribed model of instruction. Written and verbal feedback given the teacher by the peer coach reinforced "correct" behaviors and identified errors. Teacher performance was judged according to the criteria defined by the model of instruction studied. The observed teacher's responsibility was to apply the feedback to the refinement of practice in using the model.

There seemed to be three advantages in this type of peer coaching: First, from the teachers' perspective, there was an opportunity to work with colleagues toward the mastery of a model of instruction that was common to all. Most of these programs asserted that the models of instruction led to increased student learning in areas of basic skills as measured by standardized tests. Students were expected to benefit by experiencing a more consistent education in terms of discipline and teaching strategies.

Second, in many schools where peer coaching was used, teacher evaluation became more standardized as evaluators adopted the approved behaviors from the instructional skills programs as criteria for judging effective teaching.

Third, from the district perspective, a tightly linked, standardized instructional system could be projected. Teaching behaviors and related student learning were controlled through centralized administration of training and peer coaching, reinforced by a standardized system of pupil testing and teacher evaluation. In simple terms, peer coaching appeared to be a vehicle for controlling organizational uniformity.

Six disadvantages are inherent in the peer coaching models: Implementation is typically "top-down," that is, designed for the classroom but initiated outside the classroom. This gives teachers little sense of ownership of the process. Teachers are apt to feel constricted by the expectation that they must *adopt* the proposed methods, rather than *adapt* them to their classroom programs. Teachers indicate that they feel constrained by the implicit expectation that they use only the prescribed model of teaching. There is also some doubt as to the validity of the research linking the instructional skills to student outcomes on standardized tests.

At the outset of most implementations, teachers believed that learning new instructional methodologies through coaching was exclusively for their professional growth. They were dismayed when the new models of instruction became the exclusive standard by which administrators evaluated their teaching. In extreme cases, if teachers did not adhere to the standards of the new model, unsatisfactory reports would be written, even in cases where students were meeting learning objectives defined in the curriculum. Teachers felt there was not enough flexibility in the methods connected with most programs of peer coaching. They were discouraged from using inquiry or critical thinking, whose divergent outcomes were difficult to fit with behavioral objectives that they were expected to pursue.

Finally, one of the greatest problems for teachers was to be asked to judge each other's performance. To what extent teachers were disaffected by the judgment of colleagues remains unclear, but the findings clearly identify the sensitivity that most teachers have about the evaluation of their teaching. Also worth noting is that most programs of peer coaching did not emphasize the development of interpersonal communication skills needed to maintain healthy relationships between teachers and coaches. It is possible that the lack of such training added to the problems in the implementation of peer coaching.

The disadvantages of peer-coaching models can be summarized by saying that teachers appeared to be intolerant of having their powers of self-evaluation and decision-making significantly reduced. The research on these models indicates that most teachers, once the external accountability measures were removed, rejected the prescribed models and the peer coaching that supported them.

Peer Consultation toward Critical Reflection

The second general group of peer consultation types include Instructional Fine-tuning and Reflection, Reflective Practice and Innovation, and Organization Development. They differ from peer coaching in an important way. They are aimed at the development of practices selected and evaluated on standards defined by the teachers, not by external experts. Underlying these types are the humanistic and cognitivist theories of learning that place the evaluation and control of instruction in the teacher. Accordingly, the principal role of the consultant is to provide his or her partner with specific feedback as requested on aspects of teaching *chosen by the teacher* and provide support for the partner's critical reflection in planning and feedback conferences.

The general advantages of this "peer consulting toward critical reflection" group are threefold. Opportunity for change and development of new knowledge about teaching is granted to the teachers at the classroom level. Teachers learn a variety of tools for providing colleagues with objective feedback related to different learning methodologies. Teachers are given the professional freedom to experiment and test their own theories of teaching and learning without fear of reprisal from a judgmental peer or administrator/evaluator.

Conversely, these kinds of peer consultation have four disadvantages: A high degree of self-initiative is required of teachers. It is voluntary, and the numbers of teachers currently interested in this kind of professional endeavor may be a minority. This leaves those teachers with low self-initiative unaffected. Secondly, the organization of such a professional development system is loosely coupled, which translates into less administrative control over the teaching methods, teacher evaluation, and student-learning outcomes. The de-emphasis on matching teacher-evaluation strategies with standardized student testing adds to the problem of accountability. Thirdly there is little evidence to support the notion that peer consultation for critical reflection positively affects student learning. Finally, critical reflection is not a high priority in the present culture of schools in which practicality is celebrated. Altered perspectives—financial and symbolic—are required before a new kind of leadership can emerge. Many administrators currently in service may be unable to accommodate these changes.

Conclusions from Comparative Analysis

Summarizing the two groups of peer-assistance types, *coaching* and *consulting,* has highlighted some important differences in what people tend to think are all the same practices. The most striking variance is that the first group of peer-coaching types aims to change the behaviors of teachers by using a system of high structure and centralized support. Formal bureaucratic structures, including teacher-evaluation procedures and standardized pupil testing, are set in place to enforce this behavioral change. Such systems as these reflect low estimates of teachers' skills and a belief that teachers are lazy and unimaginative. They appear to be designed as a catch-net for marginal teachers, reluctant teachers, and those who simply need a high degree of structure before they can enter into anything new. In spite of all the formal accountability measures, these centralized, top-down programs do not cause long-lasting change.

The second type of assistance appears to be designed for teachers who operate from the opposite end of the spectrum, although this impression is not overtly stated by any of the program architects. The support systems in this group tend to be less formal, and they become highly dysfunctional if attempts are made to bureaucratize them. Any attempts from central administration to control the peer-consultative process usually fail abruptly. The success of peer consulting seems to be dependent on the health of the immediate culture and the shared meaning within the group. Administrators were most functional when they were able to help teachers come to some common understanding of what was going on and to support teachers in their pursuit of the goals that *they* (the teachers) defined.

On the other hand, administrators were most successful when they helped teachers work toward these goals, rather than impose externally defined criteria, such as standardized pupil assessment and teacher evaluation to guide teacher activity. The literature on peer-consultation types in the second group, however, did not provide substantial evidence that long-term change has occurred. However, the concept is relatively new, and what we predict, based on what we have observed in PQT and other programs during more than a decade, is that the peer-consultation notion, for teachers, will persist and grow.

Continuum Relating Peer Consultation Types to Other Educational Factors

To help understand how peer consultation fits into the larger educational scene, a continuum may clarify the relationship of the peer-consultation types to other educational factors and influences (Figure 5.1). This figure is intended to help establish the fit between different styles of communication, teaching, peer consulting, and leadership. One emergent idea is that there seems to be very little thought given to the relationship among these levels of operation in our North American system of education. This omission leads to circumstances, for example, where very self-directed and mature teachers might suddenly find themselves in an educational innovation that is very prescriptive and is led by a principal who is infinitely directive and judgmental. Or, conversely, laissez-faire administrators might end up in situations where they are asked to lead a very tightly prescribed instructional program. It must, however, be stated at the outset that there is no *fixed* relationship among any of the elements identified on this spectrum. It merely represents a rough assembling of understandings that may clarify the families of educational functions most closely associated with peer consultation.

At the top of the continuum are placed *Ways of Communicating*. These approximate the range of communication styles that peer consultants might use with one another. On the left side, the style is didactic—even prescriptive—and is often associated with peer-coaching techniques that inform colleagues about where they have deviated from the expected practice. Here, the colleague observer often is expected to control the assessment and flow of information. Standards are fixed and externally developed from principles created outside the teacher's classroom. On the right side are modes of communication that are nondirective and transactional in nature. Some examples of communication on this side are questioning, clarifying, and listening. The orientation in this family is communication that fosters self-evaluation and self-direction. The aim is to work toward

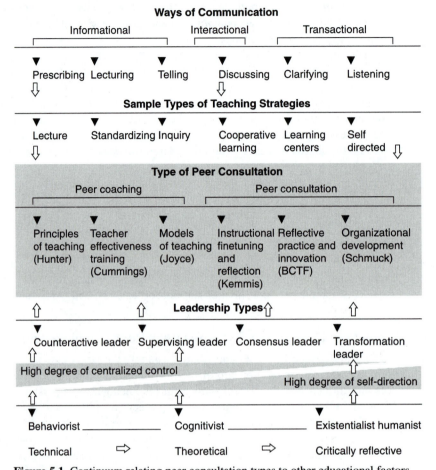

Figure 5.1 Continuum relating peer consultation types to other educational factors.

Source: Smith, Neil Stephenson, *Peer consultation as a means of professional growth.* Ph.D. Dissertation, University of Oregon, 1989.

human development with less emphasis on technical proficiency than would be found on the left side. These types of communication are more often associated with practices of peer consultation and organization development, rather than with peer coaching.

On the second level of the spectrum are *Sample Types of Teaching Strategies*. Admittedly, they have been oversimplified and stereotyped, but nonetheless, cooperative learning, self-directed learning, and learning centers are located on the right side. If implemented in a heuristic fashion, these correspond to the focus on self-direction and self-evaluation, and match closely with peer consultation for reflective practice. On the other side, the more didactic styles of teaching, for example, lecture and standardized learning, relate more to the practice of peer coaching. Although it is inaccurate to place all the peer coaching models on the didactic side of the scale, it is accurate to suggest that most peer coaching deals with directive coaching—processes that attempt to lead a teacher toward a specific model, usually some form of direct instruction. Although the architects insist that the elements of effective teaching are transferable to all types of teaching strategies, this style of coaching would not work if the peer coach could not quickly compare the observed practice to prescriptive guidelines.

On the third level, three learning theories are identified, ranging from behaviorism with emphasis on technical functions, through cognitivism, to humanism with a tendency toward critical reflection. Underlying all these is centralized control. This control is usually opposed to the amount of self-direction afforded to the learner (who may be a student or a teacher).

Leadership Types relate to peer consultation types. For example, the supervising leader would be better suited to coaching toward direct teaching models than would the transformative leader. Different leaders fit certain peer-consultation programs. Educators should consider how peer consultation and peer coaching relate to the broad spectrum of education. It could prevent "forced fits" when caught in innovations for which they are philosophically and practically ill suited.

There are drawbacks to this notion. For example, consider Teaching Strategies. The Lecture, if shaped in heuristic manner, can be a powerful catalyst for self-directed learning and discovery. Similarly, the types of peer consultation called Reflective Practice and Innovation could easily be used by a person who wants to learn more about direct instruction. We urge you to view the continuum only as a general representation of the issues raised.

THE NATURE OF PEER CONSULTATION IN PRACTICE

Why Did Teachers Choose to Become Involved?

Teachers who entered PQT typically had 10–15 years of teaching experience. This was also true in other K–12 projects, although an occasional hardy first- or second-year teacher volunteered (having experienced "mentoring" in some cases). Teachers in community colleges, vocational colleges, and medical school programs usually had fewer years of direct teaching experience, though all had some experience as teachers.

Interviews and interactions showed that many lacked confidence in their teaching abilities and were reluctant to be observed by colleagues for fear of being judged. Like weathered consumers, most entered these programs with a healthy cynicism about the underlying motivations and stability of such projects. Many felt abandoned, manipulated, insulted, or bored by previous projects to which, regretfully, they had dedicated themselves. In PQT, most were confident the 3-year partnership between the teachers' federation and the local school board was a potentially solid program. Most were committed to finding out about the philosophical and practical possibilities of peer consultation *prior* to volunteering.

Teachers felt much could be learned about their own teaching and from the teaching of their colleagues. Most preconceptions of peer consulting lacked a realistic notion of the time commitment required to make it meet their needs, and the difficulty of finding some space in busy schedules.

Teachers joined PQT and its counterparts with different goals:

1. To learn ways to collect data and confer with colleagues. Many had been involved in peer observations in the past and wanted to learn different ways to collect information that could be used with a variety of models of teaching.

2. To learn how to work with colleagues in conferences that were interesting and challenging, but not alienating. Many teachers had worked with peer observation before and had found it to be either too benign or too critical in its impact.

3. To work with colleagues in the study of teaching. They looked on the classroom, clinic, shop, or laboratory as a rich source of ideas to regenerate teaching commitment, and saw colleagues as an untapped source of professional knowledge. Most of the inservice they had experienced was apart from the realities of their situations. They saw in peer consultation a way to make the study of their own work (as teachers) a legitimate activity.

4. To reduce feelings of professional isolation. Working with a colleague or colleagues on a common project was perceived as a way to develop important professional relationships that transcend staff room chatter and, at the same time, preserve personal autonomy.

Inservice Preparation for Peer Consulting

Interviews and questionnaires reveal that only after some months of application and practice did most teachers begin to recognize two aspects that were essential for their preparation as peer consultants. One was learning to communicate with a colleague nonjudgmentally. The second was learning to select aspects of one's own teaching that are relevant and important to the practice of self-evaluation and to be able to look at them in a critical yet constructive manner.

Different sources of data reveal that a few teachers find a 5-day instructional session overly complex or unnerving (particularly undergoing the stress of microteaching) to the point that they do not trust the process enough to commit themselves to it. Medical instructors who have traditionally believed that they can "see one, do one, teach one," saw an evening and a morning in a pleasant retreat as perhaps "not enough." Subsequent monthly meetings of 2 hours at a variety of hospitals, restaurants (for breakfast), or homes proved to be instructive and satisfying.

Different generations of instructional groups operated as different subcultures within their milieus, separated not by dissimilar knowledge, but by separate training experiences. In some places, people who were influenced by one training session had difficulty integrating with groups who had attended other sessions. In others, this was not a problem. This phenomenon may present a challenge for educators. Those who are planning systems of long-term change and educational renewal should examine carefully the natural development of subcultures that can emerge from separate training sessions. The split cultures that developed in our studies tended to detract from the possibility of organizational collaboration. Yet we also found that attempts to involve everyone in processes like peer consultation all at once, even in a small family-like school, or subgroup, is not always a viable answer to this problem.

Peer Consulting: What Is It, Really?

From the outside, the popular image of peer consulting is something like this: Teachers are given time off from their classes, they observe one another, they learn from the observations and possibly learn new things from one another, and isolation is reduced. In reality, we found that peer consultation is difficult and complex. In one sense, the process does have a simple elegance. Its mechanics are logical and comprehensible. It appears to enable teachers to engage at levels of complexity suited to their needs. It seems adaptable to investigating and learning about most functions of teaching. Our research revealed that most teachers were able to complete planning conferences (or describe what they were interested in observing), observe and collect data pertinent to their colleagues, and subsequently provide requested information and supportive analysis in the feedback conferences.

However, peer consultation is also enigmatic and mysterious. Reaching a stage of harmonious operation and providing a colleague or colleagues with interactions that promote critical reflection is often a formidable challenge. Generally, the peer-consultative process is seen as a plausible means of professional development, but it requires certain conditions to function well. Three areas are especially worthy of mention: (1) levels of engagement, (2) teacher commitment, and (3) coping with time shortage.

Levels of Engagement

Teachers operated in peer consultation at different levels. In most cases they were working toward higher levels of engagement. Some maintained their activity at one level, satisfied with what it provided. First was the level of avoidance in which teachers maintained their belonging status, but in reality never became involved in practicing peer consultation. Perhaps 10 percent engaged in this dance at the edge of the pool, never getting wet, but, interestingly, never throwing in the towel. Reasons for avoidance might include low self-esteem, low trust of colleagues' abilities to observe nonjudgmentally, fear of being observed, and the perception that teaching is a "performance" rather than a dynamic process of professional decisions.

The majority of PQT teachers engaged in peer consultation at the second level. They used it for everything from making simple adjustments in their current techniques to experimenting with new theories and models of teaching. Teachers typically started with safe observations involving students' work, then moved to observations they considered higher risk, such as teacher–student interactions. Teachers at this level most commonly found (1) increased collegiality in their work, (2) increased understanding of their teaching, (3) improved abilities to analyze their own teaching, and (4) increased knowledge of the teacher-evaluation system. They were usually successful in developing skills of self-evaluation. Some were successful in their pursuit of effective dialogue with colleagues about theoretical and philosophical considerations, a luxury seldom afforded in the culture of the staff room.

At the third level, critical reflection, 10–15 percent of PQT teachers found peer consultation useful as a means to examine their teaching critically and to guide fundamental changes in how they conceived their teaching practices. With the support of colleagues, they ventured into serious examinations of their beliefs about teaching and learning. A few struggled with the transition from one paradigm of teaching to another that was entirely different.

Eight PQT teachers volunteered in the third year of the program to become part of a research group whose goal was to develop narrative descriptions of their work and to share this knowledge about their teaching with others by publishing it in provincial teachers' journals. By the spring of 1989, both of these goals had been accomplished. In the first medical teacher group, a similar goal was accomplished following their year of meetings.

There is no shortage of difficulties in learning the art and practice of critical reflection. Time limitations, conservative norms of the culture for teachers, emphasis on practicality in schools, lack of familiarity with the concept of reflection, and low self-esteem of teachers are some of the factors that work against critically reflective practice. When motivation is high and situational factors are favorable, teachers succeed in learning the skills of promoting one another's critical inquiry and self-evaluation.

The work necessary for some teachers in PQT and similar programs to succeed at the top level was not cheap. If, however, self-review and school-based development are things that we would like to nurture in preparation for the schools, colleges, and universities of tomorrow, perhaps teachers and administrators who are succeeding at breaking the norms of today represent an important foothold on new ways of functioning in teaching institutions. Moreover, if the levels of engagement represent a sequential development, then the more teachers practice peer consulting, even at the levels of fine-tuning, the more likely teachers will be prepared to work toward higher levels of reflective practice. Ideally, projects such as these, carefully studied, will help identify how higher levels of understanding teaching in classrooms, clinics, and elsewhere can be reached.

Teacher Commitment

Teachers who became engaged in the process had varying degrees of commitment. This commitment was affected by a number of important conditions and influences.

Clarity of Personal Goals.   This was a major influence on how deeply teachers became involved in peer consultation. Those who were unsure of their goals, or how well they were meeting them, had serious problems analyzing their experiences. It not only diminished their commitment but negatively affected their peers.

Clarity of Group Goals.   Almost as important as individual goals was the clarity of the goals that shaped a common purpose among teams of teachers. The whole function of organizational development procedures, where attended to, helped the group function as a healthy entity, support the structure, and ease decision-making. Ill-defined goals and an unstructured group of aimless individuals led to a quick breakdown.

Understanding Self-evaluation and Self-direction.   Many teachers, even the most confident and competent, lacked clear concepts of their own abilities and ways of assessing them, perhaps a natural consequence of the organized isolation that finds teachers in a vacuum devoid of useful feedback from colleagues.

Teachers have few reliable sources of data from professional colleagues for constructing reliable self-concepts. Related to this is a tendency by many to be caught in tension between self-determination and traditional dependence and comfort provided by deferring to authority.

This tension surfaces in teachers' comments that reflect a strong desire for personal autonomy in decisions that affect their teaching and a reluctance to take the steps necessary to realize the desire. Self-evaluation is a skill, as well as an attitude, needed to examine critically one's own strengths and weaknesses. It is not easy, nor is it commonplace, in our system of education.

Many teachers had difficulty with this in attempting to progress beyond the neophyte stages of consulting. Our educational system functions almost exclusively on evaluation by others and seems to have given teachers little preparation for self-evaluation. And in most classrooms, clinics, or offices the students are still implicitly given to believe the myth that the teacher is one whose knowledge is complete, and for whom weaknesses are never considered. The teachers' reinterpretation of their roles as experts to include being life-long learners, or models of self-reflection in the eyes of students, represents a radical departure from the traditional norms.

What has become clear is that teacher commitment to pursuing peer consultation and adopting a course of critical reflection regarding their own work must be conceived as a developmental process. For teachers to move from one extreme to the other involves major adjustments affecting the way they think of themselves as teachers and as human beings. The challenge becomes existential as well as technical and theoretical.

For many, to become genuinely reflective (and critical) of their work through peer consultation demands the support and nurture of empathic colleagues to help them sort through the more difficult questions regarding their teaching. In our study of peer consultation, the role of the trustworthy and supportive colleague was of paramount importance among all the conditions for successful consultation.

Time Shortage

For years we have heard principals and other administrator/evaluators say, "We like your observation techniques and would use them . . . if we just had time." Now, when peer consultation is discussed with teachers, we hear the same lament. There is precious little time available for all the functions we expect schools to perform these days. However, if our priorities include staff development near the top, then we can make time for this activity.

Other Factors.

There are several other factors that affect the peer-consultative process.

Relationships with Colleagues. The list of prerequisites for successful peer consultation extracted from patterns of behavior in the case studies are strikingly similar to those for a successful marriage. Teachers who shared experiences in the instructional sessions, who had similar goals, who practiced open communication in their conferences, and who were similarly committed to peer consulting, were those who seemed to thrive in the process. Conflicts in relationships were most commonly reported in areas of differing values or interpersonal communications and problems of a colleague judging a partner's work.

Most teachers perceived a marked improvement in collegial relations as a result of peer consultation. They experienced improved relations with people in their groups, and noted special differences in the depth and quality of relations with their immediate consulting partners. Many talked about the importance of having at least one other person in the school who really seemed to understand their classroom, who was willing to share in sorting out their concerns and problems, and who would also share in the successes and failures of new attempts. In questionnaires and interviews, teachers indicated no discernible impact on relations with colleagues who were not involved in their projects.

Trust Levels.   Teachers felt that trust with colleagues increased as a result of the instructional session and subsequent peer-consultation practice. Coming to understand and know others' commitment to teaching, sharing risks together, and exchanging roles in observations engendered mutual confidence and comfort among colleagues.

Teachers spoke about the competitiveness that prevails in school culture. This competitiveness often precluded sharing, responding to, and supporting colleagues' successes or changes. These teachers reported that peer consultation shifted teachers away from a spirit of competitiveness toward true collaboration.

In the interviews and questionnaires, other factors that increase intercolleague trust were mentioned, including mutual respect. As teachers began to appreciate each other's talents and personal qualities, their confidence to adventure into new territory increased. Reciprocal responsibility was another factor mentioned. Teachers emphasized that a regular exchange of roles was essential. In situations where a person wanted to be the observer, but not the teacher, tension and conflict arose. Shared risk taking was a third factor. Taking risks together, both in the inservice and in the teaching situation, seemed to increase the levels of trust. With failures came support from colleagues and a renewed sense that the process was not going to destroy confidences. Separation from evaluation systems was also an important factor; when observed by administrators, teachers avoided mistakes at all costs. No risks meant very little learning. In evaluation, flawless and simple performance became the teachers' priority.

Leadership, at School Level and Beyond.   Along with teachers' capacities for self-leadership, various types of institutional leadership interacted positively or negatively with peer consultation. In roughly half the schools, administrators demonstrated a combination of high commitment to peer consultation and an ability to facilitate teacher self-direction through collaborative leadership. This type of leadership appeared to produce a safe and productive climate for peer consulting. Teachers felt honored and supported by this approach, and felt that the decisions that they made in the classroom were trusted.

These administrators (1) were able to listen to and understand teacher's perspectives; (2) did not mix peer consultation with teacher evaluation; (3) did not act as the judge of teachers' peer consultation efforts; (4) did not try to control the content of peer consultation; (5) placed a high value on the time that teachers spent in peer consultation; (6) actively supported peer consultation in discussion with other teachers, but were careful not to proselytize about it; (7) modeled the kinds of attitudes and skills that were consonant with peer consulting, for example, risk taking, trusting others, good listening skills; (8) were able to judge their appropriate degree of direct involvement in the process, and to respect teachers' autonomy and decision-making capacities; and (9) were adept at resolving conflicts among group members.

The combination of low commitment to peer consultation and a high degree of directiveness seemed to influence the process most negatively. Three leadership types were identified in the case studies that did not fit well with the peer consultative process: (1) the cheerleader, who was interested more in the form of peer consultation than the function; (2) the supervising leader, who had a sincere interest in seeing the process succeed, but was intent on judging the teachers' work and controlling the outcomes according to the leader's personal standards; and (3) the counteractive leader, who used a low level of commitment and a high level of directiveness to actively sabotage teachers' progress.

Leadership at upper levels was also important. Teachers relied on the administration for (1) budget support and (2) symbolic support that made teachers feel that their work in the project was valued, and that peer consultation was part of the institution's long-range plans.

Teachers also played important leadership roles in implementation. Although most did not choose to become involved in administrative tasks, they played vital roles in sustaining group vision and motivating their peers, often simply through example. In situations where groups lacked strong administration and teachers had to assume the leadership responsibilities, the demands were too great. The implementation in these cases appeared to be less successful, and groups were typically more fragmented.

Peer consultation is only a part of the restructuring and reforming that needs to take place in the educational system. It is, we believe, a very important element in that process. We have observed it in public, private, and separate schools in western Canada and the northwestern states. We have seen it take place in community colleges, graduate schools, vocational colleges, and medical schools. It is surprising that in all these settings it is unusual for teachers—be they primary, elementary, secondary, college, university, professional, or otherwise—to share their hopes, concerns, aspirations, and achievements with their closest colleagues, their peers. To do so, in a nonthreatening, nonjudgmental situation that provides some feedback from the real, not theoretical or hypothetical, world is a highly desirable and useful activity for many teachers.

NOTES

1. Acheson, K. A. (1964). *The effects of feedback from television recordings and three types of supervisory treatment on selected teacher behaviors.* Stanford.

2. Smith, N.S. (1989). *Peer consultation as a means of professional growth: A study in British Columbia schools.* Ph.D. Diss., Eugene, OR: University of Oregon.

3. Shamsher, M. (1992). *Peer consultation as a means to reflective practice and classroom research: A case study of the Program for Quality Teaching in British Columbia schools.* Ph.D. Diss., Eugene, OR: University of Oregon.

4. Smith, N. S., & Acheson, K. A. (1991). *Peer consultation: An analysis of several types of programs.* Eugene, OR: Oregon School Study Council, February.

5. Acheson, K. A., Shamsher, M. & Smith, N. S. (1998). Instructional development and supervision, Handbook of research on school supervision. Firth, G. and Pajac, E. Eds. (N.Y., Macmillan).

Unit Three

Conferencing Techniques

OVERVIEW

Data recorded by an observer must be shared with the teacher. Good data badly shared may become bad data. In this unit we look at some good ways to plan observation sessions with teachers and provide them with feedback, and we consider some of the interpersonal dynamics that are involved in the process. Chapter 6 looks at styles of interpersonal communication, while Chapters 7 and 8 are addressed to the planning and feedback conferences.

OBJECTIVES

The purpose of this unit is to help you develop

An appreciation for how the differences in styles and strategies can be accommodated in conferences with teachers

Methods for planning with teachers in order to observe most effectively

Explicit techniques for providing useful feedback to teachers to aid them in analyzing, interpreting, and modifying their instructional efforts

An approach to supervision conferences consistent with the goals set forth in Unit 1

Chapter 6

Styles of Interpersonal Communication in Clinical Supervision

Author's Note

In this chapter we emphasize two fundamental personal styles: direct and indirect. They have been applied to many studies of teaching, supervising, and other forms of interpersonal communication. There are numerous other ways to categorize personal styles. We mention some of them. What we supervisors and observers say to teachers is certainly important. How we say it is probably more important.

Think of doctors, dentists, counselors, teachers, administrators, parents, and others you have known. Some may have been very competent or skillful but you didn't look forward (with pleasure) to interacting with them. Others had flaws you were willing to overlook because you believed you would gain something from being with them. Our effectiveness as supervisors, peer consultants, mentors, or colleagues can be enhanced by recognizing that we are not all the same in how we perceive what is going on.

A recent "popular" book by a talented writer is titled *What Really Matters* (Schwartz, 1995).[1] It looks at a number of organized activities that are based on differing theories and practices that explore ways to think about how our personal style interacts with someone else.

We do not choose one system for analyzing styles over all others. We do not recommend trying to change your style that took a long time to develop. We do recommend that you respect others' styles that also took a long time to develop.

In the past decade there has been much progress made in research pertaining to personality styles or traits. Over two decades and four previous publications, we have been aware of the work done by Bales,[2] Cattell,[3] Murray and Rorschach,[4] Flanders,[5] Blumberg,[6] Hersey and Blanchard,[7] Gregorc,[8] Myers-Briggs,[9] Kiersey and Bates,[10] Kiersey[11] and many others who have studied how personality styles and interaction styles affect what can happen when observers give feedback to those they observe.

Some of the most intriguing findings in these fields of investigation have resulted in the Five-Factor Model or Big 5. The names of these factors are extraversion, conscientiousness, agreeableness, openness to experience, and emotional stability. A colleague at the University of Oregon, Lewis R. Goldberg,[12] has been a prominent researcher and writer in this field for many years.

—KAA

Take my advice: don't give advice.

—Anonymous

INTRODUCTION

The techniques in the chapter on feedback conferences can be used by any supervisor or peer observer who has systematically collected observational data to analyze with a teacher or colleague. How the data are interpreted and what decisions are reached will depend to a considerable extent on the supervisor's or consultant's style. Styles of consultation can be described in many ways. A common distinction is direct versus indirect styles.

Ned Flanders differentiates direct teaching styles (i.e., lecturing, directing, criticizing) from indirect styles (i.e., accepting feelings, encouraging, acknowledging, using student ideas). Arthur Blumberg uses similar categories for supervisor behavior and has gathered some evidence that teachers prefer an indirect style of supervision. The direct and indirect behaviors an observer may record in a classroom can also be noted in a conference. They can be placed on a continuum, though no scale is intended. They are: expressing and accepting feelings; praising, acknowledging and using others' ideas, asking questions; lecturing or otherwise engaging in monologue; directing; criticizing, even antagonizing.

Another range of possible conference behaviors on the teacher's part can be constructed using the work of Robert Spaulding.[13] His words that follow can be used to classify the behavior of young children in the classroom: escape, withdraw, respond to internal stimuli, respond to external stimuli, seek help, transact, share, self-direct, and attend. For an adult who is writing a term paper (or revising a book) the list can be read from right to left as predictable behaviors. Think of them as "coping" behaviors that one may also use to survive a one-on-one conference.

The behavior of either conferee can be described with labels used by Everett Shostrom.[14] His words are: warm, sensitive, dependent, supportive, controlling, critical, strong, aggressive These characteristics can be translated into verbs that describe a range of verbal behavior the supervisor or teacher can employ: care, guide, appreciate, empathize, respect, express, lead, and assert.

One can also view the observer's actions as aversive (dominating, punishing) or supportive (approving, receptive). Setting limits and setting goals are actions that usually lie between these extremes but can be pushed toward one end or the other.

Although teachers indicate a preference for observers who emphasize the supportive, caring style, these are not the only appropriate behaviors for an observer. Doing something aversive (e.g., when a parent prevents a child from playing on the highway) may indicate a caring style at times.

In the past decade, words such as those used above plus several thousand others that could describe personality traits or factors have been subjected to sophisticated factor analysis. The result is a surprising consensus among scientists who study human personality. The Five-Factor Model, or Big 5 comprise **E,** extraversion (surgence), **C,** conscientiousness, **A,** agreeableness, **O,** openness to experience (intellect), and **N,** emotional stability (low neuroticism).

This chapter recommends several techniques usually regarded as indirect, but direct observers also can use them. Indeed, they should be used when persuasive data are shared. The techniques are concerned with listening, acknowledging, clarifying, encouraging, guiding (rather than directing), supporting, and dealing with feelings. The techniques that follow are especially useful for consultants who want conferences to be "teacher-centered." Whether an observer's essential style is direct or indirect, self-centered or teacher-centered, O, C, E, A, or N,[15] these techniques can be used to improve the quality of interaction between the conferees.

Before leaving our consideration of what has been learned about personal styles and interpersonal styles in the recent past we need to recognize some older systems with a history worth recognition in respect to this chapter. The California Personality Inventory (CPI, Gough, 1972)[16] was a factor in a study of direct and indirect styles of supervision (Acheson, 1964).[17] The sixteen category classification of Cattell entered our work in the 1970s when workshop participants were asked, "What kind of supervisor would you choose?" What they told us was that they wanted a supervisor who was fairly intelligent but not too much smarter than the supervisee. They preferred someone who was very trusting but not gullible, self-assured but not overbearing, calm but not phlegmatic.

During the life of our book other, older systems have taken on new meaning. The Enneagram, as described by Riso (1990),[18] Palmer (1995),[19] and others, has had considerable impact. Another "old" system (Jung, 1976),[20] as interpreted by Myers-Briggs (2000) has had wide use in industry and other endeavors. Interesting melds of these systems are appearing in the literature and on the Internet. They can increase our understanding of what goes on beneath our defensive behaviors and also our efforts toward growth.

COMMUNICATION TECHNIQUE 1: LISTEN MORE, TALK LESS

Many observers dominate the conversation. The teacher has little chance to identify goals and objectives, analyze and interpret information, or reach decisions about future actions. Teachers talk to students (on average) about two-thirds of the time they teach, and (we suspect) observers talk in about the same proportion to teachers. The exact ratio varies, but too many observers do most of the talking. It is difficult to attend to a teacher's concerns in a conference or encourage a teacher's plans for improvement when the observer monopolizes the conference. Avoid this tendency when applying the techniques in the remainder of this chapter.

COMMUNICATION TECHNIQUE 2: ACKNOWLEDGE, PARAPHRASE, AND USE WHAT THE TEACHER IS SAYING

Observers who insert an "I understand" or "I know what you mean" in the course of a teacher's conversation indicate that they are listening. Accurate paraphrases also show that they understand the teacher. Using the teacher's ideas can be even more convincing than merely acknowledging (hearing) or paraphrasing (comprehending) them. Applying an idea to a different situation is but one example; pointing to a logical consequence is another. Paraphrasing can be overdone if too many responses are similar, or if they are inappropriately placed. For example, if a teacher says, "The car was going 60 miles an hour," it doesn't contribute much to respond, "What you are saying is that the automobile was traveling a mile a minute." An effective paraphrase must be a genuine effort to communicate that we understand what the other person is getting at. Using the teacher's idea shows that the observer heard, understood, and is pursuing the thought. Of course, it can be pursued so far that it ceases to be the teacher's idea and becomes the observer's. Generally, however, having a person you respect use your idea is rewarding.

COMMUNICATION TECHNIQUE 3: ASK CLARIFYING QUESTIONS

The teacher's statements often need to be probed to clarify the observer's understanding and to get the teacher to think carefully about inferences and decisions. "Tell me what you mean by that" or "Can you say a little more about that?" are examples. So is "What would you accept as evidence that. . . ."

In many instances, if we do not clarify, miscommunication is the result. Occasionally someone will say, "You're absolutely right! Moreover," and then the person proceeds to say the exact opposite of what you thought you said. Of course, that could be a conscious strategy or a case of not listening at all, but a clarifying question avoids unintentional misunderstandings.

An example of paraphrasing and asking clarifying questions took place in a high school where the principal gave the faculty an administrator appraisal form to fill out anonymously. After analyzing the compiled responses, the principal said in a faculty meeting, "What you seem to be telling me in this survey is that I'm not as accessible as you would like." Several teachers said, almost in unison, "Could you tell us what 'being accessible' would look like?" To which the principal replied: "Well, I'd keep my door open more and welcome 'drop-in' chats. And if you stopped me in the hall and asked a question, I'd try to answer it briefly instead of pointing out that I was on my way to a meeting."

Having announced and clarified his intentions in public, he was destined to become "Mr. Accessible" in the next few months. Of course he had some help from wags on the faculty who could not resist asking, "Are you feeling accessible?"

Several points can be made with this example: (1) the paraphrase translated a statistic into flesh-and-blood behavior; (2) the clarifying question checked the perceptions of the subject and his observers; and (3) the public announcement of a resolution to change virtually ensured success. The same process takes place in the feedback conference. Note that the principal had objective data, analyzed and interpreted the data, made a decision, made use of paraphrasing and clarifying questions, and received verbal support in his resolve to change. These are exactly the steps we should follow in helping teachers improve their teaching.

COMMUNICATION TECHNIQUE 4: GIVE SPECIFIC PRAISE FOR TEACHER PERFORMANCE AND GROWTH

To say "That was a nice lesson" is not specific praise. Saying "That was an excellent answer you gave to Billy" or "Removing Fred from the group was an effective way to handle the problem" makes the approval explicit. It is especially important to note positive instances where the teacher has shown growth toward an avowed goal.

There is some possibility that an observer will reinforce more than was bargained for. A workshop leader received this comment from a participant on the postworkshop evaluation: "Stopping the tape recording to explain what was happening was really helpful." So the leader stopped the tape about twenty times during their next workshop, until someone sent this note: "Why don't you let the tape play long enough for us to hear what's going on?"

Again, an elderly lady who had never eaten apple pie remarked that when she was a girl, she turned down her first opportunity to do so and gained considerable attention: "Imagine that! Carrie doesn't eat apple pie." The attention was such that in subsequent situations, she felt compelled to continue her refusal, although she confessed, "I always thought I might have liked it."

Yet in our experience, the possibility of too little reinforcement for teachers is much more likely than too much. Teaching often seems a thankless task to those who toil in the schools of our nation. They seldom lack critics, however.

COMMUNICATION TECHNIQUE 5: AVOID GIVING DIRECT ADVICE

This does not say never give direct advice, just wait a while. Let teachers analyze and interpret. Often the decisions they reach will be very similar to yours. For most teachers, having their ideas for change reinforced by someone they respect is more likely to produce results than having to carry out someone else's idea. On the other hand, there are times when it is better to say what we think rather than let indirectness become manipulative.

Some people are naturally compliant, submissive, and obedient; perhaps they enjoy being told what to do. Nevertheless, our experience with teachers indicates that most of them prefer to feel responsible for their own actions. People who choose teaching as a career expect to be in charge of their classes; they expect to make professional decisions about goals, subject matter, materials, methodology, evaluation, and other aspects of the educational process.

The line between "guided discovery" and "manipulation" is a fine one. The observer must decide when "Here's the way it looks to me" is preferable to making the teacher feel that guessing games are being played.

COMMUNICATION TECHNIQUE 6: PROVIDE VERBAL SUPPORT

The emphasis of the observer is on helping the teacher identify professional goals relating to classroom performance, then obtaining valid feedback to assist in reaching those goals. It is often difficult for teachers to separate personal goals from professional goals, and it is especially difficult to separate emotional problems from professional ones. Many of the problems administrators identify as deterrents to instructional improvement by their teachers have their basis in personal aspects of the teacher's life—for example, apathy, lack of organization, or emotional instability in the classroom.

It would be convenient if we could exclude personal problems from a discussion of techniques to use in conducting conferences, but they often enter the discussion despite all efforts to stay on a professional level. Most observers have had the experience of a teacher crying at some point in a conference. Analyzing behavior is an intensely personal process that often defies a scientific or cold-blooded approach.

Hence, we need ways of dealing with these situations as they arise. It does not seem reasonable for an observer to be in tears along with the teacher, yet some expression of sympathy or empathy is in order. If the problems seem to be medical or psychiatric, the course of action is clear: seek help by referring the teacher to an appropriate specialist. Ordinary teacher observers and school administrators are not competent to make medical diagnoses ("He's an alcoholic" or "She's mentally ill"), and it is definitely not advisable for them to attempt psychiatric therapy or psychological counseling without the necessary special training and experience. Even teachers in medical schools and their observers (about teaching) shy away from diagnosing outside their specialty.

On the other hand, if the problem does not seem to require specialized, professional, medical, or psychiatric treatment, a sympathetic listener can often help a person work through a problem. In a previous edition, we quoted a university student: "You're the first one around here who has helped me!" This student had sought aid from several advisers in solving a personal problem. One faculty member took the time to listen to the particulars, then said, "It seems to me you've identified several possible alternatives. You could drop out of school and work full-time for a while, or you could take a reduced load and work part-time; and you also need to decide whether to get married now or wait." With his own alternatives outlined, the student said, "I see now what I need to do. Thank you." (He did not share his decision with the professor.)

Client-centered counseling doesn't always work out as quickly or as well, but for a number of reasons it may be an appropriate strategy for consultation with a teacher. The observer does not necessarily know more about teaching biology, kindergarten, French, or physics than the teacher; is probably not aware of as many factors in this particular classroom situation as the teacher; does not expect to spend the rest of the term, year, or career in this teacher's classroom; and will probably rely on the teacher to do most of the follow-up decisions. It is within the domain of the observer to consider what the teacher says about personal problems in the light of how they pertain to performance in the classroom.

The level of trust the two people have established is a major variable in how helpful an observer can be to a teacher with a personal problem that may be interfering with classroom effectiveness. Several factors influence trust building. We tend to trust those who trust us. We tend to trust those whose competence we respect. One way to build a teacher's confidence in our competence as observers is to demonstrate our ability to provide useful feedback and to conduct productive conferences.

In some cases, an observer needs to take full charge of the dealings with certain teachers: selecting what kinds of data will be collected and then analyzing and interpreting that information, drawing conclusions about which goals are being met and which are not, and deciding what needs to be done in the future. At the other extreme, an observer may encourage some teachers to set their own goals, select appropriate information to use in assessing the achievement of those goals, and make decisions about future efforts. As pedagogical strategies, these approaches are either didactic or heuristic. How much structure observers provide for a conference will depend on their estimate of what kind of atmosphere will provide maximum potential for the growth of a particular teacher. We have found that when teachers are given a choice of observers some choose one they know to be quite direct whereas others prefer one who tends to be indirect. Teachers who prefer the direct approach may say, "I know where she stands" or "He tells it like it is" or "I'm tired of people 'bouncing everything off the wall.'" Those who like an indirect style may say, "I feel more comfortable with Mary; she doesn't act like she has all the answers" or "Fred helps me do my own thinking and treats me like a colleague" or "I've had enough of the 'hardsell' approach."

The classroom observer is often cast in a double role: as a colleague helping to improve instruction and as an evaluator. It is sometimes awkward to deal with these two functions simultaneously. For example, to say "I'll devote the first few visits to helping you improve and save the evaluating until later" does not reassure the teacher, nor can the observer forget what has been seen. With teachers who are doing reasonably well, this need not be a problem: "I'm expecting to write a favorable evaluation anyway, so let's concentrate on some areas you'd like to work on" is one approach. Teachers on the borderline deserve to be informed of this fact, but the conference can still be positive and productive. Fair dismissal procedures also require that teachers be given early notice of deficiencies and assistance in attempting to overcome them.

In a few cases, the teacher may be in an "intensive evaluation" situation. (Some school districts encourage such a teacher to have an attorney or teachers' organization representative in attendance at any conferences with an evaluator.) Obviously, the tone of the conference will be different in the intensive case. Yet observers do not have to turn from Jekyll into Hyde. A skillful parent serves as both counselor and disciplinarian and can do so in a consistent style. Observers, too, should be able to fulfill both aspects of their role skillfully.

Dissonance theory provides a rationale for changing teachers' classroom behavior through observational feedback and teacher-centered conferences. The writings of Leon Festinger,[21] Fritz Heider, and others supply powerful insights into the dynamics of what Robert Burns expressed in poetic form as the gift of seeing ourselves as others see us. We each have an externally perceived self and an internally perceived self. We develop discomfort when we become aware of a discrepancy between what we believe to be "the real me" and what "the perceived me" seems to be doing in the eyes of others or in the information collected through systematic observation. For example, a teacher who believes that teachers should smile a lot feels that he smiles a lot; if he views videotapes of himself that show no smiles, he has dissonance. This dissonance can be reduced in several ways, such as

1. "The videotape is wrong."
2. "It was a bad day, I was nervous."
3. "It isn't really that important to smile so often."

In other words, he can (1) deny the information, (2) reduce the importance of the information, or (3) reduce the importance of the behavior. Another possibility is that he can resolve to make the perceived self more like the "real" or ideal self. That requires changing his behavior.

The goal of supervision for instructional improvement is to get teachers to change their behavior in ways that both they and their supervisors regard as desirable. In some cases only the observer (and not the teacher) sees a suggested change as desirable. Now the observer experiences dissonance. Among the options for reducing this dissonance are the following:

1. "You'll do it my way, or I'll send you to Siberia."
2. "Let's look at some more data about what is happening."
3. "Let's work on something you are concerned about."

In other words, the observer may (1) reduce dissonance by forcing compliance from the teacher, or (2) and (3) attempt to achieve consonance through increased understanding of what is on the teacher's mind.

There are times when it is necessary to force teacher compliance to the observer's demand—for example, when laws or official school policies are at stake. Most problems that observers and teachers work on are not that clear-cut. They concern ways of dealing with students; choosing strategies for teaching certain concepts, skills, or facts; finding alternative ways of managing the many variables in teaching; selecting elements of teaching style that can be modified by the teacher through the use of feedback, practice, and experimentation. It is unlikely that a teacher can eliminate a fundamental personality characteristic, such as dominance, emotional stability, or empathy. Nevertheless, a teacher can learn to use strategies that reduce the tendency to dominate or can develop classroom management techniques that reduce emotional stress. Some outward and visible signs of empathy can be observed, practiced, and incorporated into a teacher's repertoire without resorting to psychiatric therapy or profound religious conversion. Most people who choose teaching as a career have basic qualities that are compatible with the requirements of the job; systematic feedback can inform and convince those who do not.

COMMUNICATION TECHNIQUE 7: ACKNOWLEDGE AND USE WHAT THE PERSON IS FEELING

Carl Rogers reminds us that when a child attempts to do something difficult and says, "I can't," a typical parental response is, "Of course you can!"[22] The response is intended to be positive, but it denies feelings. It might not hurt to say, "It is difficult, isn't it, but you'll get it."

Researchers have found that feelings are seldom acknowledged verbally in the classroom.[23] The occurrence in conferences is less well documented, but we suspect that it is unduly limited. When the goal is to change behavior, affective aspects cannot be ignored. The emotions that can be expressed in a conference range from rage to despair, from exhilaration to depression. Clinical observers should not ignore the significant emotional content of what teachers are saying any more than they would ignore important cognitive statements.

One way to respond is to describe what you are observing: "You appear to be quite angry about that" or "This seems to make you anxious." Don't be surprised if the teacher's response is "Oh, no, I'm not really angry" or "Who's anxious? I'm not anxious." We tend to deny feelings, as if it were bad to have them, especially in a teaching situation. A psychologist once remarked, "I always knew when my mother was angry at me because she showed it immediately, and I could take that; but my father would wait to 'have a talk with me later,' and that was an agonizing experience." Expressing feelings can be healthy and helpful. After an especially satisfying performance before a large class of graduate students, the instructor was told by one student, "I enjoyed seeing that you were relishing the experience." That is a good observation to share. Telling a teacher "You appeared to be enjoying the responses you were getting" or "I shared your apprehension when Dickie volunteered" can have a desirable effect on the tone of the discussion.

COUNSELING

For many years we advised observers to avoid taking on a counseling role with teachers. We thought it best for observers to spend the limited available time helping teachers improve their instructional efforts rather than attempting to work on marital, financial, or psychological problems. We felt that the "amateur psychiatrist" would do more harm than good. In the case of serious problems, we still feel this way, but we have modified our position somewhat.

The more we work with observers, the more we recognize that it is impossible for them to separate teachers' instructional problems from their personal problems. What is needed is an approach that avoids the pitfalls of inept amateur therapy yet deals honestly with problems expressed by the teacher that have significant impact on classroom performance.

For example, if a teacher says, "I'm spending so much time fighting with my spouse that I just can't get my lessons prepared," the observer might do one of several things:

- threaten to fire the teacher if work does not improve.
- offer advice on how to improve a marriage.
- concentrate on ways of handling schoolwork at school.
- recommend a counselor.
- provide nondirective counseling.

Any of the above might work, depending on the situation and the nature of the individuals involved. An objective approach consistent with other techniques in this chapter might be the following:

OBSERVER: Here are some of the things you've mentioned that would be desirable. Let's indicate them briefly in one column. Here are some things you have identified about your current situation. Let's put them in another column. Now you can add or subtract from either list, but the essential problem is to ask what it takes to get from here to there.

It is conceivable that a conscientious supervisor might perform all the tasks of planning, observing, and giving feedback (as recorded and coded by reliable means) and still not be regarded as helpful by the teacher. We suspect that when this happens, other personality factors or interpersonal dynamics account for the discrepancy. The data we have on what teachers want from an observer suggest a fairly open and democratic approach for most teachers. Yet we can use open and democratic procedures to communicate content that is quite structured. Self-guided discovery, teacher-guided discovery, and didactic teaching are examples of procedures that lie along this continuum.

Carl Rogers, who pioneered client-centered counseling in the 1940s, argues for "person-centered" approaches in a wide range of human activities.[24] He contrasts our usual notions of power and control with another view of influence and impact.

Some Notes On Leadership: Two Extremes

Influence and Impact	Power and Control
Giving autonomy to persons and groups	Making decisions
Freeing people to "do their thing"	Giving orders
Expressing own ideas and feelings as one aspect of the group data	Directing subordinates' behavior
Facilitating learning	Keeping own ideas and feelings "close to the vest"
Stimulating independence in thought and action	Exercising authority over people and organizations
Delegating, giving full responsibility	Coercing when necessary
Offering feedback and receiving it	Teaching, instructing, advising
Encouraging and relying on self-evaluation	Evaluating others
Finding rewards in the achievements of others	Being rewarded by own achievements

For most teachers, influence and impact are needed from observers, not power and control.

MANAGEMENT

Douglas McGregor's Human Side of Enterprise suggests two approaches to management, theory X and theory Y.[25] They are not opposite poles on a continuum but two different views about work—including teaching and observing. Theory X applies to traditional management and the assumptions underlying it. Theory Y is based on assumptions derived from research in the social sciences.

Three basic assumptions of theory X are

1. The average human being has an inherent dislike of work and will avoid it if possible.
2. Because of this human dislike of work, most people must be coerced, directed, and threatened with punishment to get them to put forth adequate effort toward the achievement of organizational objectives.
3. The average human being prefers to be directed, wishes to avoid responsibility, has relatively little ambition, and wants security above all.

McGregor indicates that the "carrot and the stick" theory of motivation fits reasonably well with theory X. External rewards and punishments are the motivators of workers. The consequent direction and control does not recognize intrinsic human motivation.

Theory Y is more humanistic and is based on six assumptions:

1. The expenditure of physical and mental effort in work is as natural as play or rest.
2. External controls and the threat of punishment are not the only means for bringing about effort toward organizational objectives. Human beings will exercise self-direction and self-control in the service of objectives to which they are committed.

3. Commitment to objectives is a function of the rewards associated with their achievement.

4. The average human being learns, under proper conditions, not only to accept but also to seek responsibility.

5. The capacity to exercise a relatively high degree of imagination, ingenuity, and creativity in the solution of organizational problems is widely, not narrowly, distributed in the population.

6. Under the conditions of modern industrial life, the intellectual potentialities of the average human being are only partially utilized.

McGregor saw these assumptions leading to superior–subordinate relationships in which the subordinate would have greater influence over the activities in his or her own work and also have influence on the superior's actions. Through participatory management, greater creativity and productivity are expected, and also a greater sense of personal accomplishment and satisfaction by the workers. Chris Argyris,[26] Warren Bennis,[27] and Rensis Likert[28] cite evidence that a participatory system of management can be more effective than traditional management.

Likert's studies showed that high production can be achieved by people- rather than production-oriented managers. Moreover, these high-production managers were willing to delegate; to allow subordinates to participate in decisions; to be relatively nonpunitive; and to use open, two-way communication patterns. High morale and effective planning were also characteristic of these "person-centered" managers. The results may be applied to the supervisory relationship in education as well as to industry.

There have been at least two theory Z candidates in more recent years. One was broached in Abraham Maslow's posthumous publication, *The Farther Reaches of Human Nature.*[29] The other dealt with the success of ideas from the 1930s in the United States when they were applied to postwar Japan following WWII. Innovations such as quality circles, cooperative learning, participatory management, and shared decision making were influenced by those theories.

NOTES

1. Shwartz, T. (1996). *What really matters: Searching for wisdom in America.* New York: Bantam Books.

2. Bales, R. F. (1976). *Interaction process analysis: A method for the study of small groups.* Chicago: Midway Reprint, University of Chicago Press.

3. Cattell; See Hall, Lindsey, and Campbell, (1997). *Theories of personality.* New York: John Wiley & Sons.

4. Murray, Rorschach: See Buros, O. (1970–1975). *Personality tests and reviews* (Vol. 1 & 2). Highland Park, NJ: Gryphon Press.

5. Amidon, E., & Flanders, N. (1967). Interaction analysis as a feedback system. In *Interaction Analysis: Theory, Research, and Application* (pp. 122–124). Reading, MA: Addison-Wesley.

6. Blumberg, A. (1974). *Supervisors and teachers: A private cold war.* Berkeley, CA: McCutchan, 1974.

7. Hersey, P. and Blanchard, K. (1982). *Management of organizational behavior: Utilizing human resources.* Englewood Cliffs, NJ: Prentice-Hall.

8. Gregorc, A. F. (1986). *Gregorc style delineator.* Gregorc Associates.

9. Myers-Briggs: Quenk, N. L. (2000). *Essentials of Myers-Briggs type indicator assessment.* New York: John Wiley & Sons.

10. Keirsey, D., & Bates, M. (1978). *Please understand me.* Del Mar, CA: Prometheus Nemesis Book Company.

11. Keirsey, D. (1998). *Please understand me II: Temperament, character, intelligence.* Loughton, UK: Prometheus Books.

12. Goldberg, L. R. http://www.ori.org/scientists/goldberg.html

13. Spaulding, R. I. (1967). A coping analysis schedule for educational settings (CASES). In A. Simon & E. G. Boyer (Eds.), *Mirrors for behavior.* Philadelphia: Research for Better Schools.

14. Shostrom, E. L. (1967). *Man, the manipulator.* Nashville, TN: Abingdon.

15. Goldberg, L. R. (1990). An alternative "description of personality"; The Big Five factor structure. *Journal of Personality and Social Psychology, 59,* 1216–1229.

15. Gough, H. G. (1972). *California psychological inventory handbook.* San Francisco: Jossey-Bass.

17. Acheson, K. A. (1964). *The effects of feedback from television recordings and three types of supervisory treatment on selected teacher behaviors,* Stanford, CA: Stanford University Press.

18. Riso, D. R. (1990). *Understanding the Enneagram: The practical guide to personality types* Boston: Houghton Mifflin, January.

19. Palmer, H. (1995). *The Enneagram in love and work.* San Francisco: Harper.

20. Jung, C. (1976). In M. Fordham (Ed.), *Psychological types.* Princeton, NJ: Princeton University Press.

21. Festinger, L. (1968). *A theory of cognitive dissonance.* Stanford, CA: Stanford University Press; Heider, F. (1958). *The psychology of interpersonal relations.* New York: Wiley.

22. Rogers, C. R. (1964). personal communication, September.

23. Amidon and Hough, "Interaction Analysis," p. 137.

24. Rogers, C. R. (1977). *Carl Rogers on personal power* (pp. 91–92). New York: Delacorte.

25. McGregor, D. (1960). *The human side of enterprise.* New York: McGraw-Hill.

26. Argyris, C. (1971). *Management and organizational development.* New York: McGraw-Hill; Argyris, C. (1973). *On organizations of the future.* Beverly Hills: Sage.

27. Bennis, W. G. (1967). *Organizational development: Its nature, origin and prospects.* Reading, MA: Addison-Wesley; Bennis, W. G. (1989). *Why leaders can't lead.* San Francisco: Jossey-Bass.

28. Likert, R. (1961). *New patterns of management.* New York: McGraw-Hill; Likert, R. (1967). *The human organization.* New York: McGraw-Hill.

29. Maslow, A. (1971). *The farther reaches of human nature,* New York Viking Press.

Chapter 7

The Planning Conference

Author's Note

Educators, like professionals in other fields, are expected to "do more with less" these days. I see overburdened school administrators, university supervisors, and cooperating teachers (for preservice supervision) everywhere, and ask, "Who has the time to do high-quality clinical supervision any more?"

Under these conditions, it's tempting to sacrifice the planning phase of the supervision cycle. There might only be the quick phone call or e-mail message to say, "I'll be in your classroom to observe next Thursday at 9:50. OK?"

I think we pay a price when we shortcut the planning conference in this manner. Quality instruction and professional growth take a back seat to other priorities. None of us want this to happen, so we must be creative and generate different ways to maintain the quality and integrity of the planning conference.

Here is what has worked for me. (Perhaps it will work for you, or stimulate you to come up with something better.) I try to schedule a full hour for a planning conference when I first start supervising a teacher. That allows sufficient time for the teacher and me to get to know each other, to attempt to lay down the foundations of trust, and to use the planning techniques described in this chapter. Then, if I find myself in a time crunch following the first supervisory cycle, I can get by with a much briefer planning conference—perhaps only 5 to 10 minutes. If a face-to-face meeting is difficult to arrange, a phone conversation might suffice.

This approach reminds me of something a clinical psychologist once told me. She said that the first time she sees a new client, she takes extensive notes on everything the client says; and she fleshes out the notes in detail afterward. That is because the client's main problems and therapist–client relationship issues are likely to be revealed in the first visit. Using her notes, she can plan her therapeutic interventions accordingly. In subsequent visits, she only needs to take a few notes during or after seeing the client unless some dramatically new problem or issue arise. In clinical supervision, too, the main problems and issues are likely to be revealed in the first supervision cycle.

There is one other point about the planning conference. I find that many of us tend to talk in generalities about our work and to distort reality to maintain our self-esteem and fulfill other needs. It's hard to talk about specific details and open our work to inspection by another person. Yet, when we allow this to happen (within a supportive climate), wonderful things can happen. That is the promise, and the task, of a good planning conference.

MDG

I mean to suggest that the preobservation conference is a time for Teacher and Supervisor to reach <u>explicit</u> agreements about reasons for supervision to occur in the immediate situation and about how supervision should operate.

—Robert Goldhammer[1]

INTRODUCTION

The planning conference sets the stage for effective clinical supervision. It provides a setting in which the teacher and supervisor can identify the teacher's concerns and translate them into observable behavior. Another outcome of the planning conference is a decision about the kinds of instructional data that will be recorded during classroom observation, which is the next phase of the supervisory cycle.

Planning conferences are also valuable because they provide an opportunity for the teacher to communicate with a fellow educator about his or her unique classroom situation and style of teaching. Many teachers feel isolated in their work because they usually teach alone in a self-contained classroom. By periodically observing the teacher's classroom, a supervisor builds a set of shared experiences that he and the teacher can discuss together in their conferences. These conferences are especially important to student teachers; they might have no one in the school other than the supervisor with whom to share concerns and emerging understandings of what it means to be a teacher.

The success of a planning conference depends in large part on how much trust the teacher places in the supervisor. Trust refers to the teacher's confidence that the supervisor has the teacher's interests at heart and will not use data that emerge during supervision against the teacher. A supervisor might be technically proficient, but unless he or she also instills trust, supervision is likely to be inefficient.

Planning conferences need not be long. Twenty to thirty minutes is usually sufficient for the first planning conference unless the teacher has a particularly difficult problem to discuss or unless the teacher and supervisor are strangers to each other. Later planning conferences might require only five to ten minutes, especially if there has been no change in the teacher's goals for improvement since the preceding clinical supervision cycle of planning–observation–feedback.

Planning conferences probably are best held on neutral territory (e.g., the school cafeteria) or in the teacher's classroom. Going into a supervisor's office for a conference might make the teacher feel like he or she is being "called on the carpet."

This chapter presents various techniques that help to ensure a successful planning conference. In a sense, they constitute a set of agenda items for the conference. Therefore, you might find it helpful to prepare for a planning conference by recording certain of the techniques as your written agenda.

The techniques presented here are not highly specific prescriptions. You will need to use judgment in incorporating them into your supervisory style and in applying them to a particular supervisory situation. Our only claim is that judicious use of these techniques provides a sound base for conducting a planning conference. What you as a person contribute to this base is equally critical for success.

CONFERENCE TECHNIQUE 1: IDENTIFY THE TEACHER'S CONCERNS ABOUT INSTRUCTION

In simple terms, the major goal of clinical supervision is to help teachers improve their instruction. One step toward this goal is to use the planning conference to identify areas of instruction in which the teacher needs improvement.

A supervisor might directly ask a teacher the specific areas in which he or she would like to improve, but this is not usually effective. Many teachers have not formulated self-improvement goals and feel put on the spot when asked to do so. A more useful approach, at least initially, is to assist the teacher in identifying concerns. Teachers who can make explicit their concerns usually are able to take the next steps of examining the concerns objectively and trying out alternative methods for handling them.

There are a variety of questions that a supervisor might ask to guide the teacher's thinking about concerns, for example: "How has your teaching been going?" "Do you find you are having more success in one area than another?" "My goal is to help you do the best possible teaching. Are there any aspects of your teaching we should take a look at?"

No one question is better than another. The supervisor should be intent on helping the teacher reveal true concerns without feeling threatened. A threatened teacher is likely to clam up or reveal only "safe" concerns. For example, teachers have told us that "individualization of instruction" is a safe concern, but discipline is not a safe concern. A teacher who mentions discipline problems might be perceived as incompetent, whereas a teacher who mentions individualization is likely to be perceived as well along the road toward being a master teacher.

Some teachers insist that they have no concerns—their class is running beautifully. In some instances this may be an accurate perception by the teacher, but we would suggest that there is always room for improvement in one's teaching. A good teacher can get better.

When a teacher insists that he or she has no concerns, the supervisor probably should take the statement at face value. The supervisor might then suggest using a "wide-lens" observation technique such as video recording (see Chapter 11), so that they can look together at the teacher's instruction. An appropriate tone can be set by asking, "How about making a videotape of one of your lessons so that we can see what aspects of your teaching please you?" After the video recording has been made and reviewed in the feedback conference, the teacher is likely to become aware of areas for improvement that were not previously apparent.

Teachers sometimes find it helpful to examine a checklist or other instrument that will be used to evaluate their teaching performance. In showing the checklist to a teacher, the supervisor might ask, "Which of these areas do you think you're strong in? Which of these areas do you think we might take a closer look at as areas for improvement?"

Frances Fuller carried out a classic series of investigations at the University of Texas on teachers' concerns during training and in their professional careers.[2] She found that the concerns of preservice teachers and new inservice teachers tend to focus on the self. The concerns of experienced teachers tend to focus on the students. Fuller summarized her findings as follows.

Early teaching phase: Concern with self

<u>Covert Concerns: Where Do I Stand?</u> *When teaching starts, [student] teachers ask themselves, "Where do I stand?" "Is it going to be my class or the teacher's class?" "If I see a child misbehaving in the hall, do I handle it, ignore it, or tell someone else?" These concerns were rarely expressed in either written statements or in routine interviews unless directly elicited.*

<u>Overt Concerns: How Adequate Am I?</u> *The concern student teachers feel about class control is no secret. It is a blatant persistent concern of most beginning teachers.*

Ability to control the class, however, is apparently just part of a larger concern of the new teacher with his adequacy in the classroom. This larger concern involves abilities to understand subject matter, to know the answers, to say "I don't know," to have the freedom to fail on occasion, to anticipate problems, to mobilize resources and to make changes when failures reoccur. It also involves the ability to cope with evaluation: the willingness to listen for evaluation and to parcel out the biases of evaluators.

Late concerns: Concern with pupils

When concerns are "mature," that is, characteristic of experienced, superior teachers, they seem to focus on pupil gain and self-evaluation as opposed to personal gain and evaluation by others. The specific concerns we have observed are concerns about ability to understand pupils' capacities, to specify objectives for them, to assess their gain, to apportion out one's own contributions to pupils' difficulties and gain, and to evaluate oneself in terms of pupil gain.[3]

Frances Fuller's insights suggest the variety of teacher concerns to which the supervisor must remain sensitive. As she notes, some of these concerns are easily verbalized by the teacher. Others must be solicited through careful questioning.

CONFERENCE TECHNIQUE 2: TRANSLATE THE TEACHER'S CONCERNS INTO OBSERVABLE BEHAVIORS

Helping a teacher translate concerns into observable behaviors is one of the most important techniques of clinical supervision. For an analogy, consider the patient who visits a doctor with vague complaints of not feeling well. The doctor's first task is to develop a differentiated picture of the patient's symptoms. The doctor does this by asking questions. "What are the specific problems you've been having?" "What does the discomfort feel like?" "How long have you felt this way?" These questions are part of a diagnostic process the doctor uses—first to isolate the problem and then to prescribe a treatment.

The clinical supervisor similarly needs to function as a diagnostician in the planning conference. Suppose a student teacher says, "I'm not sure I have the confidence to be a teacher." The teacher's expressed concern is lack of confidence, but the supervisor needs to probe further. Confidence might mean something different to the teacher than it means to the supervisor.

In using the technique of translating concerns, the supervisor needs to listen for the teacher's use of words and phrases that are abstract, ambiguous, or stated at a high level of generality. These typically are concepts that are at least one level removed from observable behavior. The following are examples of teacher statements that contain abstract or ambiguous words:

"I'm afraid I'm a dictator."

"I can't get this class of students interested in learning about geography."

"There's just not enough time to cover everything I want to get across."

"Some of my students are just like wild animals."

"I'm afraid I don't project warmth."

"I wonder if I'm too critical of students."

"These kids just aren't able to understand basic algebra."

When you hear a teacher use such terms to refer to a concern, your task is to clarify the terms so that they are stated in observable form. Here are examples of questions that might help the teacher state a concern more concretely:

"Do you know a teacher who projects warmth? What does she do?"

"What kinds of things do you do that make you think you're critical of students?"

"How would you know if a student understands or doesn't understand?"

"To help me understand how much content you're trying to cover, can you start by telling me the most important information and ideas you want students to learn?"

These are not the only kinds of questions that are useful. The supervisor is free to use any questions or other techniques that help the teacher focus on abstract terms and clarify their meaning.

As a supervisor, you can judge your comprehension of a teacher's concerns by asking yourself this question: "Do I have enough information so that I can clearly observe the teacher's concern as it is expressed in his/her classroom?" Another helpful question is "Do the teacher and I mean the same thing when we use the term ———?" If your answer to both questions is a confident "Yes," this is a good indication that you are using the technique properly.

Several research studies have been done to clarify the meaning of key concepts in teaching. For example, Andrew Bush, John Kennedy, and Donald Cruickshank conducted research to determine the observable referents of teacher clarity.[4] Their approach was to ask students to list five behaviors performed by their clearest teacher. They were able to identify the following observable behaviors underlying the concept of clarity:

- gives examples and explains them.
- repeats questions and explanations if students don't understand them.
- lets students ask questions.
- pronounces words distinctly.
- talks only about things related to the topic he is teaching.
- uses common words.

- writes important things on the blackboard.
- relates what he is teaching to real life.
- asks questions to find out if students understand what he has told them.

This list is not exhaustive, but it can help teachers and supervisors work together to improve the clarity of the teacher's instruction.

Even a nonverbal concept, such as teacher enthusiasm, can be made observable through careful analysis. Mary Collins identified observable referents for enthusiasm by reviewing previous research on this variable, by her own analysis, and by consulting other teacher educators. Collins' list of observable behaviors is presented below. Using this list as a guide, she and others were able to help teachers improve their level of enthusiasm significantly in classroom instruction.[5]

Observable Referents for Enthusiasm

1. *Vocal Delivery:* great and sudden changes from rapid excited speech to a whisper; varied, lilting, uplifting intonations; many changes in tone, pitch.
2. *Eyes:* dancing, snapping, shining, lighting up, frequently opened wide, eyebrows raised, eye contact with total group.
3. *Gestures:* frequent demonstrative movements of body, head, arms, hands, and face; sweeping motions; clapping hands; head nodding rapidly.
4. *Movements:* large body movements; swings around, changes pace, bends body.
5. *Facial Expression:* appears vibrant, demonstrative; changes denoting surprise, sadness, joy, thoughtfulness, awe, excitement.
6. *Word Selection:* highly descriptive, many adjectives, great variety.
7. *Acceptance of Ideas and Feelings:* accepts ideas and feelings quickly with vigor and animation; ready to accept, praise, encourage, or clarify in a nonthreatening manner; many variations in responding to pupils.
8. *Overall Energy:* explosive, exuberant; high degree of vitality, drive, and spirit throughout lesson.

You will find examples of observable referents for other teacher concerns in Chapters 9–12. The chapters also present methods for recording classroom data about these observable referents.

CONFERENCE TECHNIQUE 3: IDENTIFY PROCEDURES FOR IMPROVING THE TEACHER'S INSTRUCTION

The first two techniques are intended to help the teacher identify concerns and translate them into observable behaviors. What happens next?

If the teacher has successfully identified some observable concerns, the stage is set for thinking about possible changes in instructional behavior. For example, consider a teacher who is worried that he or she comes across as dull and unenthusiastic. As the supervisor helps this teacher identify observable behaviors that comprise enthusiasm, the teacher is likely to ask, "I wonder how I could get myself to do those things?" The supervisor facilitates this process by thinking aloud with the teacher about procedures that can be used to acquire new behaviors.

The simplest procedure, perhaps, is for the teacher to practice the behaviors independently. The supervisor might say, "Why don't you make a list of these enthusiasm behaviors on a five-by-eight-inch card and keep it near you when you teach? In a week or so, I'll come in and make a video recording so you can see how you're doing."

Sometimes the needed procedures are more involved. For example, a teacher's concern might be how to use learning centers effectively. This involves a whole set of instructional skills. To acquire these skills, the teacher might need to do some reading and to attend workshops on learning centers.

If a teacher's concern is about changing student behavior, a sequence of procedures is needed. To illustrate, suppose the teacher is concerned that students do not pay attention during class discussions. The supervisor first helps the teacher to define "attention" as a set of observable behaviors—answering teacher's questions thoughtfully, looking at other students as they speak, initiating relevant comments and questions, and so forth. The teacher's next task is to develop instructional procedures that will bring about these desired "attending" behaviors. Finally, the teacher will need to practice these instructional procedures until they are mastered.

In brief, three steps are involved in bringing about change in students' behavior:

1. Identify the specific student behaviors you (the teacher) wish your class to use.
2. Identify the instructional procedures you will need to use to bring about the specific student behaviors.
3. Identify a strategy for learning and practicing the instructional procedures.

Bringing about change in student behavior is probably the most difficult goal a teacher can strive for, but it also yields the greatest rewards.

The following is an excerpt from a planning conference in which the goal was change in the behavior of second-grade children:

TEACHER: I'd like you to come in and take a look at Randall and Ronald. They don't do anything but play and talk.

SUPERVISOR: Are Randall and Ronald the only ones you want me to observe?

TEACHER: No. I have a real immature group this year. You might as well observe all of them.

SUPERVISOR: What do you mean by "immature"?

TEACHER: Oh, they have very short attention spans, haven't learned to settle down, and they just talk without permission.

[*At this point, teacher and supervisor decided to focus on one problem behavior—talking without permission. The dialogue continues.*]

SUPERVISOR: Can you give an example of a situation where they talk without permission?

TEACHER: Well, when I have them in a small reading group, and I ask one of them a question, any of them will speak up if they think they have the answer. Sometimes they don't even listen to the question, they just say what's on their mind. And it

> doesn't matter whether another child is already talking. They'll just ignore him and speak at the same time.
>
> SUPERVISOR: I think I have a pretty clear idea of what's happening. What do you think you can do so that only the child you call on responds, and so that if another child has something to say, he waits his turn?
>
> TEACHER: I guess I could teach them some rules for participating. Like raising their hands when they wish to speak and remaining quiet when another child is speaking.

Teacher and supervisor proceeded to discuss possible methods of teaching these rules to the children. The teacher took notes on the procedures and agreed to practice them the following week. In addition, the supervisor suggested that the teacher try praising or otherwise rewarding children when they obey participation rules in the reading group. In making this suggestion, the supervisor discovered that the teacher was unfamiliar with the reinforcement principles underlying the use of praise and other rewards in classroom teaching. The supervisor therefore suggested that the teacher might benefit from enrolling in an upcoming workshop on classroom management in which these principles would be discussed.

This example illustrates the three steps in bringing about change in both teacher and student behavior:

1. Identify the specific student behaviors desired, such as students raising hands when they wish to speak and being silent when another child is speaking.

2. Identify instructional procedures, such as teaching children the instructional rules and rewarding them for appropriate behavior.

3. Identify a strategy for learning the instructional procedure such as practice in the classroom and attending a workshop.

These steps represent but one of many approaches for helping teachers improve their instruction and develop as professionals. In Chapter 2, we describe a model of professional development that encompasses a variety of approaches, each suitable for a particular purpose. You might find it worthwhile to acquaint teachers with the model to show them the range of resources that are available to help them, no matter what their present state of professional development might be.

CONFERENCE TECHNIQUE 4: ASSIST THE TEACHER IN SETTING SELF-IMPROVEMENT GOALS

In discussing the previous conference technique, we presented the example of a teacher concerned about students speaking out of turn. The supervisor helped the teacher identify several observable behaviors of students that reflected this concern and also helped the teacher identify procedures for changing these behaviors. It seems apparent that the teacher's goal is to improve students' verbal participation behaviors in reading groups. The clinical supervision process is facilitated by making this goal explicit. By doing so, teacher and supervisor both develop a clear understanding of the direction in which the clinical supervision process is headed. It also prevents a state of confusion, with the teacher thinking, "I wonder what the supervisor expects me to be doing?"

The supervisor or the teacher can state the goal, but whoever does so should check that the other person has the same understanding of the goal and agrees with it. In the example we have been considering, the goal formulation process might occur as follows:

SUPERVISOR: To review, then, one of the things you're concerned about is students' speaking out of turn. You've picked out a number of behaviors you'd like to see your students engage in. Given that, is there a goal you would set for yourself?

TEACHER: Yes. My first goal is to reduce the incidence of students' speaking out of turn. My other goal is to have my students engage in more positive behaviors, like listening to one another and raising their hands when they have something to say.

SUPERVISOR: Those are worthwhile goals, and I'll do what I can to help you with them.

This interchange between teacher and supervisor, if done naturally and genuinely, gives structure and focus to the planning conference.

The goal-setting process needs to be adjusted for the teacher's particular situation. For teachers who are working on growth goals (rather than deficiency needs), goal-setting can be teacher-centered. Teachers who are on plans of assistance or have little insight into the teaching process might require supervisor-centered goal-setting. Even in this situation, you as the supervisor need to keep in mind the long-term goal of helping the teacher become a self-determined, intrinsically motivated professional. Thus, even if it is necessary for you to specify the goal, you should discuss your reasoning so that the teacher views the goal as reasonable rather than arbitrary or reflecting an idiosyncratic philosophy of teaching. If the discussion process is open and there is a climate of trust, we have found that most teachers will gradually "own" the goal.

CONFERENCE TECHNIQUE 5: ARRANGE A TIME FOR CLASSROOM OBSERVATION

The first four techniques involve the teacher and supervisor talking about the teacher's instruction and setting goals. Now it is time to plan for observing the teacher's instruction firsthand.

The first step in planning for observation is to arrange a mutually convenient time for the supervisor to visit the classroom. For one reason or another, there might be certain lessons the teacher does not wish you to observe or you are unable to observe because of time conflicts. The major criterion for selecting a lesson is that it should present opportunities for observing instances of the teacher's concerns and solutions to those concerns. For example, if the teacher's concern is students' responses to discussion questions, there is no point in observing a lesson in which students are engaged in independent learning projects.

Arranging a mutually convenient time for classroom observation is important for another reason. Teachers are resentful when supervisors come to their room unannounced. Indeed, our experience indicates that few things disturb teachers more than unannounced visits by a supervisor or other individual in a position of authority. Teachers need to feel that the supervisor respects them as professionals and as people with first-line responsibility for their classrooms. They are not likely to feel this way if a supervisor pops in any time he or she wishes to do so.

Arranging a mutually convenient time is important when supervising experienced teachers, but it is equally important when working with student teachers. They can be put into a state of constant tension if they know that the supervisor can enter their class unannounced and at any time. Arranging a time for observation and data collection beforehand enables the student teacher to prepare instructionally—and emotionally—for the supervisor's visit. It also gives the student teacher a sense of control over the supervisory process. Having this sense of control increases the likelihood that the teacher will use supervision for self-improvement rather than feel used by it.

CONFERENCE TECHNIQUE 6: SELECT AN OBSERVATION INSTRUMENT AND BEHAVIORS TO BE RECORDED

Teachers' participation in the planning conference largely reflects their perceptions of what occurs in their classroom. These perceptions might mirror or differ from what actually occurs. Observational data are needed to provide an objective check on the teacher's perceptions and also to record instructional phenomena that may have escaped the teacher's perception. Therefore, an important step in the planning conference is for the supervisor and teacher to decide what kinds of observational data might be worth collecting.

A wide range of observation instruments are presented in Unit 4 of this book. You will need to become familiar with them in order to help the teacher select an observation instrument appropriate to his or her instructional concerns. For example, if a teacher is concerned about nonverbal behavior, a video recording (Observation Technique 10) might be appropriate. If the concern is about a problem child in the classroom, an anecdotal record (Observation Technique 9) can be helpful. Or if a teacher is concerned about the level of commotion in his classroom, a record of students' movement patterns (Observation Technique 8) might yield useful data for instructional improvement.

The selection of an observation instrument helps to sharpen a teacher's thinking about instruction. If the teacher and supervisor use the conference only to talk about instruction, the conversation might drift into vague generalities and abstractions. Selecting an observation instrument brings the teacher "down to earth" by focusing attention on the observable realities of classroom instruction.

Either the supervisor or the teacher can suggest appropriate observation instruments and behaviors to be recorded on them. If the teacher is unfamiliar with methods of classroom observation, the supervisor might need to initiate suggestions. Once teachers become familiar with the range of instruments, however, they should be encouraged to initiate their own suggestions.

In discussing observation instruments with teachers, you might wish to stress their nonevaluative nature. These instruments are designed to collect objective data that teachers can inspect in the feedback conference and from which they can form their own judgments about the effectiveness of their teaching.

CONFERENCE TECHNIQUE 7: CLARIFY THE INSTRUCTIONAL CONTEXT IN WHICH DATA WILL BE RECORDED

A teacher who is asked to look at too many aspects of his or her instruction at once is likely to become confused. Your classroom observation might focus on the teacher's enthusiasm or classroom discipline or the at-task behavior of students, but not all three.

However, there is the risk of oversimplification. Instructional behavior does not occur in a vacuum. It occurs in a context that must be understood if the target behaviors and concerns are to be interpreted properly.

In short, you as the supervisor cannot walk into a teacher's classroom "cold" and expect to understand what is happening. Instead, we recommend that you allow time in the planning conference to ask the teacher a few questions about the instructional context of the behaviors to be recorded. Because the usual instructional context is a lesson that the teacher plans to teach, you might wish to ask the teacher such questions as:

"What content will you be teaching in the lesson that I'll be observing?"

"What are your students like, and how diverse are they?"

"What do you expect the students to learn in this lesson?"

"What teaching methods and materials will you be using?"

"Is there anything I should be aware of as you teach this lesson?"

Asking these questions indicates to the teacher that you wish to understand the teacher's classroom from his or her perspective. Your presence in the classroom during the lesson will be tolerated better because the teacher and you have a shared understanding of what the lesson is about.

NOTES

1. Goldhammer, R. (1969). *Clinical supervision: Special methods for the supervision of teachers*. New York: Holt, Rinehart & Winston, p. 60.

2. Fuller, F. F. (1969). Concerns of teachers: A developmental conceptualization. *American Educational Research Journal, 6,* 207–226.

3. *Ibid.,* pp. 220–221.

4. Bush, A. J., Kennedy, J. J., & Cruickshank, D. R. (1977). An empirical investigation of teacher clarity. *Journal of Teacher Education, 28,* 53–58.

5. Collins, M. L. (1978). Effects of enthusiasm training on pre-service elementary teachers. *Journal of Teacher Education, 29,* 53–57; Bettencourt, E. M., Gillett, M. H., Gall, M. D., & Hull, R. E. (1983). Effects of teacher enthusiasm training on student on-task behavior and achievement. *American Educational Research Journal, 20,* 435–450.

Chapter **8**

The Feedback Conference

Author's Note

As a student in the 1930s and 1940s I remember feedback as the squeal you heard from placing a microphone in front of a loudspeaker. Another example was what a thermostat sends to a furnace. The advent of computers brought new meaning to the word. Another milestone was reached at Stanford in the early 1960s when teacher interns received feedback from videotapes of their lessons in microteaching and in regular classrooms.

When given feedback from observers, students, and videotape, teachers appeared to choose students first, then videotape, and then observers (supervisors). An observer who employs the techniques discussed in the following chapter can overcome this disadvantage. Information that teachers regard as objective, free of bias, useful, and coming from a competent friend can have desirable effects.

KAA

Perhaps the best measure of whether a [feedback] conference has been useful, in Teacher's framework, is whether it has left him with something concrete in hand, namely, a design for his next sequence of instruction.

—Robert Goldhammer[1]

INTRODUCTION

Several things must take place before a successful feedback conference can occur. The teacher and supervisor should have

- established a climate of mutual trust.
- determined the teacher's concerns and self-improvement goals.
- translated the concerns and goals into observable behaviors and products.
- selected an observation instrument and types of classroom behavior to be recorded.
- discussed relevant contextual features of the classroom situation that is to be observed.
- collected and—if appropriate, summarized—the observational data.

If these things have happened, you will have laid the groundwork for a successful feedback conference.

In the feedback conference itself, the supervisor and teacher review the accuracy of the observational data. Next, they interpret the data, looking for significant patterns—especially those involving teacher behavior and its effect on students. They also try to explain the patterns, possibly invoking values, beliefs, and formal theories of human behavior.

Then, the teacher and supervisor make decisions about the next steps. These may involve trying alternative strategies, changing curriculum objectives, treating particular students differently, or setting goals to learn new instructional skills. Also, the teacher and supervisor might see the need for more observational data of the same or different sort. In fact, the feedback conference that completes one cycle of clinical supervision often initiates the planning phase of the next cycle. (Although planning can be initiated, we still recommend a separate planning conference, however brief, shortly before the next classroom observation.)

These procedures in the feedback conference are only useful if the supervisor's purpose is to help the teacher become a reflective, self-regulating individual focused on personal professional growth. Unfortunately, this is not always true of actual clinical supervision, as we find in a research study conducted by Miriam Ben-Peretz and Sarah Rumney.[2] They observed feedback conferences in Israeli teacher-education programs and discovered that the conferences were

> in most cases very one-directional, the teacher making comments and the trainee agreeing. The majority of remarks concerned shortcomings of the student teachers. For instance, the teacher would say: 'You should have taught this in a different way,' or 'I do not agree with your explanation of this word,' or 'Why didn't you follow my instructions?'[3]

Ben-Peretz and Rumney concluded from these and other research findings that, "cooperating teachers perceive the student teachers not as novice professionals but as 'students' whose primary duty is to listen and learn."[4]

It is helpful to keep in mind that preservice and inservice teachers will be on their own once the prescribed period of clinical supervision has ended. Teachers might listen to, and comply with, the supervisor's directives and recommendations, but this does not mean that they will internalize them. For this reason, we believe it is best if the supervisor and teacher get "on the same page" in terms of collecting and interpreting observational data.

For this to happen, the supervisor must understand how the teacher makes sense of classroom phenomena; conversely, the teacher must understand the supervisor's sense-making. Additionally, both must come to a shared understanding and agreement that the ultimate goal of clinical supervision is to help the teacher generate alternative instructional approaches and test them in action.

Reaching these shared understandings in planning and feedback conferences requires time. However, Ben-Peretz and Rumney found that feedback conferences led by cooperating teachers were quite brief. Ten to twenty minutes was the typical duration. Feedback conferences led by university supervisors were substantially longer (thirty to forty minutes); there was also more reciprocal communication and more generation of alternative ideas for teaching. Although Ben-Peretz and Rumney's research was limited to Israeli teacher education, our experience indicates that the same situation exists in the United States and elsewhere.[5]

Finding time for the feedback conference—and other parts of the supervisory cycle—is no easy task. Nonetheless, finding time should be a major priority, given that teachers' professional growth is at stake.

CONFERENCE TECHNIQUE 8: PROVIDE THE TEACHER WITH FEEDBACK USING OBJECTIVE OBSERVATIONAL DATA

Many teachers feel defensive as they enter the feedback conference, because they see it as an evaluation of their competence. Their defensiveness will worsen if they perceive the observational data to be subjective, inaccurate, or irrelevant. Therefore, an objective record of classroom events—such as is provided by videotaping, audiotaping, or selective verbatim—is crucial. Teachers might be surprised by what the data reveal, but they generally will accept the data as valid and instructive.

It is important to realize that observational records are never perfect. For example, videotaping provides an excellent record of classroom events, but it cannot capture everything. Furthermore, the judgment, skill, and biases of the person operating the video camera will affect the recording.

A teacher might be tempted to dismiss the observational record because of these imperfections. As a supervisor, you can acknowledge the teacher's concern, but go on to note that, while all data are imperfect, some data are better than others. If the data achieve a certain level of objectivity, there is much to be learned from them. You might wish to invoke the time-honored saying, "let's not throw out the baby with the bath water."

We have found it best to present the observational record to the teacher as soon as possible in the feedback conference. This approach is neutral and professional in tone. A statement like, "Let's look at the data we have collected," is usually sufficient. If the data are numerical or involve the use of symbols, you first might need to refresh the teacher's memory of what they mean.

During or after the teacher reviews the observational record, you can ask the teacher to *describe*—not *evaluate*—what the record reveals about the lesson. For example, suppose a teacher looks at a video recording and says, "Wow. It took me too long to get the class settled down." Your response might be, "Let's see how many minutes passed from the time the bell rang to the time instruction began." Once the minutes are known, the supervisor and teacher can discuss whether the minutes are too many and what a reasonable time limit for settling the class down might be.

As another example, consider the teacher who examines a selective verbatim (see Chapter 9) and says, "I didn't explain the Malthusian theory of population growth very well." As a supervisor, your response might be, "You're not happy with your explanation. But before we make any judgments about it, let's try to understand how you went about explaining the theory to the class. So, looking at the selective record, would you walk me through the explanation?"

By asking the teacher to focus on description, the supervisor is revealing that understanding is the priority rather than a "rush to judgment." (If the teacher's description is confused or incomplete, the supervisor can help out by clarifying particular features of the observational record or by asking clarifying questions.) This approach reduces the threat of the feedback conference for the teacher and provides a better foundation for developing a plan for improving the teacher's instruction.

Interpretation of the observational record follows naturally from a careful descriptive analysis of it. The teacher and supervisor together can look for possible causes and consequences of observed teacher behavior; theories, values, and beliefs to explain the cause-effect patterns; and alternatives to try in the future. For example, observation of students' at-task behavior during a class period might show their interest in an instructional activity waning after 20 minutes. The teacher might interpret these data as indicating a weakness in the activity or as a normal consequence of students' limited attention span. Depending on the interpretation, decisions for change will vary. If the activity is judged inappropriate, it can be modified or changed substantially in future lessons. If it is interpreted as appropriate but too long, it might merely need to be shortened.

Deciding what changes to make in future instruction can take many forms. Decisions can relate to any elements discussed in the planning conference. For example, the conferees might conclude that one or more of the following should be changed:

- the objectives of the lesson or unit.
- what the teacher does during the instruction.
- what students do during instruction.

Decisions vary in magnitude. At one extreme, the teacher might decide to leave teaching as the result of systematic observational feedback. (We have seen instances of this.) At the other extreme, the teacher might decide not to change a thing. (This has not happened, in our experience; teachers who believe they are perfect must be very rare.) More often, teachers think of several aspects of their instruction that can be changed. The teacher might decide to experiment with these changes one at a time and analyze the effects. Usually the effects can be observed by the teacher without repeated visits by a supervisor, but in some cases a supervisor will be needed.

Occasionally a teacher reaches a decision as the result of viewing data without making any comments during the feedback conference. For example, a teacher might resolve to get rid of an annoying mannerism noted in watching a videotape or to spend more time working with a particular student after analyzing observational data about the student's behavior.

We recall one teacher, who was using a low-key style during a videotaped session, display a very dynamic style during the next observation (also videotaped). The supervisor asked about the obvious and abrupt change in teaching style—a matter that had not been mentioned in the previous conference. The teacher replied, "It wasn't until after I saw that first tape that I realized how undynamic I was. I swore I'd try something much different the next time!" Such a radical change is unusual, but this teacher found he was capable of a more energetic approach to teaching—at least occasionally.

Science makes use of accurate, objective data to understand, predict, and control. Similarly, when presented with accurate, objective data rather than a supervisor's opinions and criticism, the teacher is in a position to use the data to propose changes in his or her instruction and predict their effects on students. The supervisor provides verbal feedback during this process, but it is focused on the objective record, and it emphasizes efforts to understand rather than to evaluate.

Some teachers work through the process described above and then do not follow through by making the changes in their instruction that they proposed. The infrequency of classroom observation by supervisors, colleagues, coaches, or others increases the likelihood that this will happen. Another contributing factor is lack of discussion of professional development opportunities in the feedback conference. Therefore, as a supervisor, you should have a professional-development model in mind as you review the observational record with the teacher. (One such model is presented in Chapter 2). You should also be aware of opportunities for professional development that exist in your immediate geographical area and beyond.

CONFERENCE TECHNIQUE 9: ELICIT THE TEACHER'S INFERENCES, OPINIONS, AND EMOTIONS

One way for a supervisor to open the feedback conference is to ask, "How do you feel your lesson went?" In response, cautious teachers hesitate to say, "Great!" for fear the supervisor will contradict or disagree. On the other hand, if they say, "Lousy," they run the risk of having the supervisor agree. "Some parts were good; others could be improved" is a safe answer for the teacher, but this is what the conference is about anyway.

The observer can choose a less threatening opening question, after the teacher has had a chance to inspect the information, by asking, "What aspects of the data do you want to talk about first?"

Eliciting the teacher's reactions to the data requires skill and patience. There is always a temptation to jump to conclusions about what has been recorded and observed before the teacher has had an opportunity to reflect on it. A conversation move that works well is to ask the following questions:

> "What do you see [or hear] in the observational record that you would repeat if you taught this lesson again?"
>
> "What would you change?"
>
> "What would a student want changed?"

We have asked these questions of hundreds of teachers—primary, intermediate, secondary, and college—who have examined observational data on their teaching behavior. No one has answered all the questions with "I wouldn't change a thing." If "What would you repeat?" gets no response (although it nearly always does; we find things we like in our own teaching), you can proceed to the second question, "What would you change?" If the teacher says, "Nothing," the third question, "What would a student want changed?" should provoke a more thoughtful response. The teacher can be asked to view the instruction from the perspective of different students, say, one who usually has difficulty understanding and one who is usually ahead of the rest.

These questions are phrased in a relatively nonthreatening manner to which most teachers are able to respond openly and with insight. In response to the third question, one teacher said,

> "Which student?"
>
> "What do you mean, which student?"

"Well, the slowest, the brightest, the least interested?"

"OK, the slowest."

"All right. What I see that teacher doing is talking too fast, using vocabulary I don't understand, discussing topics that don't affect me. I don't think she likes me; she almost never calls on me even when I know the answer."

This was a good insight for the teacher to develop. The anecdote points out that one function of the supervisor is to serve as a catalyst, that is, to help the teacher make productive use of the available information for self-improvement as a professional.

For most teachers, the steps in the feedback conference are reasonable and appropriate: providing objective data, analyzing and interpreting it, and drawing conclusions with the teacher taking equal part in a collaborative process. Unfortunately, some supervisors reverse the process. They provide their own conclusions and then search the observational record for evidence to substantiate the conclusions. Alternative interpretations might not even be considered.

For a small percentage of teachers, a "conclusions first" conference approach is justified. For example, it might be more effective to say, "You've been late for work twelve times this month. This has got to stop, or there will be serious consequences!" rather than to say, "Here are some data about your punctuality. Do you find anything of interest?" An alternative move might be to ask, "What do you propose to do about this record of tardiness?"

Even stronger examples can be given for medical settings where the teacher needs to point out to the student, intern, or resident that the patient being discussed is at risk of harm. In schools and colleges, there are also persons (namely, students) "at risk."

Several assumptions are involved in a procedure that encourages teachers to come to their own conclusions, based on objective data and thoughtful analysis.

- Few teachers set out deliberately to do a bad job. Most want their students to learn and develop.
- Most teachers can generate alternative teaching strategies, if encouraged to do so.
- We don't see ourselves as others see us. Being able to view our teaching from a new perspective can be an enlightening experience.
- Those insights we discover for ourselves tend to be internalized and acted on with more energy and better spirit than those we are given by others.
- Many teachers prefer a collaborative, collegial approach rather than one in which the supervisor is regarded as "superior."
- Good data can be more persuasive than mere admonishments.

At first glance, the last assumption in the above list seems questionable. How can data, in themselves, persuade a teacher to change? Yet, in our supervisory experience, we have found that this is often the case. A teacher, after studying a seating chart on which an observer has recorded which students were responded to by the teacher (and in what ways), began to understand why some students feel "turned off" and began to plan activities that create opportunities to respond in positive ways to those students. Many teachers who have analyzed charts of their direct and indirect behaviors (using Flanders's categories, which are described in Chapter 12) have modified the indirect-direct ratio. Teachers who have had access to verbal flow patterns on seating charts (who talks to whom) have been stimulated to experiment with different seating arrangements.

A high school science teacher studied observational charts that showed what percent of his students were at task for various time periods. The percentages were strikingly high, which might have been expected to please this instructor. Yet the teacher concluded that they were too high. Every year a number of students dropped this course; after the teacher saw the data, he realized he was "keeping their noses to the grindstone" so much that the course was unduly punishing. He decided to restructure the course.

Most teachers experience emotions as they teach and also as they examine the observational record of their teaching. While teaching, they might experience panic when students spin out of control or when a planned lesson ends well before the end of the class period. They might feel burned-out at the end of the school year or after years of a stressful school situation or lack of intellectual stimulation. They might experience joy when they see students get excited by a teaching activity or experience an insight. They might experience disappointment when the observational record presents them with data very discrepant from their image of themselves as a teacher. Or they might experience elation when the observational record demonstrates improvement in a troublesome aspect of their teaching behavior.

It is important for you as a supervisor to be aware that teachers have emotions, to bring the teacher's emotions into the feedback conference as appropriate, and—most importantly—to accept, without judgment, whatever a teacher might tell you about these emotions. For example, we have had preservice teachers whose field placements are not going well. They are anxious that they will fail the placement, and so they react to observational data with fear about what they might reveal. Also common among preservice teachers is anxiety about standing up in front of a class of students and having sole responsibility for their instruction.

Some anxiety can facilitate positive changes in teaching behavior, but if the anxiety is too severe, the teacher can "freeze" and be unable to process the observational data and learn from it. In this situation, it is helpful for the supervisor to surface the teacher's anxiety and discuss it. This process by itself can relieve the teacher's anxiety. Also, a frank discussion about the anxiety can suggest things that the teacher and supervisor can do to solve the problem that is producing the anxiety. For example, we have had student teachers who were very anxious about how they were perceived by the class for which they were assuming responsibility. Once this anxiety was out in the open, we were able to work with the student teacher and the cooperating teacher so that the latter could better prepare the class to accept the student teacher's legitimacy as its instructor.

As a supervisor, you should be just as aware of a teacher's positive emotions as of the negative emotions that interfere with teaching. We have seen teachers become very excited when they discover a new theory (e.g., the theory of multiple intelligences) or curriculum that increases their effectiveness with students. In supervision, we have seen teachers express pleasure at observational records that confirm their effectiveness in the classroom or that make visible a vague concern that they have had about some aspect of their instruction. It is important for you to acknowledge, validate, and reinforce these positive feelings. Indeed, these feelings are what sustain many teachers through periods of stress and stimulate them to become better at what they do.

CONFERENCE TECHNIQUE 10: ENCOURAGE THE TEACHER TO CONSIDER ALTERNATIVE METHODS AND EXPLANATIONS

Supervisors often have the strong inclination in the feedback conference to say something like, "Here's what I would do if I were you." This short-circuits the supervision process. If teaching were a straightforward physical skill, then viewing the performance and giving advice like, "Keep your eye on the ball," would be effective. Translated to advice about teaching, this tends to become "Be firm, fair, and consistent." This is undoubtedly good advice, but it does not tell what to be firm about (discipline? standards?) or what is fair and consistent for all (activities for the physically handicapped? individualized academic assignments?). Moreover, there are always reasonable alternatives for teaching anything, so any prescriptive advice might make the teacher question the supervisor's qualifications.

When change is desired, the supervisor should encourage the teacher to generate several alternatives and choose the most promising. Once the teacher has made suggestions, the supervisor can add to them. By having the opportunity to speak first, the teacher feels heard and is likely to be more receptive to what the supervisor has to say.

The ability to generate alternative methods and explanations is critically important to a teacher's potential to grow as a professional. Without this ability, teachers can get into a rut or become rigid in their thinking. In reality, human behavior is complex and is affected by many factors. Therefore, any one explanation for classroom behavior is likely to identify some relevant factors, but ignore others. By constantly considering alternative explanations, the teacher is likely to develop a richer understanding of students, themselves, and their colleagues.

As a case in point, we recall working with an inexperienced teacher at the middle-school level. The teacher was struggling with several students who would not do any seat work. His explanation was that these students were experiencing the turbulence of adolescence, one manifestation of which was rebellion against adult authority. We recommended that the teacher talk individually with each student to see whether their reluctance to do seat work might have other explanations. The teacher learned, to his surprise, that one student was earning a failing grade and figured there was no point in doing any more work in the class; his fate was sealed. Another student said that she was troubled by problems at home and could not focus on her studies. Needless to say, these alternative explanations caused the teacher to think about the students in a different way and to consider new methods for motivating them.

Some teachers hold the implicit belief—below the level of conscious awareness—that their behavior is "fixed." Even if their teaching methods do not produce the results they wish, they do not believe their behavior is amenable to change. By encouraging teachers to consider alternative methods for achieving an instructional objective or other goal, you help them question this belief.

As we explained in Chapter 1, Argyris and Schön, among other researchers, claim that professional practitioners have "espoused theories" and "theories-in-use" that guide their work. If these theories are not questioned, the practitioner is likely to develop a set of work routines that do not change over time, even if they are ineffective. One way to help practitioners—including teachers—break out of these routines is to have them generate ideas about alternative methods of behaving in a certain situation and then test them in actual practice.

For example, one of us worked recently with a team to help a group of secondary teachers consider new ways of teaching their curriculum. Observational data revealed that the teachers, in general, required students to learn a great deal of isolated facts and skills. The teachers had used this approach for so long that they could imagine no other way of approaching the curriculum. The team introduced the teachers to an alternative method of teaching curriculum content, which is called "concept-based teaching," among other names.[6]

Some teachers were skeptical about this teaching method. They thought it would be difficult to implement and would wind up confusing students. However, as they tried the method (with staff-development support), they found that they could continue teaching facts and skills they considered important, but now organized in a meaningful conceptual framework. Some students who formerly learned by rote, if at all, now had better comprehension of the curriculum and were willing to expend more effort on learning.

CONFERENCE TECHNIQUE 11: PROVIDE THE TEACHER WITH OPPORTUNITIES FOR PRACTICE AND COMPARISON

Some supervisors play a more direct role in the supervisory process by suggesting and demonstrating a particular method or technique in a classroom setting. Curriculum specialists in particular are often asked to do such demonstrations. In this situation, the teacher becomes the observer and records data to be analyzed and interpreted in the feedback conference. For example, an elementary teacher was experiencing difficulty explaining the mathematical meaning of pi and the formulas for circumference and area. She asked a mathematics specialist to take over a lesson while she observed the explanation and recorded student questions. During the feedback conference, information about the specialist's lesson was incorporated into information taken from the teacher's experience and plans.

Gerald Elgarten conducted an experiment to determine whether modeling by the supervisor facilitates the development of experienced mathematics teachers.[7] In one of the experimental conditions, a supervisor observed the teacher's lesson and identified teaching behaviors that needed to be introduced or changed.[8] The supervisor then taught the same lesson to the teacher's next class while modeling the strengths of the teacher's lesson and also the targeted teaching behaviors. The teacher observed the lesson and responded to three questions:

1. What do I [supervisor] do that you don't do too often?
2. What do we both seem to do?
3. What good things do you do that I don't seem to do?

These three questions served as the focus of the feedback conference. At the end of the conference, the teacher left with a list of teaching behaviors to practice and internalize. In another experimental condition, the teachers received similar supervision, except that the supervisor did not model the desired changes in teaching behavior by teaching a lesson.

The results of Elgarten's experiment revealed that the teachers who had the opportunity to see their supervisor teach a model lesson implemented more of the desired changes than teachers who participated in clinical supervision without this feature.

One explanation for the effectiveness of supervisor modeling is that it gives teachers the opportunity to observe good teaching techniques in a real-world context, not just hear about them. Also, supervisors undoubtedly gain credibility in the eyes of teachers if they can "practice what they preach."

Another effective strategy is to suggest that one teacher observe another in order to compare teaching styles, strategies, and techniques. If the observing teacher has some knowledge of systematic observation and recording, the feedback conference can result in a mutual sharing of ideas and perspectives. In a small group that takes turns sharing videotaped examples, the observers can learn about their own teaching vicariously while watching others.

Time for collecting observational data and providing feedback is always limited. One way to deal with this problem is for the teacher to collect some of the data. This can be done by teacher-made video or audio recordings (see Chapter 11), by students completing checklists (see Chapter 12), or by teacher aides or colleagues using one of the methods described in Unit 4.

If the teacher has collected and analyzed some of the data, the feedback conference can be more efficient. Furthermore, the performance of these tasks can be a learning experience in itself. For example, transcribing a "selective verbatim" (see Chapter 9) from a tape, charting student participation, or plotting frequencies from a student questionnaire can heighten the teacher's awareness of classroom behavior that is effective or in need of improvement.

SUMMARY OF STEPS IN A FEEDBACK CONFERENCE

The feedback conference is the last step in the clinical supervision cycle. (The first two steps are the planning conference and classroom observation.) Ideally, the feedback conference includes the following steps:

1. The supervisor displays the data recorded during the observation. This is done without evaluative comments.
2. The teacher described and analyzes what happened during the lesson as evidenced by the data. The supervisor simply helps to clarify what behaviors and events are represented by the recorded data.
3. The teacher, with the help of the supervisor, interprets the observed behavior. At this stage the teacher becomes more evaluative, because causes and consequences of classroom events must be discussed as desirable or undesirable.
4. The teacher, with assistance from the supervisor, decides on alternative approaches for the future to attend to dissatisfactions with the observed teaching or emphasize those aspects that were satisfying.
5. The supervisor reinforces the teacher's announced intentions for change by agreeing with them or helping the teacher modify the intentions if there is some disagreement.

Supervisors are often surprised at how easily these steps can be accomplished. When supplied with adequate information and allowed to act on it, most teachers can analyze, interpret, and decide in a self-directed and constructive manner. When things do not go well in a feedback conference, the difficulties can usually be traced to failure on the part of the supervisor to use effective techniques, such as those we considered in this chapter.

NOTES

1. Goldhammer, R. (1969). *Clinical supervision: Special methods for the supervision of teachers*. New York: Holt, Rinehart & Winston, pp. 69–70.

2. Ben-Peretz, M., & Rumney, S. (1991). Professional thinking in guided practice. *Teaching & Teacher Education, 7,* 517–530.

3. *Ibid,* p. 519.

4. *Ibid,* p. 525.

5. Graybeal, N. D. (1984). Characteristics of contemporary classroom supervisory process. *Dissertation Abstracts International, 45*, 07A. (University Microfilms No. AAG84-22846)

6. Erickson, H. L. (2002). *Concept-based curriculum and instruction: Teaching beyond the facts*. Thousand Oaks, CA: Corwin.

7. Elgarten, G. H. (1991). Testing a new supervisory process for improving instruction. *Journal of Curriculum and Supervision, 6,* 118–129.

8. The experiment had four experimental conditions, but we describe only two of them (the most critical for our purposes) here.

Classroom Observation Techniques

OVERVIEW

In order to have persuasive data available for feedback conferences, the supervisor needs a wide range of observation techniques and recording devices, such as the videocassette recorder (VCR) and laptop computer. These are described in this unit. Most of them are easily understood and can be used effectively after a little practice. Also, most of the techniques and devices can be used to observe either a whole class, a group of students, or an individual student. The information they provide the teacher and supervisor is a central element of the clinical supervision cycle.

OBJECTIVES

The purpose of this unit is to help you develop

A repertoire of data-recording techniques

Skill in selecting an appropriate observation method for a given teaching practice

Understanding of the strengths and limitations of different observation methods

An appreciation of the need for regular, systematic observation in doing clinical research

SUMMARY OF METHODS FOR OBSERVING EFFECTIVE TEACHING PRACTICES

In Chapter 3 we reviewed teaching practices that research has found to be effective. These practices are listed in the left column of the following list. The right column lists methods for collecting observational data on how frequently or how well the teacher uses each practice. These methods are described in more detail in the chapters of this unit: Chapter 9 (selective verbatim); Chapter 10 (seating charts); Chapter 11 (wide lens); and Chapter 12 (checklists and time coding).

Most of the effective teaching practices can be observed using methods other than those listed here. In fact, virtually any observation method can be adapted to observe virtually any teaching practice. This list only includes the method that we believe is most convenient and appropriate for each practice.

Effective Teaching Practices and Methods for Observing Them

Effective Teaching Practice	Method(s) of Observation
1. Clarity	Wide lens (audio recording)
2. Variety	Wide lens (audio recording)
3. Enthusiasm	Wide lens (video recording)
4. Task-oriented approach	Wide lens (video recording)
5. Avoidance of harsh criticism	Selective verbatim (teacher feedback)
6. Indirect teaching style	Timeline coding (interaction analysis)
7. Teaching content covered on criterion test	Wide lens (anecdotal record)
8. Structuring statements	Selective verbatim (teacher directions and structuring statements
9. Questions at multiple cognitive levels	Selective verbatim (teacher questions)
10. Praise and encouragement	Selective verbatim (teacher feedback)
11. Explicit teaching model	Wide lens (anecdotal record)
12. Discussion method	Checklist
13. Allocated time	Timeline coding (Stallings observation system)
14. Student at-task behavior	Seating chart (at task)
15. Homework	Wide lens (anecdotal record)
16. Cooperative learning method	Seating chart (at task; movement patterns)
17. Use of value statements and success to motivate students	Wide lens (anecdotal records, reflective journal)
18. Equitable treatment of students varying in achievement, ethnicity, and gender	Seating chart (verbal flow)
19. Classroom management	Selective verbatim (classroom management statements)
20. Changing strategy based on decisions while teaching	Wide lens (video recording)
21. Curriculum implementation	Wide lens (reflective journal)

Chapter 9

Selective Verbatim

Author's Note

Publicly, we are inclined to portray teachers as residents of Lake Woebegone—"They're all above average." In reality, some teachers don't live up to this accolade because of flaws in their classroom instruction. Here are examples from my supervisory experience:

- the teacher who presented so much content, and in such a disorganized manner, that it went right over students' heads.
- the teacher whose questions had a lackluster or drill-and-kill quality, leading students to think that learning is mechanical and without meaning.
- the teacher whose admonishments to students were either ignored or heeded only temporarily.
- the teacher whose directions or explanations left students in a state of confusion.

The good news is that I was able to help teachers like these by using the selective-verbatim methods described in this chapter. Assuming the teaching flaw has a verbal component (and most of them do), I only take notes on those aspects of the lesson that are relevant to it. Thus, the teacher is not overwhelmed by data in the feedback conference or by the prospect of having to improve everything about his teaching style all at once.

The selective-verbatim techniques that you'll read about here do not cover all aspects of teaching, but they do cover some of the most important—asking questions, giving feedback to students, structuring a lesson, and managing student behavior. After studying the chapter, you should be quite able to adapt selective-verbatim methodology to cover other aspects of teaching as well.

If a teacher is at all open to improving her instruction, I find that she gets a lot out of examining a selective-verbatim transcript. I might need to do a bit of cueing, but for the most part the teacher can pick out flaws on her own. Then comes one of the most rewarding parts of clinical supervision—working together to generate more effective teaching techniques and trying them out.

MDG

Except in special instances in which some quality of timing or of sound or of sight evolved as a salient supervisory issue, written data have proven most useful and most wieldy to clinical supervisors. Perhaps the greatest advantage of a written record . . . is that Teacher and

Supervisor can assimilate it most rapidly and most easily; the eye can incorporate, almost instantaneously, evidence that took a relatively long time to unfold in the lesson.

—Robert Goldhammer[1]

INTRODUCTION

The primary goal of clinical supervision is help teachers become better at facilitating students' learning. Accomplishing this goal requires that the supervisor and teacher have a shared vision of what learning means. The learning process is extremely complex, but we believe that there are some essential elements that all educators would acknowledge. These elements are expressed in the form of the following six principles:

- For learning to occur, students' attention must be directed to the information to be learned.
- For learning to occur, students must interact with the information so that it becomes personally meaningful.
- For learning to occur, students must be appropriately motivated.
- For learning to last, students must practice using the information so that it becomes stored in long-term memory and can be retrieved for subsequent use.
- Various group processes in the classroom can facilitate or hinder students' learning.
- The content of students' learning will vary depending on whether the information presented to them involves lower or higher forms of knowledge (e.g., facts versus concepts) and lower or higher intellectual operations (e.g., recall versus synthesis and prediction).

You will find in this chapter that the learning process is heavily influenced by how teachers and students *talk* to each other. In particular, you will find that a teacher's verbal communication patterns can facilitate students' learning if it incorporates the learning principles mentioned above. Conversely, muddled or negative communication patterns can detract from students' learning. Therefore, as a clinical supervisor, you can help teachers improve their instruction by a careful analysis of their communication patterns. This analysis is made possible by an observation technique called selective verbatim.

Selective verbatim requires the supervisor to make a written record of exactly what is said, that is, a verbatim transcript. Not all verbal communication is recorded, however. The supervisor and teacher select beforehand the particular types of verbal events to be transcribed; it is in this sense that the verbatim record is "selective." In this chapter we identify verbal behaviors that reflect effective or ineffective teaching and that are amenable to the selective verbatim technique.

A selective verbatim is usually made while the teacher's class is in progress, but this is not a requirement. If an audio or video recording of a class session is available (see Chapter 11), the selective verbatim can be made from the recording.

The selective verbatim should be word-for-word. For example, suppose the supervisor is recording a teacher's questions, and the teacher asks, "What do we call animals that live exclusively off plants . . . you know, we have a certain name for these animals . . .

does anyone know it?" If the supervisor writes, "What is the name of animals that live exclusively off plants?" this is not a verbatim transcription. It misses certain features of the communication that might affect students positively or negatively.

ADVANTAGES OF SELECTIVE VERBATIM

Selective verbatim has several advantages as a classroom observation technique. We mention four of them here.

First, providing teachers with a selective verbatim transcript focuses their attention on what they say to students or on what students say to them. In this way they become sensitized to the verbal process in teaching. All other levels of communication are screened out by the transcript.

Another advantage of a selective verbatim transcript, compared to a complete transcript, is that it focuses teachers' attention on just a few verbal behaviors. Teachers who are trying to improve their instruction are more successful if they do not try to change many aspects of their communication behavior at once.

Changing a few teaching behaviors might seem unimportant, but keep this in mind: small positive changes can encourage further changes, which might be more substantial. For example, we have witnessed the feeling of accomplishment teachers get when they realize that they habitually use an annoying verbal mannerism, such as "you know" or "uh," and then achieve control over it. This feeling of control and change motivates subsequent, more substantial changes in teaching behavior, such as improvement of one's questioning technique.

The third advantage of selective verbatim is that it provides an objective, nonjudgmental record of the teacher's behavior. While in the act of teaching, many teachers get so caught up in the process that they do not listen to what they are saying. Even if teachers do listen, the verbal events are so fleeting that they are unable to reflect on the impact of these events. Selective verbatim solves this problem by holding up a "verbal mirror" to teachers, which they can examine at their convenience.

Finally, selective verbatim has the advantage of being simple to use. The supervisor only needs a pencil and pad of paper. Also, the verbatim transcript can be made while the supervisor is observing the teacher's classroom. The transcript might need to be typed if the supervisor's handwriting is illegible, but no other transformation of the data is needed.

DRAWBACKS OF SELECTIVE VERBATIM

Selective verbatim is clearly a powerful tool for observation, but some problems can occur in using it. A teacher who knows in advance what verbal behaviors will be recorded might become self-conscious about using them. For example, just knowing that a supervisor will observe verbal praise might increase a teacher's use of this behavior. Even if this should happen, the teacher might gradually internalize the technique of verbal praise and use it whether the supervisor is present or not.

We find in practice that teachers generally do not become self-conscious when a selective verbatim transcript is made. As teachers realize the impact of their verbal behavior on students, they usually want to cooperate with the supervisor to learn more about what they and their students say.

Another problem with selective verbatim arises from its "selectivity." The larger context of classroom interaction is lost if the teacher and supervisor focus too narrowly on verbal behavior. For example, a teacher might look at a selective verbatim transcript of praise statements and dismiss them with, "Oh, I see I used verbal praise ten times. I guess that's pretty good." The analysis needs to go further to explore such questions as whether the praise was given to students who deserved it and whether it overemphasized extrinsic motivation for learning. In-depth analysis of this kind requires that the supervisor record, at least mentally, the entire flow of the lesson. A skillful supervisor is one who simplifies the teaching process by focusing the teacher's attention on a few aspects of teaching, yet relates these aspects to the total context in which instruction occurred.

Still another problem with selective verbatim is that the teacher or supervisor might select trivial aspects of verbal communication for observation. To avoid this problem, the supervisor and teacher should explore why each identified verbal behavior is worth recording and analyzing. If a satisfactory rationale cannot be given, they must consider whether scarce supervisory time should be used to record that particular verbal behavior.

Supervisors occasionally find that they cannot keep up with the flow of verbal interactions. It simply goes by too fast to record. When this happens, we recommend that supervisors use a symbol, such as a line, to indicate where they stopped recording temporarily. It is generally better to record a few verbal statements word for word than to paraphrase or omit part of what was said.

OBSERVATION TECHNIQUE 1: TRANSCRIBING TEACHER QUESTIONS

Question-asking is one of the most important aspects of teaching. This is what educator Mary Jane Aschner had in mind when she called the teacher a "professional question maker."[2]

Researchers have found that teachers rely on question-asking as a staple of their teaching repertoire. Almost a century ago, R. Stevens discovered that high school teachers asked almost 400 questions during an average school day.[3] Unbelievable as this figure might seem, it also has been observed in studies of more recent vintage. In the 1960s, William Floyd found that a sample of primary school teachers asked an average of 348 questions each during a school day.[4] John Moyer found that elementary school teachers asked an average of 180 questions in a science lesson.[5] In Joan Schreiber's study, fifth-grade teachers asked an average of 64 questions in a 30-minute social studies lesson.[6] More recently, S. J. Doneau found that teachers' oral questions consume from 6 to 16 percent of classroom time, depending on the grade level and subject being taught.[7] Similarly, Kenneth Sirotnik found that the most common form of verbal interaction between teachers and students is the traditional recitation—a series of rapid-fire teacher questions to test students' mastery of facts, typically those covered in a textbook.[8]

Asking a lot of questions during a lesson might seem unjustified, but research suggests otherwise. Barak Rosenshine found that asking many questions during a recitation is more effective than asking few questions.[9] This finding makes sense if we consider that the criterion of effectiveness is student performance on achievement tests, which typically assess the amount of information that students have learned. Asking more questions allows the teacher to have students rehearse more information than fewer questions would.

The centrality of questions in the instructional process leads us to recommend that if a teacher and a supervisor can observe only a single aspect of classroom interaction, it should be the teacher's question-asking behavior.

Technique

The supervisor's task is to make a written record of each question asked by the teacher. (Another approach is to use a checklist, such as that shown in Figure 12.3 in Chapter 12.) Because teachers typically ask many questions, the supervisor might ask the teacher to estimate the length of the lesson. Then the supervisor can use time sampling, which means that the supervisor observes samples of the lesson (e.g., every other 3 minutes of the lesson). Obviously, if you are planning to observe the teacher's use of questions, you will want to select a lesson in which this verbal behavior occurs with some frequency.

It seems a simple matter to decide what is or is not a question. "How many kilometers in a mile?" is obviously a question. But how about "Johnny gave a good answer, didn't he?" or "Sue, won't you stop fidgeting in your seat?" or "I'd like someone to tell me how many kilometers there are in a mile." The latter example is a declarative statement, not an interrogative, yet it clearly has the intent of a question.

To avoid confusion, we suggest a simple rule. If the teacher's statement is asked in a questioning manner or has the intent of a question, include it in the transcript. There is no harm in including ambiguous examples, but omitting them might cause a teacher to overlook a significant aspect of his question-asking behavior.

Figure 9.1 shows selective verbatim transcripts based on observation of two fifth-grade teachers. The teachers assigned students to read the same brief handout on the behavior patterns and environment of wolves, followed by a question-and-answer session to help the students review and think about what they had just read.

Data Analysis

As teachers examine selective verbatim transcripts of their questions, you can ask them to focus on different aspects of their question-asking behavior.

Purpose for Asking Questions

It is worth checking whether the teacher is aware of his or her purpose in asking questions and can make that purpose explicit. The following are purposes that reflect sound learning principles:

- Questions can focus students' attention on what is to be learned. In other words, the teacher's question serves as a cue to students that the information required to answer the question is important. This attention-directing is necessary, because students are often exposed to a lot of information in their textbook or other instructional resource. They might not know how to sort through this information to determine which of it is most important. The relevant learning principle, as we stated above, is this: "For learning to occur, students' attention must be directed to the information to be learned."

Teacher 1
1. Now, what do we know about this animal? What do you know about the wolf? You can refer back to this little ditto, if you'd like. Jeff?
2. Next?
3. Mike?
4. Heather?
5. Now Jeff just said that sometimes livestock . . . people or farmers hate them because they kill their livestock. Would livestock be small animals? What do you think?
6. Terry?
7. John?
8. Mike?
9. Terry, again?
10. Jeff?
11. Jerry?
12. Who said that, Jerry? Was there a quote or something in that article?
13. Do you remember the man's name?
14. Do you know something? Last night, after we read this article, after school, Jeff said, "Gee Mr. Edwards, I think I've seen that name, or something." He went right down to the library and brought back this book, and it's by the same man. Jeff, did you have a chance to look at that last night?
15. Jeff, does it concern itself with the wolf?
16. Does anyone have anything else to say about what we already know?

Teacher 2
1. What do you know about the Arctic and that kind of area that would lead you to believe that a dog would have to be more strong there than he would have to be, say, here? Dana?
2. Pam?
3. What kind of work does he have to do?
4. Terry?
5. Karen?
6. Why do the dogs work harder in the north than they work here? John?
7. Why don't our dogs have to work?
8. What don't we need done here?
9. Allen?
10. Doug?
11. Why do you suppose the Eskimos don't have machines? Joey?
12. Do you think so? Does anyone have another idea about why they don't, 'cause there's probably more than one idea?
13. Why would they be primitive? Pat?
14. Wanda?
15. It mentioned in the stories that wolves traveled in packs, in groups. Why do you suppose they do? What do you suppose is their reason for doing this? Joe?

Figure 9.1 Selective verbatim transcripts of fifth-grade teachers' questions.

- Teachers can use questions to motivate students to engage in learning. In a study of middle-school U.S. history classes, Ed Hootstein asked students what techniques a teacher could use to make this subject interesting.[10] One of the most-mentioned techniques was, "Use thought-provoking questions."[11] The relevant learning principle is this: "For learning to occur, students must be appropriately motivated."

- Teachers can use questions to get students to process new information and put it into their own words, so that it becomes meaningful. Questions also get students to practice using the new information. These related purposes reflect two key learning principles: "For learning to occur, students must interact with the information so that it becomes personally meaningful; and they must practice using the information so that it becomes stored in long-term memory and can be retrieved for subsequent use."

As teachers examine their selective verbatim transcript in relation to these purposes for using questions, you can expect that they will become more reflective about using questions in a purposeful manner to promote students' learning.

Cognitive Level of Question

Teachers' questions can be classified into two categories: "fact" and "higher cognitive." Fact questions require students to recall facts or information stated in the curriculum materials. In contrast, higher cognitive questions (also called "thought" questions) require students to think about the information they have studied and to state their own ideas. Questions can be analyzed into additional categories using Bloom's taxonomy[12] or other question classification system, but the two levels of "fact" and "higher cognitive" are satisfactory for most purposes.

The research literature we reviewed in Chapter 3 does not demonstrate unequivocally that higher cognitive questions are superior to fact questions. The available evidence suggests instead that an emphasis on either type of question can be effective depending on the teacher's objectives for the lesson. If the lesson's purpose is to teach or review facts and routine skills, an emphasis on fact questions probably will be effective. If the purpose is to develop students' ability to think, the emphasis probably should be on higher cognitive questions. These conclusions about the effects of questions are consistent with one of our learning principles: "Students' learning outcomes will vary depending on whether the information presented to them involves lower or higher forms of knowledge (e.g., facts versus concepts) and lower or higher intellectual operations (e.g., recall versus synthesis and prediction)."

Fact questions and higher cognitive questions are not always easy to distinguish from one another. For example, a student might be asked to recall a fact stated in the assigned reading. The student might not be able to recall the fact, but can deduce it by using higher cognitive processes and other information he or she knows. A question that is higher cognitive in form (e.g., a "why?" question) might actually be a "fact" question if the student simply repeats an idea heard or read elsewhere.

It is apparent that the first teacher in Figure 9.1 is emphasizing fact questions as indicated by phrases like "what do we know about . . . ?" "Who said that?" and "did you have a chance to look at that last night?" In contrast, the second teacher focuses on higher cognitive processes, as indicated by phrases like "What ... would lead you to believe ... ?" "Why ... ?" and "Does anyone have another idea?" One of these teachers is not necessarily more effective than the other. The first teacher might have had good reasons to emphasize fact questions, and the second teacher might have had equally good reasons to emphasize higher cognitive questions. The supervisor can identify these reasons by conferencing with the teachers about the thinking that went into their lessons.

Amount of Information

Fact questions can be classified into "narrow" and "broad," depending on the amount of information called for in the question. For example, the first teacher in Figure 9.1 asked, "What do you know about the wolf?" This is an example of a broad fact question. "Do you remember the man's name?" is an example of a narrow fact question because it asks for only one bit of information. Teachers sometimes ask a series of narrow fact questions—a teacher-centered practice that uses up class time—when one broad question might be sufficient.

Academic and Personal Questions

Teachers' questions often focus on academic knowledge and thinking. For example, in teaching about a novel, a teacher might ask such questions as, "What is the main conflict facing the hero?," "What symbols does the author use?," and "How does the setting affect the actions of the characters?" These questions reflect the traditions of literary analysis and criticism established by academic scholars.

It is also possible to ask questions that are more personally engaging, for example, "How do you think the hero will respond to this challenge?" Martin Nystrand and Adam Gamoran call these *authentic questions*, because they invite students to express their own ideas.[13]

Bracha Alpert studied a high school teacher who made extensive use of such questions.[14] Here is a sample of them:

- "Why is the [literary character] so angry ... think of what kinds of things make you angry, really angry?"
- "Do you feel sorry for any of the characters?"
- "Did you see his way as somewhat less worthwhile than hers?"

Alpert found that students in this teacher's classroom were more motivated to engage in classroom interaction, because their personal feelings and opinions were legitimated as part of the curriculum. Students of other teachers whom Alpert studied were more reluctant to participate in discussion because of a nearly exclusive emphasis on academic knowledge and thinking patterns.

The value of personal questions is supported in the learning principle: "For learning to occur, students must interact with the information so that it becomes personally meaningful." By asking personal questions, the teacher is inviting students to access their feelings and opinions—which inherently have personal meaning—and relate them to the formal academic curriculum. Ultimately, academic disciplines such as history, art criticism, chemistry, and mathematics derive from the personal experiences and curiosity of researchers and scholars. However, the human face behind academic knowledge is likely to remain hidden from students, unless teachers make it part of their instruction.

Teachers should find it worthwhile to examine selective verbatim transcripts of their questions to determine the use of academic and personally engaging questions, especially if they find that students are reluctant to answer their questions. Awareness of the distinction between academic and personal (or "authentic") questions might suggest how they can use questions differently to facilitate greater engagement by students in the learning process.

The distinction between academic and personal questions reflects recent interest in constructivist instruction as an alternative to conventional instruction, especially in science and mathematics classes. We consider constructivist instruction later in this chapter.

Redirection

Teachers can call on one student to answer each question, or they can ask several students to respond. That is, they can "redirect" the question. Redirection is a useful technique for increasing student participation and eliciting a variety of ideas for students to consider. Higher cognitive questions are redirected more easily than fact questions, because the former usually do not have a single correct answer.

Both teachers in Figure 9.1 used the technique of redirection by naming the student they wished to respond to their question. Redirection also can occur by nonverbal acknowledgment of a student who has his or her hand raised or by establishing eye contact with a student. These instances of redirection will not show up in a selective verbatim transcript. If you wish to record these instances, you can do so by writing an *R* or other symbol whenever they occur. The names of the students can be recorded, instead, if you know them.

Probing Questions

These are "follow-up" questions designed to help students improve or elaborate on their initial response to the teacher question. They are not easy to detect in a selective verbatim transcript, unless you make special note of them, such as by placing a *P* beside each one. The following is a complete verbatim transcript of the events that transpired when the second teacher in Figure 9.1 asked Questions 6 and 7.

TEACHER: Why do the dogs work harder in the north than they work here? John?

JOHN: Well, most of the dogs here don't really have to work hard.

TEACHER: Why don't our dogs have to work?

JOHN: They're house pets, and we do most of the work ourselves, and we don't need stuff like they do up there.

TEACHER: What don't we need done here?

JOHN: We don't need dogs to pull things here. We have cars, but the Eskimos don't, so they use dogs.

The teacher's two probing questions helped John give a more complete and specific answer to the initial question.

Teachers sometimes are unaware that they accept or overlook poor responses to their questions. A transcript of their probing questions provides one indication of whether this is happening. An absence of probing questions suggests lack of attention to student responses, whereas liberal use of this technique suggests that the teacher is listening carefully to what students say and is challenging them to do their best work.

Multiple Questions

The practice of asking several questions in a row can be spotted easily in a selective verbatim transcript. Note that the first teacher begins his lesson by asking two questions in succession: "Now, what do we know about this animal? What do you know about the wolf?" The same teacher also asks multiple questions in the fifth and twelfth recorded statements. The second teacher asks multiple questions in the twelfth and fifteenth recorded statements.

Teachers usually engage in this behavior when they are "thinking on their feet." They may try various phrasings and ideas before they hit upon the question they want to ask. Teachers for whom this is habitual practice should reflect on whether it is distracting or confusing to students. Teachers can avoid asking multiple questions by preparing questions in advance of the actual lesson.

Teachers also engage in multiple question-asking when they literally repeat their question. They do this because they think students did not hear them the first time they asked the question. The problem is that repeating the question might condition students not to listen carefully to the teacher the first time he or she asks a question.

OBSERVATION TECHNIQUE 2: TRANSCRIBING CONSTRUCTIVIST DIALOGUE

Educators are becoming increasingly interested in the theory of learning known as constructivism. According to this theory, individuals learn by developing their own understanding of the world. Or in other words, they learn by "constructing" their own understanding of the world. Some theorists—most notably, Jean Piaget—focus on how individuals come to understand the world by experimenting with it and developing progressively more sophisticated cognitive structures. Other theorists—most notably, Lev Vygotsky—focus on how individuals interact with each other to develop a shared understanding of the world. This theoretical approach is sometimes called *social constructivism*. In teaching methods based on social-constructivist theory, the teacher and students work together to develop a shared understanding of curriculum content.

Constructivist theory has important implications for classroom instruction. Researchers have found that many students have difficulty learning concepts like *photosynthesis* and *acceleration*, because they try to memorize definitions or the teacher's explanations without really understanding them. In fact, they might have misconceptions about these concepts, which persist despite conventional teacher instruction.

Constructivist teaching methods have been developed to deal with this problem. The essence of these methods is for the teacher to help students go through a thinking process that results in accurate, deep understanding of important concepts in the curriculum. The teacher asks students a series of questions that encourage them to formulate their own theories and predictions drawn from them; test them through actual experimentation; and use the results of the experiment to validate their theory or revise them. The hoped-for result is a rich understanding of the concept, not superficial or rote learning.

Higher-cognitive questions, which we discussed above, stimulate students to think. However, the thinking is less sustained than in constructivist teaching; and typically students do not have an opportunity to empirically test their thinking. The sustained nature of constructivist question-asking is sometimes characterized as "constructivist dialogue" or "collaborative dialogue." An example of this type of teacher–student interaction to develop student understanding is shown in Figure 9.2.

Jere Brophy compared recent research on teaching in different school subjects.[15] He found lines of research on constructivist dialogue across subjects, often within the context of inquiry models of teaching. However, the nature of the discourse that was investigated and advocated varied from one subject to another. Figure 9.3 shows Brophy's synthesis of these discourse variations.

The situation is a first-grade math lesson on measurement and equivalency. Children were asked to use a balance to determine how many plastic links equaled one metal washer in weight. The teacher is interacting with one of the children, a girl named Anna.

T: How many links does it take to balance one washer?
S: (After a few minutes of experimenting) Four.
T: If I placed one more washer on this side, how many more links do you think we would need to balance it?
S: One.
T: Try it.

Anna placed one more link in the balance tray and noticed that balance was not achieved. She looked confused and placed another link in the tray and then a third. Still no balance. She placed one more link in the tray. Balance was achieved. She smiled and looked at the teacher.

T: How many cubes did it take to balance one washer?
S: Four.
T: And how many to balance two washers?
S: (counting) Eight.
T: If I put one more washer on this side, how many more links will you need to balance it?
S: (Pondered and looked quizzically at the teacher) Four.
T: Try it.
S: (after successfully balancing with four links) Each washer is the same as four links.
T: Now, let me give you a really hard question. If I took four links off of the balance, how many washers would I need to take off in order to balance it?
S: One!

Figure 9.2 Selective verbatim transcript of a constructivist dialogue.

Source: Brooks, J. G., & Brooks, M. G. (1993). *The case for constructivist classrooms* pp. 73-74. Alexandria, VA: Association for Supervision and Curriculum Development.

Language Arts

- Discussion of the meanings of text (especially narratives) and of individuals' reactions to it.
- Discussion to enrich students' understanding of content and appreciation of literature.
- Analysis of examples of writing genres to develop understanding of the nature of their features and how these might be included in one's own writing.

Mathematics

- Mathematical argumentation: using problem contexts for developing mathematical ideas, representations, and procedures.
- Geometric inquiry, sensemaking, and problem solving within a classroom discourse that establishes ideas and truths collaboratively.

Physical Sciences

- Biological inquiry framed within the constructivist model of learning and ideas about biology as a domain.
- Analysis of physics problems and negotiation of potential approaches and solutions.
- Discussion to stimulate students to construct understandings, concept maps, and mental models of chemical phenomena in problem solving or laboratory debriefing contexts.
- Engaging in the dialectic between evidence and explanation or observation and theory that occurs in extended inquiry activities in earth system science (more in small-group than in whole-class settings).

Social Studies

- Analysis and response to historical events, with focus not just on establishing what happened but on considering connections to other events and implications for personal or civic policy decisions.
- Negotiation of learning accomplished through field studies, map-based instruction, and simulation work in geography (during subsequent debriefings).
- Thoughtful discourse around big ideas in culture studies.
- Value-based discussion of social and civic issues, especially controversial issues.
- Economics-based discussion occurring in the context of concept teaching, inquiry, or debriefing following experiential learning or simulations.

Figure 9.3 Discourse variations across school subjects.

Source: Adapted from: Brophy, J. (Ed.). (2001). *Advances in research on teaching* (Vol. 8, pp. 454–455). Oxford: JAI Elsevier.

Technique

As a supervisor, you will need to observe a lesson that is specifically designed around principles of constructivist teaching. Otherwise, you are unlikely to have any data to record. Constructivist discourse is not a routine feature of teaching, nor is it typically found in all school subjects. You are most likely to have the opportunity to make a selective verbatim transcript of constructivist discourse during a science or math lesson of a teacher who has had some preparation in constructivist theory and methodology.

As the lesson unfolds, you should make notes about any materials, media, or raw data that were used as part of the process to develop students' understanding about a concept or principle. If students took notes or made drawings, consider collecting samples to analyze with the teacher in the feedback conference. Most importantly, record all teacher questions and student responses or statements relating to efforts to achieve understanding.

Data Analysis

Because constructivist teaching usually involves many questions, you and the teacher might look at the aspects of question-asking that we discussed under Observation Technique 2. However, the main focus of analysis should be on the distinctive features of constructivist teaching.

Concrete representations of the abstract

It is difficult for students to construct their own understanding of the abstract concepts of science, mathematics, and other disciplines without access to concrete representations of these concepts. You and the teacher can examine the selective verbatim transcript to determine whether teacher questions and student statements were centered around primary source data, manipulatives, or other materials. In Figure 9.2, we see that the interactions between the teacher and student focused on a balance tray.

Telling versus asking

If a student does not understand a concept or cannot answer a question, the teacher might be tempted to offer an explanation. The alternative is to ask a question that encourages the student to keep interacting with primary source data or other materials in the search for understanding. If the selective verbatim transcript reveals instances of preemptive explanations, you and the teacher can explore ways that questioning could be used instead.

One of the most effective types of questions is a request for the student to make a prediction based on the student's existing understanding of the concept, and then to test it with the materials or primary source data. For example, in Figure 9.2, we see that the teacher asks the student to make a prediction about what will happen if one more washer is put on the balance tray: the student makes a prediction, and then the teacher says, "Try it."

OBSERVATION TECHNIQUE 3: TRANSCRIBING TEACHER FEEDBACK

Researchers have found that teacher feedback can facilitate students' learning (see Chapter 3). For example, if we are learning a new skill, we need feedback to know how well we are performing the skill. Without feedback, we might simply practice bad habits or terminate training too soon. It is probably for this reason that "correction and feedback" is an important component of the research-based "explicit teaching model" described in Chapter 3.

Praise and criticism probably are the most common types of teacher feedback. Sincere praise encourages students to learn and to keep trying if obstacles arise. Harsh criticism has the opposite effect. This aspect of verbal communication, then, is relevant to the learning principle that we stated earlier in the chapter: "For learning to occur, students must be appropriately motivated."

Technique

As the supervisor, you need to arrange with the teacher to observe a sample of classroom instruction in which there is frequent verbal interchange between the teacher and students. During instruction, you record the teacher's verbal feedback statements. It also is useful to record the immediately preceding student remark or action that prompted the feedback. Another option is to make note of the affective content: Was the verbal feedback enthusiastic in tone? Neutral? Hostile?

As with question classification, it is not always an easy matter to decide whether a particular teacher remark is an instance of verbal feedback. You will need to rely on your judgment to determine whether the remark is likely to be perceived by a student as feedback on his or her behavior. Your judgment will be sound to the extent that you closely observe students' reactions and the total instructional context when making the selective verbatim transcript.

Figure 9.4 presents a selective verbatim transcript of a junior high school teacher's feedback statements and the context in which they occurred. The lesson was organized around an article about population explosion that the students had been asked to read.

You may wonder whether to include probing questions, which we described earlier in the chapter, as instances of teacher feedback. Consider, for example, the second and third teacher utterances in Figure 9.4. We classified them as probing questions because they were intended to elicit a more specific answer from the student. At the same time, the fact that the teacher asked the questions is feedback to the students that the answer can be improved. That, at least, is our view of the situation. As an observer of classroom instruction, you will need to make your own judgment about whether to include probing questions in a selective verbatim of teacher feedback.

Data Analysis

The teacher and supervisor can examine a selective verbatim transcript of feedback statements from several perspectives, including the following.

Frequency

The simplest analysis you can make of the selective verbatim transcript is to determine the frequency with which the teacher provides feedback. You might observe teachers who provide little or no feedback to their students. These teachers tend to use a highly directive style of instruction. Their primary concern is to impart knowledge—perhaps with too little concern about whether students are "receiving" the knowledge.

Other teachers make extensive use of feedback. They tend to be more responsive to students and to encourage teacher–student interaction. In Figure 9.4, we counted ten instances of teacher feedback—a fairly high frequency for this amount of transcription.

Variety

Of concern here is whether teachers rely on a few limited forms of feedback or whether they provide a variety of feedback. John Zahorik, in a research study of teachers' feedback behavior, found that teachers' verbal feedback tends to be constricted.[16] Only a few kinds of feedback are used regularly. Zahorik found that the most frequent form of feedback to

T: All right. Could someone tell me what the report was about? Ann?

S: Well, it was about birth control.

T: Birth control?

S: Uh, population explosion.

. . .

S: It was about the population explosion, but it was also about limits. It made a lot of predictions, like we won't have room to get around, and there's not going to be any room to plant crops.

T: <u>I'm glad you remembered that the author said that these were "predictions."</u> Why do you think I'm glad you remembered that the author used the word "predictions?"

. . .

S: I also heard that they're going to have a farm under the sea, for sea-farming.

T: <u>Who's "they"?</u>

S: Well . . . the scientists.

. . .

S: And as the years go by, cars will get better and better.

T: <u>Are you sure?</u>

S: Well, I'm not certain, but pretty sure.

T: <u>Pretty sure. This is kind of what I wanted you to get out of this article. These are your opinions, your predictions of what might happen. And they sound pretty good to me, and I'll bank on them to a certain extent, but something might happen to the automobile industry so that your predictions wouldn't come true.</u>

. . .

T: Who made that statement that was quoted in the article?

S: Professor Kenneth E. F. Watt.

T: <u>Professor Kenneth E. F. Watt is saying it.</u> Do we know that what he's saying is worthwhile?

S: Well, Professor Kenneth E. F. Watt isn't the only one that is making these predictions. There's probably thousands of people making these predictions.

T: <u>Yes, that's a good point, Rodney. We can have some faith in what he's predicting because others are making similar predictions.</u>

. . .

T: Why, throughout the whole world, are there so many people having so many children? Did you ever stop to think about it? Steve?

S: When the children grow up, they want children. Then when those children grow up, then they get more children, and that goes on and on.

T: <u>Steve, I'm not sure I'm following you. Could you clarify your idea a bit?</u> Why do people want to have so many children?

. . .

T: (concluding remark) <u>I thought the ideas you had to contribute were a lot more interesting than the article itself.</u>

Figure 9.4 Selective verbatim transcript of teacher feedback.

students was simply to repeat the student's answer to a question. An illustration of this practice is the eighth teacher utterance in Figure 9.4.

Ned Flanders found that a particularly effective form of feedback is to acknowledge students' ideas by building on them.[17] He identified the following ways in which to build on student ideas:

1. *Modifying* the idea by rephrasing or conceptualizing it in the teacher's own words.

2. *Applying* the idea by using it to reach an inference or take the next step in a logical analysis of a problem.

3. *Comparing* the idea with other ideas expressed earlier by the students or the teacher.

4. *Summarizing* what was said by an individual student or group of students.

The sixth teacher utterance in Figure 9.4 is an example of acknowledgment by applying students' ideas to reach an inference.

Teacher verbal feedback also can be analyzed to determine whether there is variety in the teacher's use of praise and critical remarks.

Another perspective for analyzing variety of teacher feedback is to determine the nature of the student responses that elicited the feedback statement. Does the teacher limit feedback to the information contained in the student's answer? Or does the teacher extend feedback to include the student's feelings and opinions? This distinction between academic and personal *feedback* parallels the distinction between academic and personal *questions* that we made above.

Research conducted by Flanders and others indicates that teachers seldom acknowledge students' feelings, even though educators generally agree that feelings—and other aspects of the affective domain—are an important part of the instructional process. Flanders found that even a small increase in feedback that acknowledges students' feelings can have a noticeable positive effect on students' motivation and the emotional climate of the classroom.

Specificity

Teachers tend to give simple, nonspecific forms of feedback, such as, "Good," "Uh-huh," or "OK." Jere Brophy, among other educators, suggests that teachers should develop the habit of making their praise or criticism more specific.[18] Below is a list of guidelines that he developed for this purpose.[19] The guidelines are for praise statements, but they can be applied also to criticism and other forms of feedback (rewards, assignments to remediate academic weaknesses, etc.). You will note that Brophy's guidelines concern not just the phrasing of the praise statement, but also the characteristics of students, especially their motivational state.

Effective Praise

1. is delivered contingently.

2. specifies the particulars of the accomplishment.

3. shows spontaneity, variety, and other signs of credibility; suggests clear attention to the student's accomplishment.

4. rewards attainment of specified performance criteria (which can include effort criteria, however).

5. provides information to students about their competence or the value of their accomplishments.

6. orients students toward better appreciation of their own task-related behavior and thinking about problem solving.

7. uses students' own prior accomplishments as a context for describing present accomplishments.

8. is given in recognition of noteworthy effort or success at difficult (for this student) tasks.

9. attributes success to effort and ability, implying that similar successes can be expected in the future.

10. fosters endogenous attributions (students believe that they expend effort on the task because they enjoy the task and/or want to develop task-relevant skills).

11. focuses students' attention on their own task-relevant behavior.

12. fosters appreciation of and desirable attributions about task-relevant behavior after the process is completed.

Ineffective Praise

1. is delivered randomly or unsystematically.

2. is restricted to global positive reactions.

3. shows a bland uniformity, which suggests a conditioned response made with minimal attention.

4. rewards mere participation, without consideration of performance processes or outcomes.

5. provides no information at all or gives students information about their status.

6. orients students toward comparing themselves with others and thinking about competing.

7. uses the accomplishments of peers as the context for describing students' present accomplishments.

8. is given without regard to the effort expended or the meaning of the accomplishment (for this student).

9. attributes success to ability alone or to external factors, such as luck or easy task.

10. fosters exogenous attributions (students believe that they expend effort on the task for external reasons—to please the teacher, win a competition or reward, etc.).

11. focuses students' attention on the teacher as an external authority figure who is manipulating them.

12. intrudes into the ongoing process, distracting attention from task-relevant behavior.

OBSERVATION TECHNIQUE 4: TRANSCRIBING
TEACHER STRUCTURING STATEMENTS

In Chapter 3 we reviewed nine characteristics of effective teaching that Barak Rosenshine and Norma Furst identified in their review of the research literature.[20] One of these characteristics is the use of structuring statements, which are teacher utterances that help students focus their attention on the lesson's purpose, organization, and key points. Common types of structuring statements are:

- previews of what students will learn in the lesson.
- summaries of what did happen.
- comments that signal transitions in the lesson.
- directions for doing seat work and other tasks.
- nonverbal cues that emphasize key points in the lesson.

Rosenshine and Furst found consistent research evidence that students whose teachers make structuring statements have better academic achievement. Also, several components of Madeline Hunter's model of effective teaching (discussed in Chapter 3) directly involve the use of structuring statements, namely: anticipatory set, stating of objectives, and closure.[21] Structuring statements also can be incorporated into teachers' use of other components of Hunter's model.

Technique

It is probably best to observe a teacher's structuring statements in the context of a complete lesson. Therefore, as a supervisor, you need to speak beforehand with the teacher to determine when to begin observing and approximately how long the lesson will last. Then, during the lesson, you will make a selective verbatim of structuring statements in the order they occur. Most such statements occur at the beginning and end of the lesson, so you need to be especially observant at these times.

Structuring statements and classroom management statements, which we cover in the next section of this chapter, sometimes appear similar. You can distinguish between them in this way: structuring statements focus on the academic content of the lesson, whereas management statements focus on classroom procedures and students' personal behavior. Using this rule of thumb, we would classify the following statements as examples of structuring statements: "When you're done with the textbook problems, you can read a story silently," and "Be sure to insert page numbers when you type your project report in the computer lab." In contrast, we would classify the following statements as examples of classroom management statement: "If you talk to your neighbor one more time, I'll have to call your parent," and "Be sure to clear your desk of all objects when the bell rings." Some teacher statements might be classified one way or another; if in doubt, it's probably better to record the statement than to pass over it.

Figure 9.5 presents a composite of lessons in which teachers gave directions. We used this approach, rather than presenting the selective verbatim of one teacher, to show the variety of forms that these verbal comments can take.

1. The report we're going to read today is about apartheid in South Africa.

2. The film we just saw on how glass is made illustrates very well some of the points that were covered in the book we're using in this class.

3. Yes, electric cars are one of the really important ways we might be able to control air pollution in the future. You might want to remember that when you write your science-fiction stories.

4. Ok. Today I've shown you three different ways you can do calculations. First, you can use your hand calculator. Second, you can use the calculator that's on most computers. And third—does anyone remember what the third method is?

5. Get out your graphic organizer on social customs and, as you're reading the story, write down things relating to music, food, and clothing in Kenya.

6. We've gone through the characteristics of the preterite tense and past tense in Spanish. Now let's compare those characteristics to see how the two tenses differ.

7. Be sure to color in the object in your picture first. Then you can cut the object out and tape it on the big board. Make sure you put the picture right above the notecard that spells out the name of the object.

Figure 9.5 Selective verbatim statements involving structuring.

Data Analysis

The process of analyzing structuring statements is facilitated if the selective verbatim transcript is reviewed fairly quickly after the lesson, while the teacher can still recall whether the statements were clearly understood by the students. As with teacher feedback, the teacher and supervisor can examine the transcript of structuring statements for amount, variety, and specificity.

Another important aspect of structuring statements is their clarity. Students can get off task because they do not understand what the teacher is saying to them about classroom rules and procedures. Not surprisingly, Rosenshine and Furst found that students learn better when they have teachers who make clear verbal statements. This finding makes sense in terms of one of the learning principles that we listed at the start of the chapter: "For learning to occur, students' attention must be directed to the information to be learned." A corollary of this principle is that students will have a difficult time maintaining attention if the information is unclear, if it comes at students too quickly, or if the teacher digresses or jumps from one point to another and then back again.

As we stated above, structuring comments can take a variety of forms, for example:

1. an overview of the lesson about to be taught.
2. the objectives and purpose of the lesson.
3. cueing remarks that focus the student's attention on key points in the lesson.
4. a summary of what was covered in the lesson.

5. statements that relate the lesson to curriculum content previously covered or to events outside the classroom.

6. reinforcement of key structuring comments by repeating them in another format (e.g., through a handout, on a blackboard, or by an overhead projector).

You and the teacher can review the selective verbatim to determine the presence of these types of structuring comments, and whether the lesson could have been improved by including some of them.

OBSERVATION TECHNIQUE 5: TRANSCRIBING CLASSROOM MANAGEMENT STATEMENTS

Simon Veenman synthesized the findings of over ninety studies of the self-reported concerns of beginning teachers.[22] The most frequently mentioned concern was classroom discipline—or, as some educators call it, classroom management. While Veenman's review of research focused on beginning teachers, classroom management is undoubtedly a major concern of preservice teachers and experienced teachers as well. For this reason, problems in classroom management often are a primary focus of clinical supervision.

Classroom management has two major aspects: (1) ensuring that students learn and follow classroom rules and procedures; and (2) handling student misbehavior, which can be viewed as noncompliance with classroom rules and procedures. One way in which teachers get students to follow rules and procedures is by giving directions during the lesson. Directions are similar to structuring statements in that they focus students' attention. Teacher statements when students misbehave also can serve to refocus the student's attention on the learning task to be performed.

Figure 9.6 shows a selective verbatim transcript of a student teacher's classroom management statements in a ninth-grade science class. Most of the statements reflect efforts to refocus students' attention to the learning task. Some are intended to get a student to desist from inappropriate behavior (e.g., statements 6, 17, and 21).

Teachers' directions reflect their rules and procedures. If the rules and procedures have been taught well at the beginning of the school year or course, the directions can be briefly stated. Also, it probably is not necessary to give many directions. This is because most rules and procedures apply from one lesson to the next. This point is illustrated in Walter's Doyle's list of fifteen tasks and situations for which rules and procedures are necessary (see Chapter 3).[23] For example, item 11 on Doyle's list concerns moving around the classroom for such purposes as pencil-sharpening and getting materials. If students have been taught rules for moving around the classroom, the teacher should not need to repeat them during the lesson.

Classroom management statements can be viewed as a reflection of how well rules and procedures have been taught. In a well-managed classroom, there should be relatively few statements of this sort. However, it is unlikely that there will be no such statements, because some students will misbehave for reasons that have nothing to do with the teacher's instruction.

When observing a teacher's classroom management behavior, you should determine the teacher's management model in the planning conference. A common feature of most models is to specify consequences for inappropriate behavior, explain those consequences

1. Guys, you need to settle down.

2. Attention, get out your notebooks.

3. Attention. The quicker we get through this review, the more time you'll have to look at how your plants are doing.

4. Loosen up, guys.

5. Guys, I need for things to be quiet.

6. This is not appropriate. This is your first warning of the day.

7. Bill . . . (Teacher is trying to quiet him down)

8. Loosen up, guys.

9. You have three more minutes.

10. Guys, you should be finishing up.

11. I need everybody to go back to their regular seat now. We have to do review.

12. Listen up, guys.

13. The quicker we get through this, the more time you'll have for your bottle. Get back to your seats.

14. Alyssha . . . everybody . . . let's look at the study sheet, so we'll have time for the bottle experiment.

15. It's up to you to figure out how to finish. Ssshh.

16. If we spend the whole time reviewing, you won't have time to look at your bottles. Sshh.

17. Sshh. Guys, this is not the time to be doing this.

18. Sam, this is your warning.

19. Ryan!

20. Guys!

21. Justin . . . Teresa . . . turn around!

22. Mark! Kelly! Sam!

23. Mark, you can't be writing notes now!

24. Sshh. Guys, it really needs to be quiet in here. Kelly!

25. Guys, everybody needs to be quiet.

26. Sam, I'm calling your parents after class.

27. Guys, listen up. You're preventing people from learning.

Figure 9.6 Selective verbatim transcript of classroom management statements.

to students, and follow through on them when inappropriate behavior persists. Statement 26 in Figure 9.6 is an example of stating a consequence for inappropriate behavior. Conferencing with the student teacher whose selective verbatim transcript is shown in Figure 9.6 revealed that she did not follow through with this consequence or other stated consequences. The supervisor helped the student teacher see a relationship between the escalating misbehavior in her lessons and the failure to put consequences into effect. From that insight, the supervisor was able to explore the reasons why she stated consequences, but did not follow through on them.

Teachers can analyze their management statements to determine their level of severity and whether they were effective in accomplishing their purpose. The first five statements in Figure 9.6 seem fairly mild. The sixth statement is more severe. Statement 22 and several others with exclamation points indicate even greater severity. (The supervisor used the explanation point to indicate a sharp tone of voice or actual shouting.) In Chapter 3 we reviewed researchers' findings that effective teachers teach classroom rules and procedures systematically, monitor their use continually, and correct misbehavior unobtrusively and before it has a chance to escalate.

NOTES

1. Goldhammer, R. (1969). *Clinical supervision: Special methods for the supervision of teachers.* New York: Holt, Rinehart & Winston, p. 84.

2. Aschner, M. J. (1961). Asking questions to trigger thinking. *NEA Journal, 50,* 44–46.

3. Stevens, R. (1912). The question as a measure of efficiency in instruction: A critical study of classroom practice. *Teachers College Contributions to Education,* No. 48.

4. Floyd, W. D. (1960). An analysis of the oral questioning activity in selected Colorado primary classrooms. *Dissertation Abstracts International, 46,* C22. (University Microfilms No. AAG60-06253)

5. Moyer, J. R. (1966). An exploratory study of questioning in the instructional processes in selected elementary schools. *Dissertation Abstracts International, 27* (01), 147. (University Microfilms No. AAG66-02661)

6. Schreiber, J. E. (1967). Teachers' question-asking techniques in social studies. *Dissertation Abstracts International, 28,* 0523. (University Microfilms No. AAG67-09099)

7. Doneau, S. J. (1985). Soliciting in the classroom. In T. Husén & T. N. Postlethwaite (Eds.), *The international encyclopedia of education: Research and studies* (pp. 407–413). Oxford: Pergamon.

8. Sirotnik, K. A. (1983). What you see is what you get—consistency, persistency, and mediocrity in classrooms. *Harvard Educational Review, 53,* 16–31.

9. Rosenshine, B. V. (1987). Explicit teaching. In D. C. Berliner & B. V. Rosenshine (Eds.), *Talks to teachers* (pp. 75–92). New York: McGraw-Hill.

10. Hootstein, E. W. (1993). Motivational strategies and beliefs of social studies teachers in a U.S. history course for middle school students. *Dissertation Abstracts International, 54* (04A), 1216. (University Microfilms No. AAG93-22026)

11. *Ibid,* p. 56.

12. Bloom, B., Engelhart, M., Furst, E., Hill, W., & Krathwohl, D. (1956). *Taxonomy of educational objectives: The classification of educational goals. Handbook 1: Cognitive domain.* New York: David McKay.

13. Nystrand, M., & Gamoran, A. (1991). Instructional discourse, student engagement, and literature achievement. *Research in the Teaching of English, 25,* 261–290.

14. Alpert, B. (1991). Students' resistance in the classroom. *Anthropology & Education Quarterly, 22,* 350–366.

15. Brophy, J. (Ed.). (2001). *Advances in research on teaching* (Vol. 8). Oxford: JAI Elsevier.

16. Zahorik, J. A. (1968). Classroom feedback behavior of teachers. *Journal of Educational Research, 62,* 147–150.

17. Flanders, N. A. (1970). *Analyzing teaching behavior.* Reading, MA: Addison-Wesley.

18. Brophy, J. (1981). Teacher praise: A functional analysis. *Review of Educational Research, 51,* 5–32.

19. *Ibid.* Copyright © 1981 by the American Educational Research Association. Reprinted by permission of the Publisher.

20. Rosenshine, B. V., & Furst, N. (1973). The use of direct observation to study teaching. In R. M. W. Travers (Ed.), *Handbook of research on teaching,* (2nd ed., pp. 122–183). Chicago: Rand McNally.

21. Hunter, M. (1979). Teaching is decision making. *Educational Leadership, 37,* 62–67.

22. Veenman, S. (1984). Perceived problems of beginning teachers. *Review of Educational Research, 54,* 143–178.

23. Doyle, W. (1986). Classroom organization and management. In M. C. Wittrock (Ed.), *Handbook of research on teaching* (3rd ed., pp. 392–431). New York: Macmillan.

Chapter **10**

Seating Chart
Observation Records

Author's Note

One of the first things I notice in a teacher's classroom at the start of a lesson is how quickly the lesson starts. In some classrooms, there's a minute or so of shuffling about, but then the teacher and students get to work. In other classrooms, the lesson gets off to a slower—and perhaps haphazard—start, as the teacher makes last-minute preparations and several students wander in late.

I see similar differences as the class period ends. Some teachers and their students work almost up to the last minute. Others allow more time for students to wind down and get ready to depart the classroom.

These variations in on-task time don't concern me greatly. However, I do get a bit alarmed when I see an entire class of students not engaged in a learning activity for many minutes at a stretch or a few students doing nothing productive for long stretches at a time. These things happen in classrooms. I've seen it. My colleagues have seen it.

The reason I get alarmed is this: while administrators, parents, and other might disagree about certain aspects of instruction, they are united in their belief that when class is in session, students should be working on some productive activity. In other words, they had better be *on task*. Student teachers who can't keep their students on task run the risk of not being recommended for a teaching license. Inservice teachers who can't keep their students on task are at risk of being put on a plan of assistance or not having their contract renewed.

For this reason, I think it's essential that supervisors know how to collect on-task data (or, as we call it in this chapter, *at-task* data). Teachers need to know how much of the time the class as a whole is on task and whether any students are significantly off task. If a problem is detected, the teacher and supervisor should make it their top priority.

The first part of this chapter shows you how to collect at-task data. The last part of the chapter, which is about how to observe classroom movement patterns, also might reveal something about at-task behavior: Are students and the teacher milling about purposively or aimlessly?

It's fairly obvious whether the teacher's class is on task or off task. I don't think it's so obvious whether the teacher is attending to *all* the students in the classroom. For one reason or another, a teacher's attention might be pulled too much to the brightest students or to those who have behavior problems. Quiet students and those with a particular characteristic might get less attention than they deserve. Verbal-flow and movement-pattern observations, both presented in this chapter, can help teachers and supervisors detect whether this is a problem.

Writing these words deepens my appreciation of the artistry of teaching. Getting a whole class of students to work productively during an entire lesson, while also attending equitably to individual students' needs, is no easy feat!

MDG

These seating chart techniques look simple, but they're not. True, all the supervisor gives you to look at is a seating chart with lines and arrows all over it. But they tell you a lot about what happened in your lesson. You can see that your teaching is following a definite pattern. Then the question you need to ask yourself is, "Is this a good or a bad pattern, something I want to change or something I want to keep on doing?"

—Comment of a high school teacher

INTRODUCTION

Several techniques for observing teacher and student behavior make use of seating charts. That is why they are called *Seating Chart Observation Records (SCORE)*.

A principal advantage of SCORE techniques is that they are based on classroom seating charts. Teachers often use seating charts in class, so they find it easy to interpret SCORE data.

SCORE techniques have several other advantages. They enable the supervisor to condense a large amount of information about classroom behavior on a single sheet of paper. They can be created on the spot to suit the individual teacher's concerns. They are easy to use and interpret. Moreover, they record important aspects of classroom behavior, such as students' level of attentiveness and how teachers distribute their time among students in the class. A special benefit of SCORE techniques is that they enable the teacher and supervisor to spotlight individual students in the class, while at the same time observing what the class as a whole is doing.

SCORE techniques have a few limitations. They help the teacher focus on particular classroom events and behaviors, but unless these are viewed within the total context of instruction, the teacher might draw simplistic conclusions from the data. Another hazard is that the teacher or supervisor might select trivial behaviors for observation. Also, classroom behavior occasionally will "speed up" or become chaotic to the point that you cannot record data fast enough. When this happens, you might need to modify or temporarily abandon the data collection process.

In using SCORE techniques, the supervisor and teacher should keep in mind that the classroom is a primary arena for students to develop the knowledge, skills, and understandings they need to lead productive, meaningful lives. To use classroom time effectively for this purpose, teachers need to understand the learning process—in particular, the six learning principles that we stated at the beginning of Chapter 9. In summary form, the principles state that learning is affected by:

- students' level of attention.
- students' level of motivation.
- opportunities for students to find personal meaning in the curriculum.
- opportunities for students to practice newly learned information.
- group processes among classroom members.
- whether the curriculum's focus is lower-cognitive or higher-cognitive.

The SCORE techniques that we present in this chapter highlight some of these aspects of the learning process. You might wish to develop SCORE techniques of your own to highlight other aspects.

OBSERVATION TECHNIQUE 6: AT-TASK BEHAVIOR

The at-task technique was developed in the 1960s by Frank MacGraw at Stanford University.[1] MacGraw devised a system of classroom observation that used a 35 mm, remotely controlled camera. From the front corner of the room the camera took a picture of the total class every 90 seconds, using a wide-angle lens. The photos were developed and enlarged. The observer was then provided with a set of pictures of a classroom during a given time period (e.g., twenty pictures to represent a 30-minute lesson).

A variety of results were obtained. Some looked like the films once shown in nickelodeons: the students gradually move from a position of sitting erect at their desks to a position of sleeping with their heads on their desks, back to a position of sitting and looking attentive. Other collections of pictures showed students working feverishly on matters that had nothing to do with the task at hand, or vacant from their seats talking to their neighbors, or engaged in a variety of actions the teacher regarded as inappropriate.

The data obtained from the pictures were valuable to the teacher in understanding individual students. However, this method of collecting data was expensive and time-consuming, so experiments were conducted using alternative methods. Ultimately a paper-and-pencil technique was developed to provide much the same data as the 35 mm camera. This paper-and-pencil technique has come to be known as an at-task analysis. A completed at-task chart is shown in Figure 10.1.

As we discussed in Chapter 3, researchers have found a strong link between students' at-task behavior and their learning. The higher the rate of students' at-task behavior, the more they learn.

This finding comes as no surprise if we consider the learning principles summarized at the start of the chapter. If students are at-task, they are directing their attention to the information to be learned and are engaged in practicing it so that it gets into long-term memory. Furthermore, if students are at task, it suggests that they view the new information and instructional activities as meaningful. Conversely, if students are off task, it suggests that the information and activities are unclear or insignificant.

Researchers have studied at-task behavior (sometimes called *engaged time* or *on-task time*) in classrooms. They calculate an at task percentage, which is the amount of time that students, on average, are at-task divided by the total amount of time allocated for instruc-

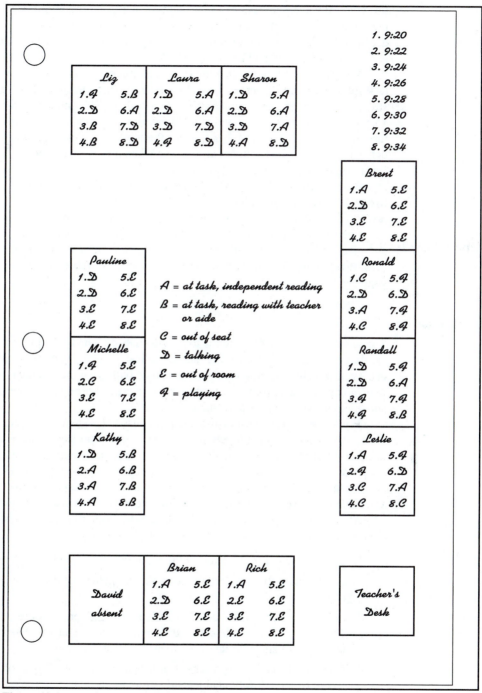

Figure 10.1 At-task seating chart.

tion (typically a lesson). For example, suppose a lesson is 50 minutes. The observer would record how much of that time each student is at task, sum the at-task time for all the students, and divide by the number of students to get a mean at-task time. Suppose that mean is 42 minutes. Dividing 42 by 50 equals 84 percent, which is the at-task percentage.

A large-scale study of elementary school students conducted in the 1970s found at-task rates between 70 percent and 75 percent.[2] This means that for every hour of instructional time, students typically were at task for 45 minutes and were off task for 15 minutes. Off-task behavior included interim activities (e.g., sharpening pencils and turning in papers), waiting for help from the teacher, socializing, daydreaming, and misbehaving. Students had a higher at-task rate when they were in teacher-led groups (84 percent) than during seat work (70 percent).[3]

We have found similar at-task rates in middle and high schools. However, an effective teacher can achieve higher rates—90% or better. Students are most likely to get off task at the beginning and end of a lesson and when a seat work assignment or group project is unclear and uninteresting. Teachers who can get a class period started right away and give students an engaging task for the last few minutes of the period can achieve a high at-task rate. Giving students an interesting, achievable task also contributes to this goal.

Technique

The intent of at-task observation is to provide data on whether individual students actually are doing the task or tasks that the teacher indicates are appropriate. Therefore, before you can use this technique, you must be acquainted with what the teacher expects the students to be doing during a given classroom period. In other words, the teacher—not the supervisor—defines what constitutes at-task behavior.

Typical at-task behaviors are reading, listening, answering questions, doing seat work, and working cooperatively to complete a group project. Lessons in which one task is expected of all students usually present no problem. However, in lessons in which students are able to do a variety of tasks, some preparation is necessary before the supervisor can use the at-task technique. If the variety of tasks is too complex, the teacher and supervisor might choose to limit the observation to one group or section of the classroom.

A record of students' at-task behavior can be made in several ways. In the procedure we use, the supervisor completes the following seven steps:

1. Stations herself in a section of the room where she is able to observe all students.
2. Constructs a chart that resembles a seating pattern of the students in the room that day.
3. Indicates on the chart each student's name, gender, or some other characteristic. The purpose is to guide subsequent analysis of the data to determine whether certain types of students act or are treated differently.
4. Creates a legend to represent at-task behavior and each type of inappropriate behavior observed. A typical legend might be:
   A: At task
   S: Stalling
   R: Schoolwork other than that requested by the teacher

O: Out of seat

T: Talking to neighbors

5. Systematically examines the behavior of each student for a few seconds in order to determine whether the student is at task, that is, doing what the teacher considers appropriate. If so, the supervisor indicates this by marking *1.A* in the box on the seating chart meant to represent the student. Figure 10.1 indicates that this is the first observation; the letter *A* refers to at-task behavior. If the student is not at task, the supervisor indicates this by recording 1S, 1R-, 1O, or 1T (using the legend created in step 4).

6. Repeats step 5 at 3-minute or 4-minute intervals for the duration of the lesson. The supervisor uses the same letter legend to indicate observed behavior, but changes the number to indicate the sequence of observations. For example, *3.A* in a box indicates that the student was at task during the supervisor's third observation.

7. Indicates the time at which each set of observations was made. This is marked somewhere on the chart (e.g., see upper right-hand corner of Figure 10.1). The supervisor also might find it helpful to record the classroom activity that the teacher was conducting at each time of observation.

We advise you to follow a few precautions in using the at-task technique. First, avoid forming too many categories for observation. Step 4 (above) lists five categories—at task, stalling, other schoolwork than that requested by the teacher, out of seat, and talking to neighbor. This is probably as many categories as you would want to form. Adding more categories complicates the observation process greatly, and it becomes increasingly difficult for the teacher to interpret the resulting data. In many classroom observations, two categories are sufficient: at task and off task.

In using the at-task technique, supervisors can become overly concerned about the accuracy of their observations. This can be avoided by keeping in mind that observation of at-task behavior requires a moderate degree of inference. The expression on a student's face might be interpreted as thoughtful reflection about what the teacher is saying or as daydreaming. We suggest you think probabilistically. If you think it is more likely that the student is engaged in thoughtful reflection than in daydreaming, use the at-task category. If you think it is more probable that the student is daydreaming, indicate this by using one of your off-task codes. It is helpful to tell the teacher that the completed chart is, to an extent, subjective. Thus, the teacher should look for general patterns rather than question the accuracy of a few isolated observations.

The at-task chart in Figure 10.1 has one box for each student in the class. The students are identified by name on the chart. If the feedback conference occurs fairly soon after the observation, the teacher should have no difficulty matching students with the boxes, even without names. However, if the feedback conference is delayed, you should consider putting students' names in the appropriate boxes of the seating chart. This is a problem if the teacher does not have a prepared seating chart to assist you and if you don't know the students' names. A simple solution is for the teacher to have students say their names aloud at the beginning of the class period while you jot them down. The student's first or last name should be sufficient.

Some supervisors use several different colored pencils or pens to record at-task data. The seating chart can be one color, and the at-task observations can be a different color. The result is a clearly organized display that is easy for the teacher to study and interpret.

Example

An elementary school principal observed a first-grade teacher's reading class. The decision to do an at-task seating chart grew out of a planning conference between the teacher and the principal. Part of this conference is reproduced below:

TEACHER: Would you come in and do an at task in my classroom? Randall and Ronald do nothing but play and talk. I would like to see just how much they really work.

PRINCIPAL: Are Randall and Ronald the only ones you want me to observe?

TEACHER   No. I have a real immature group this year. You might as well observe all of them.

PRINCIPAL: What do you mean by "immature"?

TEACHER: Oh, they have short attention spans, haven't learned to settle down, and they are all talking without permission. In other words, this first grade doesn't really know how to settle down and do some work.

PRINCIPAL: Do they seem to understand what you have planned for them?

TEACHER: Yes, but they have a hard time settling down to work. Ronald moans and groans most of the time or plays.

PRINCIPAL: What kinds of behavior should I observe for the at task? What categories should I use?

TEACHER: Before I forget, remember some of my children are out of the room for music at the time you're coming.

PRINCIPAL: That's right. I'll put it on my checklist so I won't forget it.

TEACHER: Check to see if they're out of their seats, talking, playing, or at task. They will also be reading to my aide or to me.

PRINCIPAL: I'll make a note of the reading aide, and I'll see you tomorrow.

For the purpose of this observation, at-task behavior was defined as independent reading in a workbook at one's seat (A) or as reading with the teacher or aide (R). The principal also recorded several other categories of behavior: out of seat (S), talking (T), out of room (O), and playing (P). The categories are shown in Figure 10.1, together with the completed at-task seating chart.

Data Analysis

Figure 10.2 provides a convenient summary of the observations recorded on the seating chart (Figure 10.1). The teacher can see at a glance how many children were engaged in each category of behavior—either at a particular point in time or summed across all the time samples. The last column indicates the average percentage of students who engaged in each category of behavior during the class period. For example, 6 percent of the children were out of their seat on average during the lesson. The numerator used to derive this percentage is the total of six children (see total column) who were out of their seat across the eight observations that were made of the lesson. The denominator (96) is the eight observations multiplied by the twelve children in the class. Dividing the numerator (6) by the denominator (96) gives the mean percent (6 percent).

Behavior	9:20	9:22	9:24	9:26	9:28	9:30	9:32	9:34	Total	%
A. At task, independent reading	4	1	2	2	2	4	2	0	17	18%
B. At task, reading with teacher or aide	0	0	1	1	2	1	1	2	8	8%
C. Out of seat	1	1	1	2	0	0	0	1	6	6%
D. Talking	5	8	2	0	0	2	2	3	22	23%
E. Out of room	0	1	5	5	5	5	5	5	31	32%
F. Playing	2	1	1	2	3	0	2	1	12	13%

Figure 10.2 Summary of at-task data from Figure 10.1.

Analysis of at-task data is illustrated by the feedback conference that occurred between the principal and the first-grade teacher. Part of this conference is reproduced below:

TEACHER: Let's see. Randall was at task once. Ronald was, too. Here is a shocker! Liz, Laura, and Sharon do a lot of visiting. I can see where I need to do some changes in the seating.

PRINCIPAL: That may solve some of your talking and visiting problems.

TEACHER: Boy, from 9:20 to 9:36, five of my students are out to music. This only leaves seven to work with. Gee, I only worked with two children, and the aide worked with one.

PRINCIPAL: It seems as though quite a few of your students are gone at one time.

TEACHER: Yes, I should try to work with these students before they go to music.

PRINCIPAL: That's a good idea! In that way you can usually have them read to you every day.

TEACHER: Maybe I could ask the aide to have Kathy only read a few pages and then listen to someone else.

PRINCIPAL: That sounds great!

TEACHER: This doesn't solve my problem with Randall and Ronald. Since Brian and Rick go to music, maybe I could put Ronald at Rick's desk. This way I can get a direct view of him. This also would separate the two boys.

PRINCIPAL: This sounds like a good step. Maybe you'll want to keep the boys apart permanently in the classroom.

TEACHER: I sure hope this works. If not, I'll find something else.

PRINCIPAL: I'm sure you will. You seem to have some good ideas already.

TEACHER: I could even have the aide work with Ronald and Randall in reading and have her play some phonics games with them. This would help expand their attention span, too.

PRINCIPAL: You're really getting some good ideas. It will be interesting to see how they work out. Maybe I could come back and do an at-task again.

TEACHER: Yes, I'd like to see if some of my ideas will help the children settle down, especially Ronald and Randall.

This interaction between the principal and teacher illustrates the importance of at-task data in clinical supervision. The data focus the teacher's attention directly on the degree to which students are engaged in productive classroom behavior. If students are not at task, the teacher knows that there is a problem that needs correction. As illustrated in the above conference excerpt, the teacher and supervisor can develop solutions once the problem has been diagnosed.

In inspecting Figures 10.1 and 10.2, you might have noted how much the students' at-task behavior changed from one observation to the next. This is characteristic of young children. Except for those who left the room, the children were likely to change from one category of behavior to another with each observation. For example, Leslie varied back and forth among behavior categories A, C, D, and F within the 14-minute (9:20 to 9:34) period of observation.

OBSERVATION TECHNIQUE 7: VERBAL FLOW

Verbal flow is primarily a technique for recording who is talking to whom. It also is useful for recording categories of verbal interaction—for example, teacher question, student answer, teacher praise, student question.

Verbal flow is similar to selective verbatim methods (see Chapter 9) in that both deal with classroom verbal behavior. The difference is that selective verbatim methods are concerned more with the actual content of the verbal communication, whereas verbal flow focuses on who the initiators and recipients of the verbal communication are and the kinds of communication in which they engage.

We reviewed in Chapter 3 a research study by Gregg Jackson and Cecilia Cosca, who found that teachers in the Southwest directed significantly more verbal behavior toward Anglo students than toward Chicano students. Research has identified other forms of bias in teacher verbal behaviors as well. Michael Dunkin and Bruce Biddle reached the following conclusions about one such bias in their review of research:

> *The majority of both emitters and targets [of verbal behavior]—whether they be teachers or pupils—are located front and center in the classroom. Thus, pupils who are located around the periphery of the classroom are more likely to be spectators than actors in the classroom drama. It could be, then, that if the teacher wants to encourage participation on the part of a quiet pupil or silence on the part of someone who is noisy, she need merely move the pupil to another location in the room!*[4]

Although teachers tend to talk more to students seated closest to them, other location biases can occur. For example, one teacher found that he had a tendency to acknowledge more questions from students seated to his right than from students seated to his left. After learning of this tendency, the teacher realized that, in talking to a class, he usually looked to the right side of the classroom. Thus, students seated to this side were in the teacher's central line of vision, whereas students to the left were in his peripheral vision. It occurred to the teacher how frustrated students to his left might be if they had questions, but could not ask them because they were out of his line of sight. With this new awareness, the teacher made a conscious effort to distribute eye contact equally to all parts of the classroom. This led to a more equal distribution of verbal behaviors.

Verbal flow is a valuable observation technique because it helps teachers discover (1) biases in their own verbal behavior, and (2) differences between students in verbal participation. Verbal flow is particularly appropriate when the lesson involves discussion, question-and-answer recitation, or other methods that require many verbal interchanges between teacher and students. It is not appropriate for observing instruction low in verbal interaction (e.g., lecture and independent study).

Technique

As with other SCORE methods, the first step in recording verbal flow is to make a classroom seating chart. Because of the many seating patterns that occur in classrooms, a standard form generally is not feasible. Instead, you sketch a seating chart on a blank sheet of paper.

Each student is represented by a box on the chart. You can put the students' names in the appropriate boxes, or if you wish to focus on a particular characteristic, you can just indicate the characteristic. For example, the teacher might suggest in the planning conference that you label each student as male or female; talkative or quiet; high-achieving, average, or low-achieving. The advantage of this kind of chart is that teachers can more easily determine whether they respond differentially to students who vary in these characteristics.

Arrows are used to indicate the flow of verbal interaction. The base of the arrow indicates the person who initiates a verbal interaction, and the head of the arrow indicates the person to whom the comment is directed.

The teacher is an exception to this procedure. Because the teacher usually initiates most of the verbal interactions, it would be awkward to have an arrow leading from the box that designates the teacher to each student to whom a comment is directed. Arrows would be crisscrossing one another as they made their way from the teacher's box to boxes situated at diverse points on the seating chart. The problem is avoided by placing the arrow completely within the student's box. The base of the arrow should come from the general direction of the teacher to indicate that it was the teacher who initiated a comment or question.

You can keep the verbal-flow chart visually simple by marking notches in the arrow to indicate repeated interactions of the same kind. This notching method is illustrated in Figure 10.3. In box A, a separate arrow is used to record each interaction. Analysis of these data indicates that the teacher directed four comments to the student, and the student directed two comments back to the teacher. The same data are recorded in box B by two arrows. The arrow indicating the teacher-initiated comment has three notches on it. The arrow indicates one comment, and each notch represents an additional comment, for a

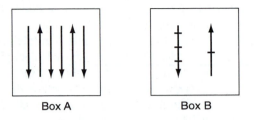

Box A   Box B   **Figure 10.3** Verbal-flow chart.

total of four teacher-initiated comments. Similarly, box B indicates a total of two student-initiated comments.

The standard verbal flow chart can be elaborated by using additional categories of observation, such as the following:

→ +	teacher praise or encouraging remark
→ −	teacher criticism or reprimand
→ F?	teacher fact question
→ T?	teacher thought question

Student verbal behaviors also can be differentiated. For example, consider these categories:

→ C	student volunteered a relevant or correct response
→ I	student volunteered an irrelevant or incorrect response
→ ?	student question
→ }	student comment directed to the class as a whole

The teacher and supervisor should decide during the planning conference what categories of verbal interaction are to be observed. It is advisable to form no more than a few categories. Otherwise, the recording and interpretation of verbal flow data become unwieldy.

Some supervisors prefer to use an alphabetic notation system rather than arrows. Letters of the alphabet indicate discrete categories of verbal interaction, for example:

Q	teacher question
P	teacher praise
C	teacher criticism
r	student volunteered a relevant or correct response
x	student volunteered an irrelevant or incorrect response
q	student question

Teacher and student behaviors are easily distinguished by the use of uppercase and lowercase letters.

Either arrows or alphabetic notation will get the job done. The choice of one or the other is a matter of preference.

Example

The assistant principal of a high school, one of whose responsibilities is teacher supervision, was asked by a first-year English teacher to determine which students were contributing to classroom and small-group discussions. The teacher's purpose was not to use the supervisor's data to evaluate the students, but to learn how she was influencing students' participation and how nonparticipating students could be encouraged to join the discussion.

The teacher and assistant principal agreed that a verbal-flow chart was an appropriate technique for collecting the data. The assistant principal arranged to visit the teacher's class at a time when a discussion was scheduled.

The verbal-flow chart made by the assistant principal is shown in Figure 10.4. Horizontal lines are used to indicate empty desks. Students' gender is indicated by an M or F. The supervisor recorded verbal-flow data using four categories: teacher question, student response, teacher positive response, and teacher negative response. Because some students talked among themselves, the supervisor decided to record this behavior by drawing an arrow between the students engaged in such talk. The period of observation was 22 minutes.

Data Analysis

Verbal-flow data can be analyzed from various perspectives, including the six learning principles that we emphasize in this book.

- A student's learning is affected by (1) level of attention and (2) motivation, which in turn are affected by whether the teacher interacts directly with the student and gives him or her opportunities to speak. Verbal flow data can indicate whether the teacher interacts with a particular student and whether that student has the opportunity to speak.

- A student's learning is affected by (3) opportunities to find personal meaning in the curriculum and (4) to practice what he or she has learned. Verbal interaction is an important way in which students search for meaning and practice new information. Verbal-flow data can indicate whether verbal interaction is occurring in the classroom and which students are engaging in it.

- A student's learning is affected by (5) group processes among classroom members. Verbal-flow data can indicate whether students engage in relevant dialogue with each other and whether the group process is democratic in the sense that all students have equal opportunity to be part of the verbal interaction.

- A student's learning is affected by (6) whether the curriculum's focus is lower-cognitive or higher-cognitive. As we illustrated above, the teacher's emphasis on lower-cognitive or higher-cognitive learning can be determined by coding the teacher's questions in the verbal-flow chart by the symbols $\rightarrow$ **F?** and $\rightarrow$ **T?** or similar notation system.

Certain of these learning principles can be highlighted by analyzing verbal flow data from particular perspectives. We describe the three most common perspectives next.

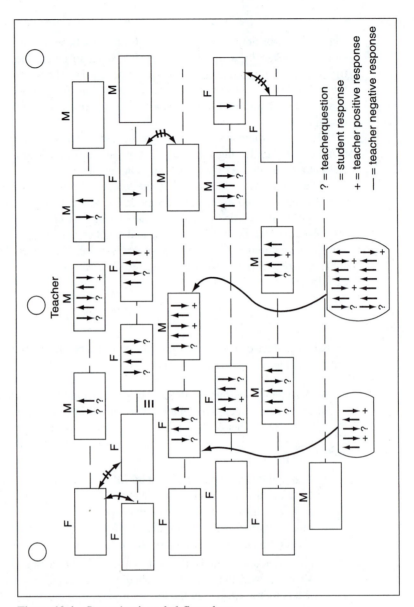

Figure 10.4 Supervisor's verbal-flow chart.

Seat-Location Preferences

As we mentioned, some teachers direct more of their attention to students seated in a certain part of the room. This is quite apparent in the teacher's verbal-flow chart. As she put it, she suffers from tunnel vision. You can see in Figure 10.4 that she asked most of her questions of students seated directly in her line of sight. Students on either side of her line of sight were ignored. It is interesting to note that these students were more likely to talk among themselves.

On seeing the verbal flow chart, the teacher commented that she might solve the problem of "tunnel vision" by seating students closer together, using the available empty seats. Another possibility is to place students in a circular seating arrangement so that everyone has eye contact with everyone else.

Student Preferences

In Figure 10.4, students are identified by gender. This coding system makes it easy to determine whether the teacher interacted equally with boys and girls, and whether she used each category of verbal behavior equally with them.

The verbal-flow chart indicates that thirteen girls and eleven boys were present for the lesson. Of the twenty questions asked by the teacher, twelve (60 percent) were directed to boys, and eight (40 percent) were directed to girls. Of the twelve positive responses by the teacher, eight (66 percent) were directed to boys and four (33 percent) were directed to girls. The two negative responses by the teacher were both directed to girls. Nine of the thirteen girls (70 percent) and four (36 percent) of the eleven boys did not participate in the lesson. These data suggest a gender bias favoring boys.

You might also note in Figure 10.4 that two students, a boy and a girl, dominated the participation. (The assistant principal needed to create additional boxes to contain their data, as indicated by the somewhat oval boxes connected by long arrows to the two students.) Thirty percent of the total number of questions asked by the teacher were directed to these two students. Moreover, these two students accounted for nearly half the student responses.

Verbal Behavior Preferences

Verbal-flow charts can be inspected to determine how frequently teachers and students use certain behaviors and whether they emphasize certain behaviors more than others. One comparison of interest in Figure 10.4 is the teacher's use of positive verbal responses to students' comments relative to her use of negative verbal responses. Of the teacher's fourteen responses, all but two were positive. The two negative responses were directed toward girls near the periphery of the classroom.

Another possible comparison in Figure 10.4 is the number of student verbal responses followed by a teacher positive response versus the number of student verbal responses not followed by a teacher positive response. There were thirty-two student responses in the lesson. Of these, twelve (38 percent) were accompanied by a teacher positive response. This is a relatively high percentage, compared with teachers' usual practice.

OBSERVATION TECHNIQUE 8: MOVEMENT PATTERNS

Another use of seating charts is to record how the teacher and students move around the classroom during a lesson. We call this SCORE technique "movement patterns." The supervisor's task is to record how the teacher and individual students walk from one section of the room to another during a given time interval. This focus on movement differentiates movement patterns from the other SCORE techniques presented in this chapter: at task, which focuses on students' level of attentiveness and engagement in classroom tasks; and verbal flow, which focuses on the nature and direction of verbal communication in the classroom.

Many teaching situations, especially in primary and elementary school, require teachers to make decisions about where to position themselves in the classroom. For example, as students file into class after recess, the teacher needs to decide whether to stand by the door, at the desk, or elsewhere. When students are engaged in seatwork or group projects, the teacher must decide whether to stay at the desk or move around the room checking on students' work.

The nature of the teacher's movement patterns can affect students' attentiveness, motivation to perform learning tasks, and ability to practice and find meaning in new information. The teacher who "hides" behind a desk might experience more discipline problems than the teacher who checks on students as they work at their desks. The teacher who always stands in one position while speaking to the class might not hold students' attention as effectively as the teacher who moves about for dramatic emphasis or to illustrate a concept on the blackboard or wall chart.

Teachers' movement patterns in the classroom sometimes reveal a bias. Some prefer one part of the classroom over another, perhaps because certain students are seated there. Others tend to stand some distance away from students' seats while speaking to the class. This can create difficulties for students who do not see or hear well, and it might provide an excuse for some students to engage in off-task behavior ("the teacher can't see what I'm doing").

Students' movement patterns can reveal whether they are at task. Sometimes it is necessary for students to move about the classroom to complete an assigned activity. At other times, though, students move about to avoid an assigned task or because they have no assigned task. The latter situation often occurs when students finish their work early in the class period; they mill around to find a classmate to engage in conversation or to find another activity.

Movement patterns can be recorded during any lesson, but the technique is most useful when the teaching situation contains the potential for movement about the classroom. For example, seat work and group projects provide situations where the teacher needs to move about, and where students do move about even when they don't need to. On the other hand, the showing of a film or a question-and-answer recitation constrains teacher and student movement. There is not likely to be much movement behavior to record.

Technique

The seating charts used in other SCORE instruments often consist of interconnected boxes, as in Figure 10.1. To record movement patterns, each student and the teacher should be represented by self-contained boxes. Also, the seating chart should represent the physical layout of the classroom, including aisles and desks or tables where students might congregate.

Figures 10.5 and 10.6 show seating charts used to record movement pattern data. Teacher or student movement from one point in the room to another is indicated by a continuous line. The line for each person originates at the point where that person was located in the room when the supervisor began observing. The teacher and students are likely to move from one point to another, stop for a while, then move to another. Each stopping point should be represented by an indicator—for example, an arrow ($\longrightarrow$), a circle ($\ominus$), or x ($\divideontimes$).

Figure 10.5 uses circled numbers to indicate stopping points. This physical movement chart shows that the teacher started the lesson standing at the front of the classroom, next moved to the student designated by box 1, and then proceeded to student 13.

A single line with a different symbol at each end can be used when a person goes from his desk to another location and then returns to his desk. For example, in Figure 10.6 the teacher went from her desk (designated by O) to Wes's desk and then returned to her desk. In contrast, Keith went from his desk to the teacher's desk and then returned.

You might wish to indicate the pattern of movement at different points in the lesson. A supply of different colored pencils is useful for this purpose. For example, you might record the first 10 minutes in yellow, the second 10 minutes in green, and so on. If the teacher plans to divide the lesson into different activities, this can form the basis for color coding. The first activity might be direction-giving, followed by small-group projects, followed by whole-class question-and-answer. Movement during each activity can be recorded with a different colored pencil. This technique helps the teacher analyze the pattern of movement that occurred at different stages of the lesson.

So many students occasionally mill about in the classroom that you will not be able to record all their movements. When this occurs, you can suspend data recording for a few minutes. (Make a note that you did so somewhere on your movement pattern chart.) Another possibility is to limit your observation to only certain students in the classroom.

Example

The movement pattern chart in Figure 10.6 was recorded in a high school typing class. The teacher worried about whether he ran "too loose a ship." He didn't think that students should be "chained to their desks" during the entire class period, yet he wanted to instill in students a sense of discipline and self-control. He and the supervisor agreed that a movement pattern chart might be a good method for recording the level of orderliness in the classroom. The supervisor observed and recorded the class's movement behavior for approximately 30 minutes.

Data Analysis

At first glance a movement pattern chart such as the one shown in Figure 10.6 looks like a hopeless maze. However, if the teacher and supervisor isolate the behavior of one person or one section of the room, they usually can make helpful inferences from the chart.

The first thing that caught the teacher's eye was the door leading into the classroom. Six students entered or left the classroom after the lesson had begun. One student who was not enrolled in the class (indicated by a "?") apparently entered the classroom, talked to several friends, and then left. The teacher thought that the mystery student probably was wandering about during his free study period. Two students (Janice and Keith) left the

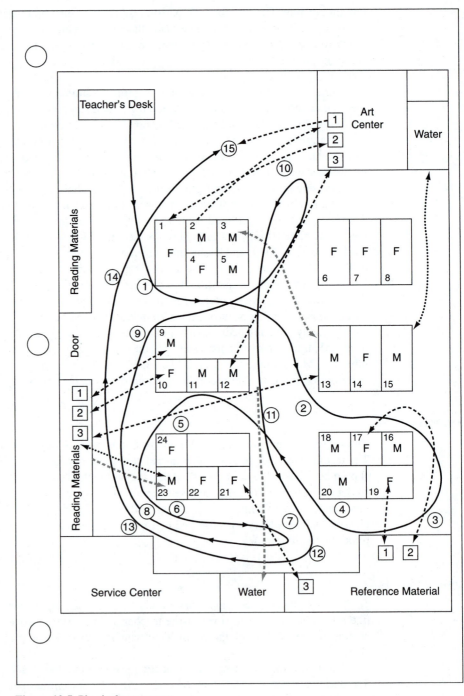

Figure 10.5 Physical movement.

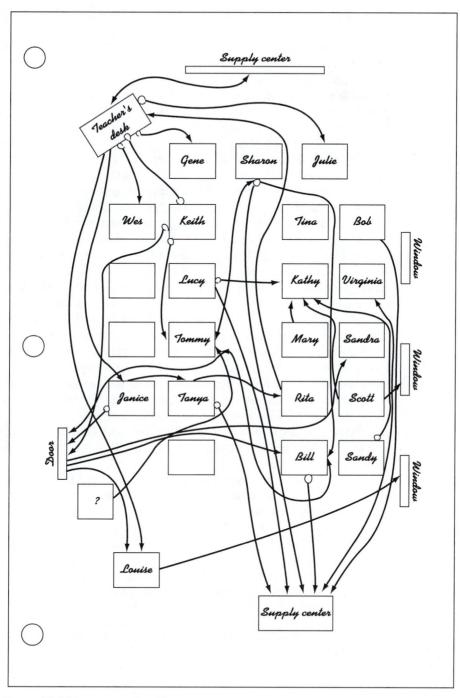

Figure 10.6 Movement pattern chart.

class while it was in session and then returned. The teacher did not realize this had happened.

After inspecting these data, the teacher decided he needed to monitor students' entry and exit behavior more closely. Also included in this resolution to himself was the decision to give students some ground rules about leaving class while it is in session. The teacher then focused his attention on his own movement behavior. He recalled that he had gone to the blackboard at the start of the lesson to write down key terms relating to typing business letters. Keith then came to his desk to ask a question. Next the teacher decided to check on students' progress, so he visited a few students (Lennie, Wes, Gene, and Julie), each time returning to his desk to catch up on some paperwork. Finally, he decided he should circulate a bit; this is reflected in a large loop starting and ending at his desk. Although he did not stop at every student's desk, he felt he got to each area of the classroom so that if a student desired to speak with him, the student could get his attention easily. The teacher generally felt satisfied with his movement pattern in this lesson.

He and the supervisor next turned their attention to the supply center. Six students (Tanya, Lucy, Sharon, Bill, Virginia, and Bob) went to the center for supplies during the observed part of the lesson. After seeing these data, the teacher wondered whether he should ask students to get any necessary materials at the start of the lesson. This procedure might create a more orderly class and might help students become more organized and systematic in their approach to typing. The supervisor suggested that the teacher experiment with this procedure and see for himself whether it produced the desired effects.

Finally, the teacher looked at other student behavior. He noted that several students had visited with each other, and four of them (Lucy, Mary, Scott, and Sandy) had congregated around Kathy's desk. Two students (Scott and Lennie) had gone to the window to see what was happening outside. The supervisor told the teacher that most of this kind of classroom movement occurred near the end of the observation period. The teacher realized then that he had an activity planned for students who finished early, but had forgotten to relay it to them because he was preoccupied with some paperwork he wanted to complete during the lesson.

Summing up his inferences from the movement chart data, the teacher felt that he might make a few changes that would create a more orderly class without losing the relaxed atmosphere he valued.

NOTES

1. MacGraw, F., Jr. (1966). The use of 35-mm time-lapse photography as a feedback and observation instrument in teacher education. *Dissertation Abstracts International, 26* (11), 6533. (University Microfilms No. AAG66-02516)

2. Borg, W. R. (1980). Time and school learning. In C. Denham & A. Lieberman (Eds.), *Time to learn* (pp. 33–72). Washington, DC: U.S. Department of Education.

3. Rosenshine, B. V. (1980). How time is spent in elementary classrooms. In C. Denham & A. Lieberman (Eds.), *Time to learn* (pp. 107–126). Washington, DC: U.S. Department of Education.

4. Dunkin, M. J., & Biddle, B. J. (1974). *The study of teaching*. New York: Holt, Rinehart & Winston, p. 226.

Chapter 11

Wide-Lens Techniques

Author's Note

Many observers "just make notes" when they visit a classroom. These may be accurate and useful for the teacher. They may also be subjective and biased. Teachers may encourage that behavior in a planning conference, "Oh, just watch everything," or "Do whatever you like." For most teachers, observations are rare, especially ones that promote professional development. Therefore, we need useful ways to look at the big picture when that is called for.

In the following chapter techniques are discussed that can lead to systematic analysis of broader aspects of the teaching process. We need to guard against the tendency to ride a hobbyhorse, such as noting instances of gum chewing, whispering, and daydreaming, at the expense of recording information that can be more useful to the teacher.

These wide-lens techniques have also been called global scan. They should be in the repertory of a skilled observer.

KAA

It was a shock to listen to the audiotape of my lesson. I never knew before how I sounded when talking to students. The idea of audiotaping lessons is good. After all, students have to hear you talk, so you might as well know how you sound to them. Just listening for a few minutes to the audiotape helped me learn quite a few things about how I communicate. I'm ready now to have myself videotaped. I want to see what that's like!

—Comment of a preservice secondary teacher

INTRODUCTION

The advantage of the observation techniques described in Chapters 9 and 10—selective verbatim and observation using seating charts—is that they enable the teacher and supervisor to focus on a few teaching behaviors. Other classroom "noise" is screened out. But sometimes it is the "noise" (i.e., what you didn't plan to observe) that is most interesting. For example, an unanticipated teaching event might occur and strike you as noteworthy because of its effect on the class. Or perhaps the teacher does something that makes you wonder, "Why did he do that?"

In situations such as these, wide-lens techniques are probably the most appropriate method of observation. We characterize them as "wide lens," because they capture and record a large number of teaching phenomena. By contrast, selective verbatim and observation using seating charts are "narrow lens."

Wide-lens techniques make few prior assumptions about what is important or effective in teaching. For this reason, they provide a good starting point in supervising teachers who are defensive or not ready to select particular teaching behaviors for improvement. After reviewing wide-lens data, the teachers might be more ready to reflect on their teaching, identify specific teaching behaviors for focused observations, and set self-improvement goals.

If a teacher finds it difficult to engage in meaningful reflection, you can remind the teacher of the fundamental principles of learning that we present in this book. In summary form, the principles state that learning is affected by (1) students' attentiveness, (2) whether they can find personal meaning in the information being presented, (3) motivation, (4) opportunities to practice using new information, (5) group processes in the classroom, and (6) whether the teacher focuses on lower-cognitive or higher-cognitive processes.

OBSERVATION TECHNIQUE 9: ANECDOTAL RECORDS AND SCRIPT TAPING

Anecdotal records are an easy way to record classroom interaction using a wide lens. The basic technique is to make brief notes of events as they occur in the classroom. This is a favorite technique of anthropologists, who are highly trained in the process of making ethnographic notes that describe what happens in a culture. In fact, the process of making good anecdotal records in supervisory observations is similar to the process of preparing ethnographies because a teacher's classroom and his or her students constitute a small-scale culture—complete with rituals, norms, values, and artifacts.

We use the term *anecdotal record* to describe this technique because it suggests informality and reminds the teacher and supervisor that the record is not complete. Like any other classroom observation technique, the anecdotal record provides a selective set of data for the teacher to examine.

Madeline Hunter, the developer of the teaching model called Instructional Theory into Practice (see Chapter 3), developed a similar note-taking method for recording classroom observations. She called her method *script taping*.[1] A script tape is virtually identical to what we refer to as an anecdotal record. It is the supervisor's set of notes of what happened and what was said during a lesson.

Hunter claimed seven advantages for the use of script taping in the supervision process:

1. The only materials required are paper and pencil.
2. It can be used to record virtually anything that occurs in a classroom.
3. Events are recorded in a temporal order, making it easy to determine how teacher behavior affects student behavior, and vice versa.
4. It is relatively unbiased, if used by a trained observer.
5. The script tape can be "played back" to the teacher in any location and at any time following the observation.
6. The script tape can be scanned quickly to find any part of the lesson.

7. Script tapes are easily stored.

Videotapes and audiotapes (see Observation Technique 10) also have advantages. They provide a more compelling and complete record of a lesson, but they are not as easy to make and use in a feedback conference as a script tape.

Technique

Anecdotal records have a wide focus, but you and the teacher will need to decide just how wide to open the lens. You can make anecdotal observations of the teacher, one student, one group of students, the whole class of students, or everyone in the class (teacher, students, teacher aides, etc.). The wider the lens, the more behaviors can be observed. As you narrow the lens, you will have a narrower set of behaviors to observe, but you will also have the opportunity to make more intensive descriptions of these behaviors.

Anecdotal records usually consist of short descriptive sentences. Each sentence summarizes a discrete observation. It is helpful to start each sentence on a separate line, and every so often record the time that an observation was made. Thus the teacher can get a sense of the temporal flow of the events that were recorded.

The sentences should be as objective and nonevaluative as possible. Instead of writing, "Students are bored," you might write, "Several students yawn; Jane looks out window." Instead of writing, "Teacher does good job of giving directions," you might write, "Teacher gives directions for recording status of jar experiment. Asks if students understand. Most of class nod or say yes." If you make evaluative comments in your anecdotal record, the teacher is likely to react to the evaluation rather than to what occurred. If your comments are descriptive and neutral, teachers can more easily draw their own conclusions about the effectiveness of the lesson.

Carolyn Frank described an activity that supervisors and teachers can use to develop skill in distinguishing between objective description and interpretation.[2] The activity is called n*otetaking/notemaking*. The first step is for them to observe a classroom lesson (or possibly a photo or video depicting a lesson). During and after the observation, they write their notes in two columns: a "notetaking" column for descriptive notes and a "notemaking" column for interpretive notes. The observers then compare their two columns of notes to determine whether each note is placed in the appropriate column and whether the interpretations in the notemaking column are grounded in the descriptions in the notetaking column. This activity can be recycled with new classroom events to improve proficiency. Figure 11.1 shows an example of notetaking/notemaking notes made by a student teacher who observed a bilingual fourth-grade classroom.

Teacher and student behaviors are not the only events to observe and describe in the anecdotal record. You also should be alert to the context of the teacher's lesson, for example:

"The room is warm. Wall thermometer reads 78 degrees."

"Teacher shows map to class. Map is faded. Names of countries are
    difficult to read."

"Lesson is interrupted by announcement over intercom."

"One of the fluorescent lights starts to hum loudly."

Notetaking	Notemaking
A child is working at the computer. There are fourteen students working at their desks. Six students are working with another teacher (aide) in the back of the room. It is an English reading/writing group she is working with—speaking only in English. I see a mother working with one child only and she is helping the student with something in English. There is a baby in a carriage nearby the mother. I hear classical music playing very lightly. I can only hear the music every once in a while when the classroom is really quiet. I stand up and move around the room to see what the children at their desks are working on. They are writing scary stories. The baby makes a funny noise with her lips and everyone in the class laughs and stares for a few seconds, even the teacher. I look at the group working with the teacher and on the board I see: 5) Yo *quiero* a mi perrito 6) Yo voy a *querer* mucho ami perro 7) Vamos a *moler* la tortilla	The class seems to be really self-directed. The children are really on task and each has their own thing that they are working on. I am not used to seeing students split up into different groups for Spanish and English readers because in my class they are Spanish readers, but it is really good for me to see this because it happens in a lot of upper grade settings, and I will be working in an upper grade bilingual setting next placement. I really like the idea of putting on music during work times. I know that when I hear classical music it really helps me to relax and calm [sic] as well as focus. I think that it has this same effect on the students in this class. I'm noticing more and more that I really cherish the laughter in a classroom when it comes from a sincere topic or source. It is also nice to see the students *and* the *teacher* laughing. It's good for students to see their teacher . . .

Figure 11.1 Example of the notetaking/notemaking method.

Source: Frank, C. (1999). *Ethnographic eyes: A teacher's guide to classroom observation.* Portsmouth, NH: Heinemann. pp. 11-12.

"Several students arrived late, with one coming in 10 minutes after class started."

"Some students had not done their homework."

An anecdotal record of these contextual phenomena can help the teacher interpret certain behaviors of students (or of the teacher) that occurred during the lesson.

The anecdotal record consists of handwritten notes made by the supervisor as he or she sits unobtrusively somewhere in the classroom. Anthropologists often make handwritten ethnographic notes, too, but they have the option of using a portable audio-recorder. They simply make an audio-recorded description of each observation on the spot. This option is not usually available to supervisors, because they and their audio-recorder are likely to be situated too close to the teacher and students.

Unless you have good handwriting, the anecdotal record will be difficult for the teacher to read and analyze. The preferred practice is to have your notes typed, so that the teacher has a neatly typed transcript to reflect upon in the feedback conference. Also, a typed transcript has a more objective, neutral appearance than a set of handwritten notes.

However, if you are pressed for time, you can get by with handwritten notes for the feedback conference—so long as they are legible.

Example

Madeline Hunter provided the following example of a script tape:

> *Opn p. 43 I'm ask ver hd-use mark to find ans whn fnd sho me w/ sig who has lots of pets Every had mark on rt ans Who can't see Mr. Sleeper (wrong ans) that rt if askd who sees but can't see. Now just rt.[3]*

In unabbreviated form, the script tape recorded the following teacher statement:

> *Open your book to page 43. I'm going to ask some very hard questions. Use your marker to find the answer. When you have found the answer, show me with the signal (thumbs up). Who has lots of pets? Everyone had the marker on the right answer. Who can't see Mr. Sleeper? (A girl gave the wrong answer.) That would be right if I asked who sees Mr. Sleeper, but I asked who can't see Mr. Sleeper? (Same child responds correctly.) Now you're just right![4]*

This example illustrates Hunter's preference for abbreviations as a way to record as much as possible of what happens in a classroom. Of course, the disadvantage is that only the observer can make sense of the script tape, and so the observer must read back parts of the lesson on which he or she wishes the teacher to focus, or rewrite the script tape in unabbreviated form.

In our experience, we have found it possible to record at least the main events of a lesson in neat handwriting and with only minor abbreviations. The advantage is that the teacher can read the script tape without assistance. This allows the teacher to get an overview of the entire lesson and to share control of the feedback conference by initiating comments and questions based on the script tape.

Jane Stallings, Margaret Needels, and Georgea Sparks provide an example of an anecdotal record that resulted from observing a child who was proving to be a management problem for the teacher being supervised.[5] The supervisor made 60 pages (!) of handwritten notes about the child over a 2-day period. The following is a partial summary of the information contained in the notes:

> *On the first day, Billy had wandered about the room 57 times. Since the school day was 5 hours long, this was about 10 times an hour. Billy had fallen off his chair 14 times, picked his nose 17 times, rubbed his eyes 23 times, received 13 smiles and 27 reprimands—mostly to stop falling off his chair and pay attention. Billy had initiated conversations with other children 44 times, but the interactions were only 1 or 2 sentences long. Billy spoke to everyone who passed his seat, tried to trip 3 people, succeeding twice. Billy was rejected 15 times by other children who were involved in some activity and was physically pushed away from a group of 3 who were working on a mural. During recess, he put a blanket over his desk, took his reading workbook and disappeared underneath. He stayed there for 5 minutes.[6]*

The second day's observations were similar, and the picture that emerged was of a hyperactive, highly distractible child who needed help in screening out the myriad distractions in the classroom.

This information was useful in working with the child's parents, reading specialist, and school psychologist to plan an educational program for the child.

Figure 11.2 presents a sample of an ethnographic protocol made by a professionally trained ethnographer. It represents the rich description possible with this method. Anecdotal records made by clinical supervisors do not usually have the same amount of detail, although this is possible if the supervisor becomes proficient in quick note taking.

You will observe in Figure 11.2 that the ethnographer does not focus on any particular child or type of teacher behavior. The ethnographer instead records any salient event as it occurs. In this particular protocol the salient events seem to relate to the teacher's management and direction-giving techniques. The teacher can review the protocol to determine whether he or she wishes to maintain or change these techniques.

OBSERVATION TECHNIQUE 10: VIDEO AND AUDIO RECORDINGS

Video and audio recordings are among the most objective observation techniques. They enable teachers to see themselves as students see them. Another advantage of recordings is their wide focus. They pick up a great deal of what teachers and students are doing and saying, and also the "feel" of classroom interaction, which includes emotional climate and nonverbal behavior.

Not too many years ago video and audio recorders were expensive and bulky. Their cost is now well within the reach of most schools. Unfortunately, they are used infrequently in clinical supervision even when the equipment is available. Video recorders are much more likely to be used in the coaching of school sports. Athletes and their coaches spend hours analyzing video recordings of games and individual player actions. Shouldn't we spend a fraction of our supervisory time with teachers reviewing recordings of their classroom interaction?

Protocol Number: 06
Name of Researcher: Gail
Date of Observation:
Subject of Observation:

2nd Grade Class, Open
1. Classroom, with two team teacher
2. and two other adults.
3. This is a joint observation with
4. Elizabeth. I will be observing two
5. reading groups today, simultan-
6. eously, including 9 children. Out of
7. the nine children, 2 are girls, 7 are
8. boys.
8:30 Noise level 2
10. At 8:30 the noise level is 2. The
11. children have just been let into the
12. classroom, taking their coats off
13. and wandering around the room.
14. Several boys are in the corner
15. fighting, and some girls are sitting
16. on the floor playing a puzzle. The
17. teacher is walking back and forth in
18. the back of the classroom not at-
19. tending the children. The noise
20. continues and the children are run-
21. ning around. There is much con-
22. fusion in the room. Two teachers
8:35 23. stand at the desk talking to one
24. another. At 8:35, Mrs. Tyler
25. leaves the room. The team teach-
26. er stays seated behind the class-
27. room at her desk. At 8:40 Mrs.

28. Tyler comes back into the room.
29. She walks to the desk at the far
30. left hand side of the classroom,
31. which is a round table, and sits
32. on the edge. She says "Blue
33. Group, get your folders and go up
34. in the front. Green Group, come
35. here." Noise levels drop to 1, and
36. the children begin to follow her
37. orders. She says, "Anybody lose
38. a quarter?" No one responds, and
39. she repeats the question again
40. with irritation in her voice. She
41. says I know someone found.
42. someone lost a quarter because
43. it was found in the coat room.
44. Look in your pockets and see."
45. No one says anything.
46. She now stands up and pulls a
47. pile of workbooks from across
48. the table over to her. They are
49. the   reading workbooks.
50. She opens one of them on the
51. top and says, "Ah Daniel!" She
52. says this with a loud sharp voice.
53. She continues, "Your work yes-
54. terday was not too bad but you
55. need some work. Evidently there
56. are still some words you don't
57. understand." She thumbs through
58. the rest of his lesson. Danny is
59. standing at the outside of the cir-
60. cle around her, not listening to

61. what she is saying. Mrs. Tyler
62. now stands and gives instructions
63. to the Green Group. She tells
64. them to go through 8 through 13,
65. reading the two stories between
66. those pages and to go over the
67. work in the workbooks that she is
68. about to give back. She tells them
69. that they may seat any place but
70. not together and she says, "And I
71. don't want any funny business."
72. She now opens the next work-
73. book which is Nicole's. She tells
74. Nicole that she is having the
75. same problem that Danny is hav-
76. ing without specifying further.
77. Nicole looks up at her with an ex-
78. pectant look on her face. She
79. then looks at a third book and
80. says "Michelle, you're having the
81. same problem." She says,
82. "Snatch means to grab. Beach,
83. what does it mean?" Michelle
84. doesn't answer. She has her fin-
85. ger in her mouth and looks anx-
86. ious. The teacher closes the
87. workbook and pushes it to
88. Michelle. Michelle takes it and
89. walks away, with Nicole. Teacher
90. then opens the next workbook
91. and says, "Mike, I don't appreci-
92. ate all these circles. She points

Figure 11.2 Example of an ethnographic protocol.

The portable video recorder is often used in microteaching, which was developed at Stanford University in the 1960s.[7] In microteaching, the teacher practices a few specific teaching skills in a scaled-down teaching situation involving a 10- or 15-minute lesson with five or so students. The microteaching lesson is videotaped and played back to the teacher so that his or her teaching performance, especially the use of target skills, can be analyzed.

Teachers almost invariably find that the video recording, whether made in a microteaching situation or regular classroom, provides an important self-learning experience. However, there are several problems to avoid. First, supervisors must be careful to arrange the video recording equipment so that it does not interfere with the lesson. This is best done by setting up the equipment ahead of time, before the students enter the classroom. Second, our experience indicates that teachers, when first exposed to a videotape of themselves, tend to focus on the "cosmetics" of their performance (e.g., physical appearance, clothes, and voice quality). In fact, a study by Gavriel Salomon and Fred McDonald revealed that in a videotape replay situation, 58 percent of teachers' self-observations were concerned with physical appearance, and only 18 percent were focused on teaching behavior.[8] This is a natural reaction. Ways to deal with it are suggested later in this section.

Another problem is that some teachers initially are anxious about the prospect of being videotaped. This problem can be alleviated by allowing teachers to experiment with the equipment before the classroom lesson is to be videotaped. Another helpful procedure is to allow teachers to keep their own videotape or show them how to erase it. This calms any fear that the video recording might get into the "wrong hands."

Although video recordings appear to be a more powerful observational tool than audio recordings, this may not be so. Teachers sometimes are captivated by the image on the TV screen and do not listen to what is being said. Audio recordings have fewer distracting cues, and so it is easier for teachers to concentrate on the verbal interaction. Research has shown that video and audio feedback are equally effective in helping teachers improve their use of verbal teaching skills.[9]

Technique

The first step in making audio or video recordings is to obtain equipment that is in good working order. Older videocassette recorders (VCR) typically include a TV camera with a built-in microphone and viewer, a tripod, a separate recording machine, and cables for connecting the various components of the system. New VCRs consist of a single, lightweight piece of equipment, although we recommend that you also use a tripod to hold the camera steady while recording.

Some VCRs record onto digital tape that can be downloaded directly into a computer. The teacher and supervisor can watch the recorded lesson on the computer screen, or additional equipment can be employed so that the recording can be viewed on a TV screen.

One advantage of digitizing the lesson is that computer software can be used to edit it. For example, the software can be used to cut out unwanted parts of the recording or to add subtitles. Editing of this type usually is unnecessary if the only individuals viewing the tape will be the teacher and supervisor. However, editing might be desirable if the tape is to be viewed by a group, as might happen in a professional development workshop.

(Miriam Sherin described how "video clubs" can be set up so that teachers can observe and learn from one another's practice.[10]) In this use of a recorded lesson, it is necessary to check and follow legal requirements for obtaining prior written permission from the students and teacher (and any other individual in the camera's view).

Audio recorders are much simpler than VCRs to set up and operate. Many self-contained models of audio recorders include a built-in microphone and operate on batteries.

The recording process becomes more complicated as the size of the class increases. If you plan to record a regular classroom situation, it is a good idea to experiment beforehand with various camera and microphone placements in the classroom to get the best sound and camera angle. The microphone built into a audio or video recorder is likely to have a small pick-up range. As the focus of supervision is usually the teacher, we suggest that you place the microphone fairly close to the teacher. By doing so, you can record everything the teacher says and some of what students say. Another option is to use a wireless microphone that can be attached to the teacher's shirt pocket or other item of clothing.

Teachers can learn to make their own video recordings, but in many situations it is more helpful if you, the supervisor, are present to make the recording. You might find it best to set up the camera on a tripod or other stationary base; then, change the lens focus and turn the camera to follow the teacher as the lesson proceeds. Cameras with a zoom lens allow you to make close-up recordings of events that interest you or the teacher.

An efficient procedure is to have teachers play back the entire recording for themselves. They can share insights about their teaching performance with you during the feedback conference. At this time you can select a short segment—or segments—of the recording (perhaps 3 to 5 minutes) for more intensive analysis. You will find that even a brief segment can yield important insights into the teacher's skill level and teaching style.

The wide focus of video or audio recordings is both a strength and weakness. The insightful teacher will be able to observe many different aspects of teacher behavior and student behavior. Some teachers will notice only a few aspects, however, and might focus on the "cosmetic" features mentioned earlier. Your role in the feedback conference is to guide the teacher's observations, encouraging the teacher to draw inferences whenever possible, but also drawing the teacher's attention to significant classroom phenomena if they are being overlooked. The learning principles that we presented earlier in the chapter can be helpful for this purpose.

Example

Many teacher education programs have a required course on teaching strategies. Often, one requirement of the course is for the teacher to participate in microteaching sessions in which they practice several different teaching methods. They make an audio or video recording of their lesson for later analysis. They might also be required to make a transcript covering several minutes of the verbal behavior that was recorded. This procedure ensures that teachers listen carefully to what was said in the lesson.

Figure 11.3 presents a partial transcript made by a preservice teacher who had presented a poetry lesson using the lecture method. This example shows that an audio recording and transcript made from it provided a rich source of feedback to the teacher on his teaching behavior.

CI 314

0:00 OK, um, what I want to talk about is, uh, a poem by Denise Levertov,
called "Living." (pause) And the reason I wanted to talk about this
is because I think it's something that I can cover in 10 minutes, and
uh, well, not in, not entirely but it's short enough to go over the
basics, and, uh, Denise Levertov I, I think is, is . . . one of the
0:30 greatest of living poets, and not, not as well known as she should be.
This poem in particular I think is, is, uh, one of her greatest poems,
and it's not as well known as many, many poems that aren't nearly as
good. (pause) Um, what I want to do is, is, is approach the poem in
1:00 terms of how it's organized . . . 'cause that's one way to get a grip,
a grasp on a poem and Uh, not so much talk about what it says as, as
the way it's, the way it's set up, um, and I, I don't think that's the
only way to read a poem, in fact I don't think it's a very complete
way but it's, um, it can lead you farther into a poem sometimes than
1:30 just talking about what it's about. And so let me just start with the
way it sounds to me: "The fire in leaf and grass/ so green it seems/
each summer the last summer.// The wind blowing, the leaves/ shivering
in the sun,/ each day the last day.// A red salamander/ so cold and so/
easy to catch, dreamily// moves his delicate feet/ and long tail. I
hold/ my hand open for him to go.// Each minute the last minute."
2:00   (Pause) OK, um, it seems to me that that poem holds together
very well. It's, it's a very tightly knit poem. Um. But it's not
held together in any of the, the traditional ways: it's not, it doesn't
have a rhyme scheme, there's no beat or rhythm that carries you along.
2:30 And so if you look at it – Well, does everybody agree that, that, it
doesn't, it doesn't seem like a fragmented poem? It goes, it goes
along, and I think it builds, builds very strongly towards its conclusion.
  Um . . . to start with, to start with the smallest units, just to
3:00 look at the sounds of the poem, and the way it . . . the way the sounds
hold together – Starting in the first line: the, the first significant
word is "fire." And you see that the "f" sound is repeated immediately
in "leaf." And the "r" sound in "fire" carries forward into "grass,"
which then carries you forward into "green" again, and then down to the
3:30 "r" ending in "summer" and "summer" which is repeated. And then you
see these, the "r" sound particularly you find again down in the poem
down in the the uh, "shivering" which repeats the "er" sound from
"summer"--and that turns up again in "salamander" in the last, next
to last triplet. And then the, when you get into "leaf" the, the
4:00 "ea" sound from "leaf" is repeated twice in the next line in "green"
and in "seems"--and in "each" and in "leaves" in the next, the next
stanza, and then, then you hear it again in "each"--in "easy"--in
"dreamily"--in "feet"--and then again in "each" in the last line.
4:30   (Pause) And, um . . . these, these sounds (pause) are, um--well,
the, uh, the tying together of the, of the poem through the, through
the, uh, the sounds in the words goes on throughout the poem. For
instance: if you look for the "o" sound, you don't see it until you
get into the poem, but it turns up towards the end. If you move down
5:00 toward, to the third verse, it starts coming in very strongly, in this
in a line "so cold and so/ easy to catch"--then it turns up again
in "I hold my hand open for him to go." And these, these are,
these are, these are the significant sounds in the poem. And this,
this technique that Levertov relies on very, very strongly in a lot
5:30 of her writing is called "assonance." Um. I--does, everyone know
what the meaning of assonance is? There's, there's two, uh,
basic techniques used, but a lot of modern poets--assonance

Figure 11.3 Transcript of lecture microlesson.

Teachers may also be asked to write an analysis of their lesson based on the transcript and other feedback data. Figure 11.4 presents the first part of an analysis written by the preservice teacher who taught the poetry lesson, accompanied by the instructor's comments in the margin. It illustrates that the process of teaching a lesson and audio-recording it for later analysis is a powerful technique for helping the preservice teacher see areas for instructional improvement.

Teachers, including the one discussed here, tend to criticize themselves too severely in their initial encounters with a recording of their teaching performance. The supervisor

It wasn't a disaster. I think the students in the group and I learned some things about poetry from it. ↓

I would rate this lecture <u>as a disaster</u>, and this
for two main reasons which are not unrelated:
nervousness and poor organization. A sudden attack
of stage fright was for some reason quite
unexpected, and because I hadn't anticipated it I
hadn't written out any more than a general outline
of the points I wanted to cover. This, as it turned
out, was not enough to see me through. Some of the
faults in this lecture, such as the astonishing
number of "um's," "uh's," and stuttering repetitions
(e.g., "What I want to do is, is, is approach the
poem . . .") are simply signs of nervous excitement;
having heard tapes of myself in conversation, I know
these mannerisms are not always present, at least
not to this degree. These I can only expect to
correct by calming down a bit, but this I think I
will be able to do if I correct some of the more
fundamental mistakes I made this time around.

The most important thing missing from this lecture
is an introduction. Immediately upon hearing the
first questions after I finished, I was made aware
that I had left out the necessary background for
reading the poem. And even though biographical
information about the author, for instance, was not
what I was mainly concerned with, it would have
given students <u>some</u> context, which is a necessary
preliminary to any appreciation. A preliminary
statement of what the poem is <u>about, or perhaps
simply some lead-in remarks about summer days and
why some moments seem more alive than others, would
have been very useful.</u> And although before the
lecture I had wanted not to seem too schematic,
afterwards I realized that I needn't have worried;
and I now regret not having outlined ahead of time
the areas I was going to cover.

Yes. This would help. A good technique →

It now seems to me, also, that I went at the poem
exactly backwards: for some reason I began with the
smallest details, the sounds of the poem, and went
on to its larger structure before talking about its
over-all theme. This is absolutely perverse; it is
almost as if I had been trying to keep the main point
a secret until the last possible moment. Clearly, it
would have been better to begin with the most
general statements, and to proceed to the more
particular ones only after these landmarks had been
mapped out.

I feel that, even so, using a blackboard would have
improved things immeasurably. Not only could I have
communicated better by writing down a few terms like
"assonance" and by marking the repetitions of sounds
rather than simply listing them; but also I think it
would have helped simply to get everyone's eyes and
attention (not least of all my own) away from the
handout sheet <u>and out into a more central meeting
place.</u> I even think that just having something to do
with my hands would have put me more at ease.

nice phrase →

I only asked questions twice in the course of the
lecture, and both questions were almost rhetorical,
being put in such a way as to actually discourage a
response: the <u>first</u> one beginning "does everyone
agree . . ." and the second one beginning "does
everyone know . . ." There were several other places
in the lecture where a question would have been in
order; and all of the questions should have been
less leading, more open to genuine answers. This
constricted questioning is, again, at least partly a
function of nervousness; as is the fact that I
forgot to ask for questions at the end.

Figure 11.4 Lecture microlesson analysis.

can ameliorate excessive self-criticism by reassuring teachers that flaws in their teaching performance are commonplace and can be eliminated with practice.

OBSERVATION TECHNIQUE 11: JOURNAL WRITING

In Chapter 1, we mentioned that reflective teaching is an important recent development in teacher education and clinical supervision. Reflective teachers, among other things, are aware of the dilemmas inherent in teaching, are aware of their belief systems and feelings and how they affect teaching, consider choices among instructional strategies, and evaluate the effect of those choices.[11]

Reflection is not the same thing as observation of actual teaching behavior, nor do they stand in opposition to each other. In fact, the two can complement each other well. Teachers can reflect on the basis of what they remember about a lesson, but they also can reflect—perhaps more effectively—based on observational data collected during a lesson.

Journal writing is an effective supervisory technique for encouraging the development of reflectivity in teachers. The technique simply involves having teachers keep a regular journal in which they record their teaching experiences and raise questions about their teaching. Just as a video- or audiotape records the external reality of teaching, so journals record the internal reality of teaching. Although teachers can be asked to limit their journal entries to certain kinds of perceptions, they generally are left free to record whatever they wish. For this reason we classify journal writing as a wide-lens technique.

Journal writing has been used primarily in preservice clinical supervision. In that context, researchers have found that this technique helps prospective teachers become more reflective and less custodial in their attitudes toward students.[12] It seems likely that journal writing would have similarly positive effects in inservice clinical supervision.

Technique

Willis Copeland suggested that the effectiveness of journal writing depends on two factors.[13] First, teachers need to be taught explicitly how to keep a reflective journal. Simply telling them to keep a journal is not sufficient. Second, teachers need to receive thoughtful feedback about the content of their journal entries from their supervisor.

With respect to the first element, teachers need guidance about the kinds of content to include in their journal entries. One approach is to tell teachers to record problems and dilemmas that occur in their day-to-day teaching. Teachers also can be asked to report attempts to solve the problem or dilemma, and the effectiveness of their solutions. These journal entries can provide the basis for discussion in supervisory conferences.

Another approach to journal writing is for teachers to focus on a particular teaching strategy or curriculum. For example, teachers can be asked to record their experiences in implementing a teaching method (e.g., project-based learning) or a new curriculum adopted by the school district.

Whatever the content focus of the journal, teachers should be allowed to describe relevant contextual factors. This means that teachers are not limited to what happens in their classroom. They can reflect on what is happening in the school, community, or the students' family that affects instruction.

All the other observation techniques described in this book stress objectivity on the part of the observer. Journal writing is an exception. Teachers should be encouraged to record not only what happened in the classroom, but also their beliefs, feelings, insights, and evolving philosophy of education. This inner reality is important to understanding a teacher's behavior in the classroom.

The confidentiality of the journal will certainly influence what teachers are willing to record in it. Therefore, the supervisor should make explicit whether the journal is the property of the teacher, and whether its contents will be shared with persons other than the supervisor.

The scope of the journal should be negotiated with teachers. For how long a period of time is the journal to be kept? Are entries to be made daily, weekly, or whenever the teacher wishes? Should entries be made for each class period during the school day, or just for selected periods? Journal writing requires effort, and so the teacher and supervisor should decide on a scope that is appropriate to, but does not exceed, the goals of clinical supervision for the particular teacher.

It is common practice in preservice education for the supervisor to write comments on the margins of teachers' journal entries. It seems unlikely that supervisors of inservice teachers would follow this procedure, though, because it puts teachers too much in a student role. Instead, the supervisor can read the journal and mark entries, or make notes about entries that he or she wishes to discuss with the teacher. Another option is for only the teacher to read the journal, and for the teacher to decide which parts of the journal he or she wishes to talk about during the conference.

We can imagine a supervision process that is built entirely around the teacher's journal writing. The teacher and supervisor discuss what the content of the journal entries should be; the teacher makes journal entries; and the teacher and supervisor meet periodically to discuss problems, insights, beliefs, and feelings recorded in the entries.

This approach undoubtedly has value, but it also has the limitation that it might not correspond to what is actually happening in the teacher's classroom. Therefore, we recommend a process in which journal writing and direct classroom observation complement each other. For example, a journal entry can reveal a concern (see Conference Technique 1 in Chapter 7) that leads to direct classroom observation by the supervisor. Discussion of the observational data in a feedback conference can stimulate the teacher to engage in reflection, which he records in his journal. In this way, the supervisory process is informed both by the objectivity of observational data and the personal meaningfulness of recorded reflections.

Example

Frances Bolin presented examples of journal writing by a student teacher in the preservice program in Childhood Education at Teachers College, Columbia University.[14] The teacher, assigned the pseudonym Lou, kept a daily journal in which he reflected on his student teaching experiences and also a weekly journal in which he recorded reflections about his student teaching, his supervision, and the total preservice program. Lou's supervisor read the journal entries, wrote responses to them, and referred to them in supervisory conferences.

One of Lou's journal entries concerned classroom management:

Sometimes I am not sure how "strict" I should be with the kids as a student teacher. Max [Lou's cooperating teacher] said he wants me not to be so timid. My timidness comes from not knowing the disciplinary boundaries at [the school]. Since I didn't know, I didn't really react. I am by no means timid, as the kids [I have worked with every summer] will attest. Now that I know what the system of discipline is I can implement it.[15]

The supervisor might help Lou with his management concerns by collecting data on students' at-task behavior (see Observation Technique 6) while Lou is teaching them. The data might indicate that his management style is fine as it is. If modification is needed, Lou can try different (possibly "stricter") management techniques, and the supervisor can collect more at-task data, which will provide Lou with feedback on the techniques' effectiveness.

Another of Lou's journal entries concerns creativity in teaching at the open space school where he is student teaching and creativity in a traditional school, which he prefers:

Maybe I am just old fashioned [sic]. I guess it depends on the kids and the school. Who said that a teacher in a typical, traditional school can't be creative and try new things. I hope that no matter what type school I work in I will be creative and not fall into a mold.[16]

In this journal entry and others, Lou expresses the view that creative teaching is important to him. The supervisor can respond to these entries by helping Lou clarify what he means by creative teaching (see Conference Technique 2 in Chapter 7). The supervisor then can collect observational data on Lou's use of creative teaching behaviors in the setting of the open space school. In the feedback conference, Lou and the supervisor can review the data and consider whether the same creative teaching patterns would be possible in a traditional school.

OBSERVATION TECHNIQUE 12: PORTFOLIOS

There is much more to teaching than what can be directly observed in the classroom. Portfolios serve a useful purpose in that they provide data on the totality of a teacher's work and professional competence. Dorothy Campbell and her associates describe this purpose well: "A portfolio is an organized, goal-driven documentation of your professional growth and achieved competence in the complex act called teaching."[17]

A portfolio can include various kinds of evidence attesting to a teacher's instructional skill, subject-matter knowledge, or philosophy of education. In this respect, portfolios provide the widest lens on teaching of any technique presented in this chapter. Also, portfolios can be tailored to reflect the unique personality and qualifications of a teacher.

Once teachers learn how to create a portfolio of their own work, they are in a good position to teach the process to others. In fact, one of the recent developments in classroom teaching is to have students create portfolios to document their learning processes and accomplishments.[18] Students need instruction in portfolio construction for it to be effective. Teachers who have already created their own portfolio are well-positioned to provide this instruction.

Because of these advantages, portfolios are becoming increasingly popular in preservice and inservice teacher education. For example, they are a key feature of the National Board for Professional Teaching Standards, which provides a process for conferring "master teacher" status on a teacher.[19] A key step in the process is for the teacher to assemble a portfolio. The portfolio consists of several different entries, each of which asks for direct evidence of some aspect of the teacher's work and an analytical commentary on that evidence. There are four different classroom-based entries, two of which ask candidates to videotape classroom interactions, and two of which ask candidates to collect student work of particular kinds. In all four classroom-based entries, candidates are required to write a detailed analysis of the teaching reflected in the videotape or student work.

Work Samples

Work samples are an important recent development in teacher-portfolio methodology. Like portfolios in general, work samples provide evidence of a teacher's competence. However, work samples focus on a specific domain of competence, namely, a teacher's ability to foster student learning under actual classroom conditions. This approach to observing teacher performance is becoming increasingly important as much of the United States moves toward standards-based schooling, statewide testing of students' achievement of standards, and legislative mandates that hold schools accountable for student-learning gains.

Andrew McConney, Mark Schalock, and Del Schalock have undertaken an R&D program to standardize work samples and measures of student-learning gains that can be used across different grade levels and school subjects.[20] In essence, they ask teachers to design and teach a unit of instruction, typically 3 to 5 weeks in duration. The work sample comprises a portfolio that documents ten steps of the design and teaching process. The ten steps are shown in Figure 11.5. McConney and colleagues also have created procedures that teacher educators can use to assess how well the teacher has performed the steps.

You will note in Figure 11.5 that six of the ten steps (3, 4, 6, 8, 9, 10) make explicit reference to teachers' assessment and interpretations of student learning gains. This emphasis is apparently different than what is typically found in teacher education programs, according to a research study by Stephen Koziol and colleagues.[21] They analyzed evaluation instruments used in teacher education programs at eleven research universities on the assumption that these instruments reflect what the programs consider most important in teaching. The researchers concluded that the teacher education programs overemphasize "management and the appearance of a smooth-running classroom over an attention to substantive teaching."[22] Substantive teaching includes the ability to facilitate students' learning of the curriculum.

It is too early to know whether work samples will become a prominent component of teacher portfolios, or perhaps a substitute for them. However, we believe that this is a likely scenario, given the current political and public support for standards-based schooling.

If work samples do achieve a position of prominence, supervisors will be called on to help teachers develop the skills needed to bring about student learning gains that can be demonstrated on externally developed (or, in some cases, teacher-developed tests). This is

1. Define the sample of teaching and learning to be described.
2. Identify the learning outcomes to be accomplished within the work to be sampled.
3. Prior to instruction, assess students' status with respect to the postinstruction outcomes to be accomplished.
4. Develop instruction and assessment plans, that align with proposed learning outcomes and the current status of students with respect to the proposed outcomes.
5. Describe the context in which teaching and learning are to occur.
6. Adapt the desired outcomes and the related plans for instruction and assessment to accommodate all students and the demands of the teaching-learning context.
7. Implement a developmentally and contextually appropriate instructional plan.
8. Assess the postinstructional accomplishments of learners, and calculate each student's growth in learning.
9. Summarize and interpret the growth in learning achieved (or lack thereof) for the class as a whole and for selected groups within the class.
10. Examine and reflect on student growth in learning in light of the preinstructional developmental levels of students, targeted learning outcomes, the context in which teaching and learning occurred, and personal professional effectiveness and development.

Figure 11.5 Steps in creating a work sample.

Source: McConney, A. A., Schalock, M. D., & Schalock, H. D. (1998). Focusing improvement and quality assurance: Work samples as authentic performance measures of prospective teachers' effectiveness. *Journal of Personnel Evaluation in Education, 11*, 343–363 (quote on pp. 346–347).

no easy task. Among other things, teachers will need to learn how to align externally mandated standards with their curriculum, instruction, and assessment.

Research by Gerald Tindal and Victor Nolet has found that this type of alignment is problematic for teachers.[23] Depending on the teacher, concepts that are included in the curriculum might, or might not be included in instruction or on tests. Most troubling is the situation in which key concepts are tested, but are not taught well (or not taught at all) or are not represented adequately in curriculum materials. Supervisors and teachers can review a work sample together to check for these alignment problems and design new instructional units that have better curriculum-instruction-assessment alignment.

Teachers also will need to develop technical skills to create valid, reliable tests that can be administered at different points in time to document learning gains. Performance assessment is a promising methodology for this purpose.[24] Among other characteristics, performance assessment emphasizes:

- students' ability to do something (as opposed, for example, to marking correct answers on traditional multiple-choice tests).
- realism (e.g., having students demonstrate reading ability by asking them to read lengthy passages).
- open-ended tasks that require demonstration of higher-cognitive skills.
- scoring rubrics in which each point on the rubric scale describes a meaningful level of learning accomplishment.

Portfolios—or more specialized work samples of the type described above—can provide observable data about teachers' design of a performance assessment, interpretation of students' scores on it, and its alignment with standards, curriculum materials, and daily instruction.

Technique

As a supervisor, you can leave the planning of the portfolio entirely to the discretion of the teacher or plan it jointly. Another option is for groups of teachers to work with each other in planning their portfolio. If the portfolio is to be used as part of a supervisory process, you most likely will want to specify the products that you wish to see in the portfolio, how the products are to be organized, and criteria for judging their quality.

You should discuss with the teacher whether the portfolio is to have a one-time use or whether it will have multiple uses over time.[25] For example, preservice teachers might assemble a portfolio that can be used to assess their readiness for student teaching. The same portfolio might be used to introduce a preservice teacher to potential cooperating teachers for a practicum or student-teaching placement. As preservice teachers gain experience, they can revise the portfolio to include better examples of their capabilities and accomplishments. The revised portfolio might be submitted when applying for an initial teaching position. The portfolio might be revised further as the teacher's career advances; he or she might use it when applying for promotion and tenure or a new position.

We see, then, that portfolios can serve different purposes and can have different audiences. For this reason, you might recommend to teachers that they maintain a collection of their best work in a loose file or other container. They might well collect more than they will ever use in a particular portfolio. However, they will have a range of materials through which they can search for products that best suit a particular portfolio need.

Experts on portfolio creation recommend that teachers organize their portfolios around a set of teaching principles, goals, or standards, such as those of the National Board for Professional Teaching Standards or other professional group.[26] Once the portfolio's organization is decided, the teacher is faced with the task of selecting products that illustrate their expertise or position with respect to each principle, goal, or standard. It is possible that the same product can be used for more than one principle, goal, or standard.

The products to be included in the portfolio can be of various types. A range of possibilities is listed in Figure 11.6.[27] However, it is important not to include every possible product in the portfolio. The key is to include only those items that are relevant to the teaching principles, goals, or standards that are used to organize the portfolio. If a product is lengthy, the teacher should consider excerpting it. In fact, the teacher's organization of the portfolio and selectivity with respect to included products makes a statement in itself about the teacher's expertise and judgment in communication.

The final portfolio should include not only products, but also descriptions and analyses of the products. For example, if a science teacher includes a five-page essay that articulates his or her philosophy of science instruction, the essay should be preceded by a brief statement explaining when, where, and why it was written. The statement provides the supervisor or other reader with a context—an advanced organizer—for understanding the role that the essay plays in the teacher's professional work and development.

Action research projects, e.g., a report describing an action-research project that one has conducted and its impact on one's professional development.

Assessment results, e.g., test information illustrating skill in designing, administering, scoring, and interpreting tests that assess particular types of student learning.

Certificates, e.g., licenses, endorsements, diplomas, transcripts, or workshop documents recognizing completion of a course of study or set of professional requirements.

Curriculum materials, e.g., documents, handouts, exercises, videotapes, resource guides, or computer software created for use in instruction.

Evaluations, e.g., reports of student teaching performance; letters of recommendation from supervisors, cooperating teachers, and university instructors; and feedback from students.

Honors, e.g., letters, awards, and scholarships acknowledging personal merit or contributions to education.

Journals, e.g., a student-teaching journal demonstrating the ability to reflect on one's own teaching.

Lessons or other units of instruction, e.g., a detailed analysis of a lesson or longer instructional unit, including plans, instructional delivery, classroom management, and student learning.

Literature reviews, e.g., a synthesis of the literature to demonstrate expertise about a particular topic.

Media competencies, e.g., a list of the types of media equipment that one can operate or computer software that one can use for instruction or personal productivity.

Observational records, e.g., an organized set of notes or case study illustrating skill in observing and reflecting on the behavior of a particular type of student or classroom event.

Parent interactions, e.g., correspondence or records of in-person or phone interactions with parents demonstrating the ability to involve parents in the schooling of their children.

Philosophy, e.g., a course paper or other written statement explaining one's general philosophy of education or position on an educational issue or practice.

Photographs, e.g., photos of one's classroom layout, bulletin boards, and décor.

Professional organizations and committees, e.g., a list of organized groups of which one is a member and their role in one's professional life.

Student contracts, e.g., individualized educational plans (IEPs) in which one has participated, and statements describing modifications of instruction to accommodate particular student needs.

Videotapes, e.g., a video and accompanying analysis of a lesson that one has taught.

Work experience, e.g., a chronological list of all places of employment and relevant volunteer experiences.

Figure 11.6 List of possible products for inclusion in teacher portfolios.

The teacher will need to decide where to position descriptions and analyses of the products, and also how to physically organize everything. One option is to create a separate document in which each product is listed, described, and analyzed. This document could be in the first section of a three-ring binder, followed by the products—separated by from each other by binder dividers. This approach makes it easy for the supervisor to get an overview of the portfolio, to focus on the descriptions and analyses, and to examine the products as desired. If the products are of different sorts (e.g., videos, photos, game boards, pages of text), the teacher might consider using a file-folder system to organize and store them. Another option is to create an electronic portfolio with a website address.[28]

As a supervisor, you can study the portfolio for evidence of competence or growth across a wide range of teaching and professional behavior. Of course, it is desirable to have a planning conference with the teacher beforehand so that you have a focus for the study of portfolio. If the portfolio is organized around particular goals, principles, or standards, the process of deciding on a focus should be relatively easy.

Example

Dorothy Campbell and associates presented examples of portfolio products created by different preservice teachers. Each product illustrates one of the set of teaching standards developed by the Interstate New Teachers Assessment and Support Consortium (INTASC—see Chapter 2). One of the standards involves communication skills: "The teacher uses knowledge of effective verbal, nonverbal, and media communication techniques to foster active inquiry, collaboration, and supportive interaction in the classroom."

A preservice teacher, Nicole, decided that clarity is particularly important when communicating with kindergarten children. Her initial practicum experiences demonstrated to her that vague, indefinite statements have an undesirable impact on children at this grade level. Therefore, she worked on developing her skill in making clear statements, and she chose to document her growth by the following portfolio entry:

Standard six: Communication skills

I have included a lesson plan and a video of the same lesson in my portfolio to document how I achieved lesson clarity by utilizing effective verbal communication techniques. I have highlighted aspects of my lesson plan that indicate the techniques I used to achieve clarity and foster productive, active learning and collaboration. In this lesson, I planned for lesson clarity in a variety of ways. In the beginning, I demonstrated and discussed the entire process of terrarium construction. Later, when the students were in their carefully planned, heterogeneous learning groups, I reviewed the steps again using a picture and word chart to which they could refer. We also discussed the various jobs that could be shared among the group members and the value of allowing everyone to help. However, rather than assigning jobs, I allowed the groups to negotiate the assignment of these jobs. As my video shows, the children were successful in following directions and did an excellent job of sharing responsibilities.[29]

The supervisor can study this analysis and accompanying products, and then hold a postconference with Nicole to discuss them. The supervisor might note that there is a research literature on teacher clarity (see Chapter 3), including studies of how teachers use different techniques to achieve clear communication with students. Nicole could compare her techniques with those cited in the literature and consider goals for further development of her communication skills.

NOTES

1. Hunter, M. (1983). Script-taping: An essential supervisory tool. *Educational Leadership, 41,* 43.

2. Frank, C. (1999). *Ethnographic eyes: A teacher's guide to classroom observation.* Portsmouth, NH: Heinemann.

3. *Ibid.*

4. *Ibid.*

5. Stallings, J., Needels, M., & Sparks, G. M. (1987). Observation for the improvement of classroom learning. In D. C. Berliner & B. V. Rosenshine (Eds.), *Talks to teachers* (pp. 129–158). New York: Random House.

6. *Ibid,* p. 144.

7. Allen, D. W., & Ryan, K. (1969). *Microteaching.* Reading, MA: Addison-Wesley.

8. Salomon, G., & McDonald, F. J. (1970). Pretest and posttest reactions to self-viewing one's teaching performance on video tape. *Journal of Educational Psychology, 61,* 280–286.

9. Gall, M. D., Dell, H., Dunning, B. B., & Galassi, J. (1971, February). *Improving teachers' mathematics tutoring skills through microteaching.* Paper presented at the annual meeting of the American Educational Research Association, New York.

10. Sherin, M. G. (2000). Viewing teaching on videotape. *Educational Leadership, 57,* 36–38.

11. Richardson, V. (1990). The evolution of reflective teaching and teacher education. In R. T. Clift, W. R. Houston, & M. C. Pugach (Eds.), *Encouraging reflective practice in education* (pp. 3–19). New York: Teachers College Press.

12. Zeichner, K. M., & Liston, D. P. (1987). Teaching student teachers to reflect. *Harvard Educational Review, 57,* 23–48.

13. Copeland, W. D. (1986). The RITE framework for teacher education: preservice applications. In J. V. Hoffman & S. A. Edwards (Eds.), *Reality and reform in clinical teacher education* (pp. 25–44). New York: Random House.

14. Bolin, F. S. (1988). Helping student teachers think about teaching. *Journal of Teacher Education, 39,* 48–54.

15. *Ibid,* p. 50.

16. *Ibid,* p. 51.

17. Campbell, D. M., Cignetti, P. B., Melenyzer, B. J., Nettles, D. H., & Wyman, R. M. (2001). *How to develop a professional portfolio: A manual for teachers* (2nd ed.). Boston: Allyn and Bacon.

18. Rolheiser, C., Bower, B., & Stevahn, L. (2000). *The portfolio organizer: Succeeding with portfolios in your classroom.* Alexandria, VA: Association for Supervision and Curriculum Development; Danielson, C., & Abrutyn, L. (1997). *An introduction to using portfolios in the classroom.* Alexandria, VA: Association for Supervision and Curriculum Development.

19. The Internet home page for the National Board for Professional Teaching Standards is http://www.nbpts.org/. Teaching standards in different certification fields and portfolio requirements can be found at this website.

20. McConney, A. A., Schalock, M. D., & Schalock, H. D. (1998). Focusing improvement and quality assurance: Work samples as authentic performance measures of prospective teachers' effectiveness. *Journal of Personnel Evaluation in Education, 11,* 343–363.

21. Koziol, S. M., Minnick, J. B., & Sherman, M. A. (1996). What student teaching evaluation instruments tell us about emphases in teacher education programs. *Journal of Personnel Evaluation in Education, 10,* 53–74.

22. *Ibid.,* p. 69.

23. Tindal, G., & Nolet, V. (1996). Serving students in middle school content classes: A heuristic study of critical variables linking instruction and assessment. *Journal of Special Education, 29,* 414–432.

24. Hambleton, R. K. (1996). Advances in assessment models, methods, and practices. In D. C. Berliner & R. C. Calfee (Eds.), *Handbook of educational psychology* (pp. 899–925). New York: Macmillan.

25. Various uses for a professional portfolio are discussed in: Martin, D. B. (1999). *The portfolio planner: Making professional portfolios work for you.* Upper Saddle River, NJ: Prentice-Hall.

26. Campbell *et al., op. cit.;* Burke, K. (1997). *Designing professional portfolios for change.* Arlington Heights, IL: IRI Skylight Publishing; Wolf, K., Lichtenstein, G., & Stevenson, C. (1997). Using teaching portfolios in teacher evaluation. In J.H. Stronge (Ed.), *Evaluating teaching: A guide to current thinking and best practice* (pp. 193–214). Thousand Oaks, CA: Corwin Press.

27. Additional possibilities for portfolio products are suggested in chapter 5 of Campbell *et al., op. cit.* In addition, the teacher and supervisor should consider portfolio products that are subject-specific—for example, the types of artifacts that Eric Pyle identified in science instruction: Pyle, E. J. (1998). The role of

classroom artifacts in the clinical supervision of science. *NASSP Bulletin, 82,* 70–76.

28. We have found that if you have the interest and basic computer skills, you can learn how to create your own website without much difficulty. For specific information, see: http://www .edsupport.cc/mguhlin/workshops/portfolio/

29. Campbell *et al., op. cit.,* pp. 34–35.

Chapter 12

Checklists, Rating Scales, and Timeline Coding

Author's Note

One of the most interesting books I've read in recent years is *The Measure of Reality,* by Alfred Crosby. His argument is that the development of quantitative thinking was the key factor that transformed Western civilization and gave birth to the Renaissance. Mechanical clocks, coordinate maps, musical notation, double-entry booking, and perspective painting were invented during this period of time. What made all of them possible was the ability to take a complex phenomenonon—time, geography, music, business, painting—and analyze it into uniform, countable units (i.e., *quanta*). Take away quantification, and much of civilization as we know it today would disappear.

So what does this have to do with clinical supervision? The answer is that, like scientists and professionals in other fields, some educators have attempted to analyze the complex phenomenon of teaching into units that can be tallied or rated on numerical scales. You would have experienced this approach if you ever rated a university instructor on a standardized end-of-course evaluation form, rated teachers on a standardized licensure form, or examined teachers' performance on competency tests, such as the Praxis examinations of the Educational Testing Service (ETS).

In this chapter, you'll read about various quantitative observation techniques and how they can be used in clinical supervision. My experience has been that they are powerful techniques, but many teachers and supervisors don't wish to use them. The educators whom I've known tend to be more holistic than analytical in their thinking, and much more oriented to learning by interacting with people than by poring over numerical data.

I believe that the education profession needs to keep stressing and developing its moral commitments to society and its students. But I also believe that teaching will not advance as an art and a science unless we subject it to quantitative analysis. Of course, you will need to form your own judgment about this matter. I invite you to read this chapter and consider whether the techniques of quantitative observation described in it can help teachers improve their instruction.

MDG

> *In almost any natural situation, particularly in one as phenomenally complex as a class-room, one perceives selectively. . . . The problem is not that perceivable <u>phenomena vary</u> in their duration and size and volume and other sensible characteristics but is, rather, <u>to see</u> things as they are objectively in their natural relationships, in their natural proportionalities, not as they are reflected by our mental fun mirrors.*
>
> *—Robert Goldhammer[1]*

INTRODUCTION

The observational methods described in the previous chapters do not predetermine what is to be observed. For example, in using selective verbatim, SCORE techniques, or video recordings, the teacher and supervisor jointly decide the categories of behavior to be observed. However, in certain situations, you might prefer a more structured observation instrument. This type of instrument has predetermined categories of teaching behavior. Unless prohibited by the instrument's author or publisher, you also have the option of modifying and adding categories to the instrument to suit your purposes.

This chapter presents a sampling of these instruments.[2] Some are forms that students complete to give feedback to their teachers. Others are forms that the supervisor completes while observing the teacher's classroom behavior.

As with the observation techniques presented in other chapters of this book, you should examine the techniques described below to determine whether they reflect principles of learning that you consider important. Our review of research and theory suggests that students' learning is most affected by their (1) level of attention and motivation, (2) whether they can find personal meaning in the information being presented, (3) opportunities to practice using new information, (4) group processes in the classroom, and (5) whether the teacher focuses on lower-cognitive or higher-cognitive processes.

OBSERVATION TECHNIQUE 13: STUDENT RATING SCALES

In the process of attending class, students are constantly observing their teacher's behavior. Having students record their observations is useful in clinical supervision, because teachers often are very concerned about how their students perceive them—even more than they are concerned about how supervisors perceive them!

Pupil Observation Survey Report

This student-administered checklist was developed in the 1960s, but is still useful in clinical supervision.[3] It measures the extent to which the teacher

1. is friendly, cheerful, admired.
2. is knowledgeable, poised.
3. is interesting and preferred to other teachers.
4. uses strict control.
5. uses democratic procedures.

These five dimensions are measured by thirty-eight items that should be comprehensible to students in fifth grade and higher.

A short version of this instrument, called *Student Evaluation of Teaching*, is available. It is shown in Figure 12.1. The first five items measure, in order, the five dimensions listed

STUDENT EVALUATION OF TEACHING

D. J. VELDMAN and R. F. PECK

TEACHER'S LAST NAME: _____

SUBJECT: _____

SCHOOL: _____

CIRCLE THE RIGHT CHOICES BELOW

Teacher's Sex: M   F

My Sex: M   F

My Grade Level:

3 4 5 6 7 8 9 10 11 12

DO NOT USE

CIRCLE ONE OF THE FOUR CHOICES IN FRONT OF EACH STATEMENT.
THE FOUR CHOICES MEAN:

F = Very Much False
f = More False Than True
t = More True Than False
T = Very Much True

This Teacher:

F f t T   is always friendly toward students.

F f t T   knows a lot about the subject.

F f t T   is never dull or boring.

F f t T   expects a lot from students.

F f t T   asks for students' opinions before making decisions.

F f t T   is usually cheerful and optimistic.

F f t T   is not confused by unexpected questions.

F f t T   makes learning more like fun than work.

F f t T   doesn't let students get away with anything.

F f t T   often gives students a choice in assignments.

Figure 12.1 Pupil observation survey.

above. The second five items also measure, in order, the same dimensions. For example, the first item ("is always friendly toward students") and sixth item ("is usually cheerful and optimistic") measure the first dimension listed above ("is friendly, cheerful, admired").

One way to summarize the data yielded by this checklist is to count the number of students in the class who circled each response option (F f t T) in each item. Another way is to score each item (e.g., $F = 0$, $f = 1$, $t = 2$, $T = 3$) and then compute the mean score for each pair of items that measure the same dimension.

Other Student Rating Scales

Figure 12.2 presents a series of items that students can rate to give their teacher data on several important dimensions of classroom instruction. You are welcome to use or adapt as many of these items as you wish. You also can use whatever rating scale you prefer. One possibility is the rating-scale format used on the *Student Evaluation of Teaching* form (described above). Another option is a scale with these five points: *never seldom sometimes often always*.

My teacher:

Clarity and task orientation

- explains things clearly.
- gives clear directions.
- makes it clear what we're supposed to learn.
- does not digress from the content we're supposed to learn.

Classroom management

- treats students fairly.
- knows how to manage students so they don't disrupt the class.
- is good about praising us when we deserve it.
- unfairly criticizes or punishes us.
- has reasonable classroom rules.

Learning and assessment tasks

- gives tests that evaluate us on what we've actually studied.
- gives tests that are too difficult.
- gives reasonable homework assignments.
- helps us review what we studied so we're prepared for the test.
- get us to think, not just learn facts.
- gives us worksheets and other class activities that are useful.

Motivating students to learn

- varies activities in order to hold our attention.
- gives us choices for projects, homework, and other assignments.
- is enthusiastic during class.
- teaches only from the textbook.
- does things to arouse our curiosity.
- makes the things we're studying interesting.
- makes it fun to learn.

Orientation to students

- talks too much.
- asks us good questions.
- lets us talk about our own ideas.
- listens carefully to what we have to say.
- answers our questions when we raise our hand.
- gives special help to students who need it.
- understands us.
- makes it comfortable for us to be in his/her classroom.
- does not have class "favorites."
- makes it possible for us to get to know each other.

Figure 12.2 List of items on which students can rate their teacher's behavior.

OBSERVATION TECHNIQUE 14: OBSERVER-ADMINISTERED CHECKLISTS

There are several published checklists that observers can use to record data on teachers' use of various teaching methods. For example, Bruce Joyce and colleagues present rating checklists for observing teaching strategies organized into three models: information processing, social interaction, and personal.[4]

Clinical supervisors sometimes construct their own checklist for recording observations of classroom behavior. For example, the following are descriptions of several checklists that we constructed for our own use in supervision. You are invited to use them as is or adapt them for your particular purpose.

Questioning Behaviors

In Chapters 9 and 10, we showed how selective verbatim and seating chart observational records can be used to capture important aspects of teachers' question-asking behavior in the classroom. A checklist also can be used for this purpose. Advantages of the checklist format are that it is relatively easy to use and a substantial number of teacher behaviors can be recorded on it. In contrast, the advantage of selective-verbatim and seating-chart procedures is that, although fewer questioning behaviors are observed, they are recorded more completely.

The checklist shown in Figure 12.3 is organized around three types of questioning teacher behavior. The first set of behaviors is important because they usually produce increased student participation in the lesson. For example, the first behavior in the checklist

```
Behaviors That Increase Student
Participation
1. Calls on nonvolunteers
2. Redirects question
3. Praises student responses
4. Invites student-initiated questions

Behaviors That Elicit Thoughtful Responses
1. Asks higher cognitive questions
2. Pauses 3-5 seconds after asking a
   question
3. Asks follow-up questions to an initial
   response

Negative Behaviors
1. Reacts negatively to student response
2. Repeats own question
3. Asks multiple questions
4. Answers own questions
5. Repeats student's answer

Strong Points of Lesson

Suggestions for Improvement
```

Figure 12.3 Checklist for questioning behaviors.

is calling on nonvolunteers to respond. Teachers are likely to call on students who raise their hands and who customarily give good answers to their questions. Yet nonvolunteers often make good contributions if the teacher takes the initiative to call on them.

Student participation also can be increased by redirecting the same question to several students. The teacher might invite additional responses to a question by a nod acknowledging a particular student or by a statement such as "Does anyone have a different idea?" or "Would someone like to add to what Susie said?" Praising answers is a technique that helps students feel that their answers are worthwhile; as a result, they are encouraged to speak up when other questions are asked. Another good technique is to ask students whether they have any questions of their own about the lesson content. The teacher might choose to answer these student-initiated questions directly or call on other students to answer them.

The second category in the question-and-answer checklist refers to the cognitive level of the teacher's lesson. Educators generally agree that students should not just recite back the facts they have learned. (This is done by asking simple fact questions of the Who, What, Where, When variety.) Students also should be encouraged to think about the curriculum content. This goal is accomplished by asking higher-cognitive questions, which are questions that cannot be answered simply by looking in the textbook. The student must think in order to generate an original response. Among other intellectual operations, higher-cognitive questions might require the student to compare and contrast, state possible motives or causes for observed phenomena, draw conclusions, provide evidence, make predictions, solve problems, make judgments, or offer opinions.

Asking a higher-cognitive question might not be sufficient to elicit a thoughtful response. One helpful behavior listed in Figure 12.3 is to pause several seconds before calling on a student to respond. This gives students time to think. It also encourages all students in the class to generate an answer, because they do not know whom the teacher will call on to respond.

Another technique on the checklist for eliciting thoughtful responses is to ask follow-up questions after the student has given an initial answer to a question. For example, the teacher might ask, "Did you agree with the jury's verdict?" and the student might respond, "No, I didn't." The teacher can follow up by asking the student to support his position (e.g., "Why didn't you agree?"). Follow-up questions also can be used to encourage a student to clarify a vague answer (e.g., "I'm not sure I understood what you said. Can you re-state your answer?"), to generate additional ideas (e.g., "Can you think of other ways of solving the energy crisis?"), or to challenge the student (e.g., "That's a good idea, but have you considered possible adverse consequences that might occur if your idea were put into practice?"). Follow-up questions can be used, too, to prompt a student who is unable to respond to the initial question.

The first two categories in the checklist in Figure 12.3 refer to the "do's" of question-asking. The third category refers to the "don'ts." Teachers should avoid reacting negatively to student responses by making critical remarks (e.g., "That doesn't make any sense at all") or by showing annoyance. Critical behavior only increases the likelihood that the student will volunteer no response in the future. The second negative behavior, repeating one's question, is to be avoided because it wastes class time and encourages students not to listen carefully the first time the teacher asks a question.

The third "don't"—asking multiple questions—refers to the practice of asking several questions in a row before settling on a question to which a response is invited. Teachers tend to do this when they are unsure of the lesson content or if they are inclined to think aloud. Multiple questions also waste class time, and they are likely to confuse students. The final "don't" is repeating student answers verbatim. A better practice is to praise the answer, extend the answer by adding new information, or invite another student to build on the answer.

The bottom two headings of the checklist provide an open-ended opportunity for the observer to comment on strong points of the lesson and teaching behaviors not on the checklist, but which the teacher also might wish to improve.

Expository Behaviors

Researchers have found that teachers on average do two-thirds of the talking in elementary and secondary classrooms.[5] The percentage is probably higher in some settings (e.g., college teaching) and lower in others. Much of this "talk time" is spent in presenting new concepts and information to students, or in explaining difficult parts of the curriculum. We have found that some teachers say they rarely engage in this type of expository teaching when, in fact, they do. In fact, expository teaching (explaining, lecturing, demonstrating) is fine, if done properly.

The checklist and rating form shown in Figure 12.4 is designed for analyzing various aspects of a teacher's expository behavior. Research evidence supporting the effectiveness of these behaviors is presented in Chapter 3.

You will note that the form is in two parts. The first part includes behaviors that can be tallied each time they occur. The tallies are counted to determine how often the teacher used a particular expository behavior during the lesson. Some of these behaviors are techniques for increasing the meaningfulness of the curriculum content—for example, using examples, advance organizers, concept maps, and graphic organizers.[6] Other behaviors are techniques for involving students so that they do not sit passively while the teacher talks. For example, asking students if they have questions about the lesson is an example of a technique that usually creates student involvement.

The second part of the form shown in Figure 12.4 is a list of teacher behaviors rated by the observer. Some of the rated behaviors concern how well the teacher organizes the subject-matter content. For example, repeating key points and summarizing them at the end of the lesson is a technique that helps students organize the various ideas presented in the lesson as "more important" or "less important."

The largest category of behaviors on the form relates to the teacher's skill in delivery. Speech is the primary medium in expository teaching, and so the teacher's mastery of oral delivery determines in large part how well the curriculum content is conveyed to students. The enthusiasm in the teacher's voice, the clarity of the teacher's remarks, the avoidance of nervous gestures and filler phrases—all contribute to the effectiveness of the lesson.

As in the Checklist for Questioning Behaviors (Figure 12.3), this checklist can be augmented by including space for additional comments about the strong points of the lesson and suggestions for improvement.

BEHAVIORS TO BE TALLIED

Meaningful Content
1. Relates lecture content to content already familiar to students
2. Gives example to illustrate concept
3. Gives explanation for generalization or opinion

Student Involvement
1. Asks students if they have questions
2. Directs question to students
3. Has students engage in activity

BEHAVIORS TO BE RATED

	good	needs improvement
Organization		
1. Lecture has clear organization and sequence	5	4 3 2 1
2. Uses blackboard, handout, etc., to show organization of lecture	5	4 3 2 1
3. Tells students what (s)he expects students to remember from lecture	5	4 3 2 1
4. Repeats key points and summarizes them at end	5	4 3 2 1
5. Avoids digressions	5	4 3 2 1

	good	needs improvement
Delivery		
1. Speaks slowly and clearly	5	4 3 2 1
2. Conveys enthusiasm	5	4 3 2 1
3. Avoids reading from lecture notes	5	4 3 2 1
4. Avoids filler phrases such as "you know"	5	4 3 2 1
5. Avoids nervous gestures	5	4 3 2 1
6. Maintains eye contact with students	5	4 3 2 1
7. Uses humor	5	4 3 2 1

Figure 12.4 Checklist and rating form for expository behaviors.

Constructivist Teaching Methods

We discussed constructivist theories of teaching and learning in Chapter 3. In brief, constructivist theorists believe that learners develop (or, in their term, *construct*) their own understandings of the world. These theorists also believe that students in conventional classrooms often acquire new knowledge and skills, but without understanding what they are learning.

Educators who subscribe to constructivism have developed various teaching methods to promote student understanding. Jacqueline and Martin Brooks organized these methods into a list and contrasted them with conventional teaching methods. We organized their list into a checklist form in Figure 12.5. The observer can place a check in one of the two checkmark columns to indicate the presence of a particular method of instructional planning or classroom instruction. (The first checkmark column is for constructivist methods; the second is for traditional methods.)

You can use the checklist as it appears in Figure 12.5 or adapt it. For example, you might include additional methods or omit some. You can use an all-or-nothing checkmark to indicate a method's use or a rating scale indicating various levels of use.

Methods for Accommodating Student Diversity

Carol Ann Tomlinson compiled a list of methods that experts recommend for differentiating instruction so that the needs and interests of all students in a classroom are met.[7] Tomlinson contrasted these methods with a list of methods found in classrooms where students are treated as if they were homogeneous. We reorganized the lists into checklist form in Figure 12.6 (note that it parallels Figure 12.5 in format.)

The terminology used in Figure 12.6 is in common use, except perhaps for *learning profile options*. According to Tomlinson, a learning profile has to do with how a student

CONSTRUCTIVIST CLASSROOMS	√	√	TRADITIONAL CLASSROOMS
• Curriculum is presented whole to part with emphasis on big concepts.			• Curriculum is presented part to whole, with emphasis on basic skills.
• Pursuit of student questions is highly valued.			• Strict adherence to fixed curriculum is highly valued.
• Curricular activities rely heavily on primary sources of data and manipulative materials.			• Curricular activities rely heavily on textbooks and workbooks.
• Students are viewed as thinkers with emerging theories about the world.			• Students are viewed as "blank slates" onto which information is etched by the teacher.
• Teachers generally behave in an interactive manner, mediating the environment for students.			• Teachers generally behave in a didactic manner, disseminating information to students.
• Teachers seek the students' points of view in order to understand students' present conceptions for use in subsequent lessons.			• Teachers seek the correct answer to validate student learning.
• Assessment of student learning is interwoven with teaching and occurs through teacher observations of students at work and through student exhibitions and portfolios.			• Assessment of student learning is viewed as separate from teaching and occurs almost entirely through testing.
• Students primarily work in groups.			• Students primarily work alone.

Figure 12.5 Checklist for constructivist teaching methods.

Source: Brooks, J. G., & Brooks, M. G. (1993). *The case for constructivist classrooms.* Alexandria, VA: Association for Supervision and Curriculum Development, p. 17.

DIFFERENTIATED CLASSROOMS	√	√	TRADITIONAL CLASSROOMS
Planning • Teacher analyzes how students in the class differ and plans accordingly. • Student readiness, interest, and learning profile shape instruction. • Excellence is defined in large measure by individual growth from a starting point. • Focus on multiple forms of intelligences is evident.			**Planning** • Student differences are ignored in planning phase of instruction. • Coverage of texts and curriculum guides drive instruction. • A single definition of excellence exists. • A relatively narrow sense of intelligence prevails.
Curriculum • Key concepts and principles are the focus of learning. • Multiple materials are provided.			**Curriculum** • Facts and skills out-of-context are the focus of learning. • A single text prevails.
Instruction • The teacher facilitates students' skills at becoming self-reliant learners. • Students are frequently guided in making interest-based learning choices. • Many learning profile options are provided for. • Many instructional arrangements are used. • Multi-option assignments are frequently used. • Time is used flexibly in accordance with student need. • Multiple perspectives on ideas and events are routinely sought. • Students help other students and the teacher solve problems.			**Instruction** • The teacher directs student behavior. • Student interest is infrequently tapped. • Relatively few learning profile options are taken into account. • Whole-class instruction dominates. • Single-option assignments are the norm. • Time is relatively inflexible. • Single interpretations of ideas and events are sought. • The teacher solves problems.
Assessment • Students are assessed in multiple ways. • Assessment is ongoing and diagnostic to understand how to make instruction more responsive to learner need. • The teacher works with students to establish both whole-class and individual standards for grading.			**Assessment** • A single form of assessment is used. • Assessment is most common at the end of learning to see "who got it." • The teacher provides whole-class standards for grading.

Figure 12.6 Checklist for methods of accommodating student diversity.

Source: Adapted from page 16 of: Tomlinson, C. A. (1999). *The differentiated classroom: Responding to the needs of all learners.* Alexandria, VA: Association for Supervision and Curriculum Development.

learns. Students vary in their learning profile. For example, some students need to talk about new concepts in order to learn them, whereas other students learn better alone. Some students learn analytically (details first and then the big picture), whereas others learn holistically (big picture first and then the details). To be effective, teachers need to include instructional *options* that accommodate these different learning profiles.

A quick inspection of the checks in the two columns will reveal the extent to which the teacher is using differentiated teaching methods to accommodate student diversity. The form can be adapted, if you wish, by adding or subtracting items or by indicating degrees of use (e.g., "used rarely or to a minor degree," "used sometimes or to a moderate degree," "used regularly or to a significant degree").

Of the methods presented in Figure 12.6, perhaps the most critical is flexible/inflexible use of time. In Chapter 3, we reviewed research evidence demonstrating that the teacher's allocation of time affects students' learning. Teachers who allocate more time for instruction on a particular topic give students more opportunity to learn that topic. Because students learn at different rates, allocating more time for slower learners increases their opportunity for academic success.

OBSERVATION TECHNIQUE 15: TEACHER EVALUATION RATING SCALES

The purpose of observation in the clinical supervision cycle is to collect *objective data* about the teacher's classroom behavior. In teacher evaluation, however, the supervisor collects *evaluative data* for the purpose of judging the teacher's competence. Observation instruments used for this purpose generally consist of evaluative rating scales. The observer makes a check or circles a point on the scale that corresponds to his or her rating of the teacher's performance. States and school districts have developed formal scales of this type to evaluate whether a teacher has sufficient skills to be certified or to be offered continued employment.

We are describing these scales here, even though they are deliberately evaluative rather than objective. One reason for doing this is that they provide a contrast that can help you better understand the objective, neutral nature of other observation instruments presented in this section of the book. Another reason is that there might be occasions in clinical supervision when it is appropriate to use evaluative observation instruments. For example, the supervisor might be working with a teacher to help him or her prepare for an upcoming evaluation. Use of the rating instrument that will be used in the evaluation can help the teacher prepare for it and defuse some of the anxiety associated with being evaluated.

A typical teacher evaluation instrument contains ten to fifteen items. Most of them typically concern the teacher's classroom behavior, for example:

1. teaches accurate content.
2. makes learning outcomes explicit to students.
3. includes both lower-cognitive and higher-cognitive objectives in instruction.
4. uses curriculum materials and technology that are appropriate to the lesson objectives.
5. motivates students to achieve the lesson objectives.

6. uses a variety of teaching strategies.

7. demonstrates effective classroom management.

8. gives students adequate feedback on their performance, and reteaches if necessary.

9. maintains a positive, cooperative classroom climate.

10. adjusts instruction appropriately for unexpected events and time constraints.

11. assesses student progress and achievement regularly and in a manner consistent with curriculum objectives.

These items are only illustrative. A review of the literature on effective teaching (see Chapter 3) will suggest other items that can be used instead of, or in addition to, those listed above. The most important consideration is that the evaluator have a rationale for each item included in the instrument. It is also important to make the rationale explicit to the teacher being evaluated. This can be done by showing the teacher the instrument and explaining it prior to the observation visit.

Other items in teacher evaluation instruments typically involve qualities of professionalism, such as these:

1. prepares coherent, complete lesson plans.

2. demonstrates ethical, professional behavior.

3. contributes to colleagues' development and to the school as an organization.

4. communicates effectively with parents and other members of the community.

5. demonstrates continued professional development.

The supervisor obviously would need to make observations outside the classroom context in order to rate these items validly.

Some teacher evaluation instruments include "indicators" that clarify what is meant by each item. It is helpful both to the teacher and the supervisor if these indicators are stated as observable behaviors. For example, consider the item stated above, "Motivates students to achieve the lesson objectives." Indicators of what is meant by this item might include

- exhibits enthusiasm (varied voice inflection, lively facial expressions, energetic body movements).

- praises and acknowledges students when they demonstrate interest or give a correct response.

- relates the curriculum content to phenomena within the range of students' experience and interest.

These indicators increase the credibility and comprehensibility of the items. They also help teachers identify what they can do to improve their ratings on individual items.

An important element of an evaluative rating instrument is the scale itself. A typical scale includes five or seven points, with an appropriate descriptor at key points on the scale, for example:

Low Competence	Average Competence	Exceptional Competence	NA
1 2	3 4 5	6 7	

	Unsatisfactory		Satisfactory		Excellent		NA
	1	2	3	4	5		

You will note that the scales include an "NA" (not applicable) option. This is because some items on the instrument might not be appropriate for a teacher's job description.

Each item on the instrument is accompanied by a scale like the ones illustrated above. The supervisor need only circle the appropriate point on the scale for each item.

OBSERVATION TECHNIQUE 16: THE FLANDERS INTERACTION ANALYSIS SYSTEM

The Interaction Analysis System developed by Ned Flanders is one of the best-known techniques of classroom observation. It was widely used in teacher training and in research during the 1960s and 1970s. Less use of it is made now as other conceptualizations of effective teaching have come into prominence. Nonetheless, the Interaction Analysis System records important aspects of teaching that are not included in other observation systems. Therefore, clinical supervisors should consider learning how to use the system.[8]

The Flanders Interaction Analysis System has two principal features: (1) verbal-interaction categories; and (2) timeline-coding procedures for using the categories to make classroom observations.

Categories of Verbal Interaction

The verbal-interaction categories are shown in Figure 12.7. With the exception of category 10 (silence or confusion), all categories pertain to a specific type of verbal behavior. Any verbal statement by a teacher or student is classifiable by one of the ten categories. This is true irrespective of grade level, subject area, or teacher and student characteristics. Indeed, one of the major appeals of interaction analysis is its universality. For example, a first-grade reading group and a graduate-level seminar could be compared for similarities and differences using the system.

Three kinds of interaction categories are shown in Figure 12.7. Some verbal behaviors are responses, either made by a teacher to a student (categories 1, 2, and 3) or by a student to a teacher (category 8). Other verbal behaviors are intended to initiate communication. Either a student (category 9) or the teacher (categories 5, 6, and 7) can play the role of initiator. Categories 4 and 10 are considered neutral with respect to the response/initiation distinction.

Another way of grouping the ten categories into larger units is to consider who is the speaker during a particular verbal interchange. In a classroom situation, the speaker is either the teacher or a student. (An observer might wish to modify the Interaction Analysis System to accommodate a class that has an aide or other person in addition to the teacher.) Figure 12.7 shows that the first seven categories are used to code teacher statements. Categories 8 and 9 are for coding student talk. Category 10 reflects confusion or the fact that no one is speaking at a particular point in time.

The most critical distinction in Flanders' approach to interaction analysis is between response and initiation. If you think about the way in which you communicate with others, you will realize that you do one of two things: (1) respond to what someone else

Teacher Talk	Response	1. Accepts feeling. Accepts and clarifies an attitude or the feeling tone of a student in a nonthreatening manner. Feelings may be positive or negative. Predicting and recalling feelings are included. 2. Praises or encourages. Praises or encourages students; says "um hum" or "go on"; makes jokes that release tension, but not at the expense of a student. 3. Accepts or uses ideas of students. Acknowledges student talk. Clarifies, builds on, or asks questions based on student ideas.
		4. Asks questions. Asks questions about content or procedure, based on teacher ideas, with the intent that a student will answer.
	Initiation	5. Lectures. Offers facts or opinions about content or procedures; expresses his own ideas, gives *his own* explanation, or cites an authority other than a student. 6. Gives directions. Gives directions, commands, or orders with which a student is expected to comply. 7. Criticizes student or justifies authority. Makes statements intended to change student behavior from nonacceptable to acceptable patterns; arbitrarily corrects student answers; bawls someone out. Or states why the teacher is doing what he is doing; uses extreme self-reference.
Student Talk	Response	8. Student talk—response. Student talk in response to a teacher contact that structures or limits the situation. Freedom to express his own ideas is limited.
	Initiation	9. Student talk—initiation. Student initiates or expresses his own ideas, either spontaneously or in response to the teacher's solicitation. Freedom to develop opinions and a line of thought; going beyond existing structure.
Silence		10. Silence or confusion. Pauses, short periods of silence, and periods of confusion in which communication cannot be understood by the observer.

Figure 12.7 Flanders interaction analysis categories (FIAC).

No scale is implied by these numbers. Each number is classificatory; it designates a particular kind of communication event. To write these numbers down during observation is to enumerate, not to judge, a position on a scale.

Source: Based on: Flanders, N.A. (1970). *Analyzing Teaching Behavior.* Reading, MA: Addison-Wesley, p. 34.

has said by listening or by offering a comment that directly relates to the other's communication; or (2) take the initiative by such means as putting forth an idea, giving a direction, or criticizing what someone else has said or done.

When teachers make a responsive comment (categories 1, 2, or 3), they are said to be using an "indirect" style of teaching. You will note that these indirect behaviors are also associated with positive affect—accepting feelings, praising, and acknowledging students' ideas. When teachers initiate a verbal interchange (categories 5, 6, or 7), they are said to be using a "direct" style of teaching. According to Flanders, a teacher question can be either direct, as in a narrow or specific question, or indirect, as in a broad or open question.

Student verbal behavior is summarized in two categories. Students are either responding in a narrow way to the teacher (category 8), or they are expressing personal ideas and opinions (category 9). Flanders and other researchers have found consistently that a teacher's use of an indirect style of teaching (categories 1, 2, 3) encourages students to offer their own ideas and opinions (category 9). In contrast, a teacher's use of a directive style (categories 5, 6, 7) has been found consistently to channel students' ideas and behavior to meet teacher expectations (category 8).

This brief glimpse into interaction analysis reveals that it is both simple and complex. All classroom communication is coded into just ten categories, yet the resulting data lend themselves to sophisticated analyses of the teacher's behavior. For example, the teacher and supervisor can analyze how the intent of a teacher's communication changes from minute to minute in a lesson. These changes might reveal a teacher's characteristic way of interacting with students. One teacher's routine might be to ask a question (category 4), elicit a narrow student response (category 8), and respond in turn by asking a new question (category 4). This is a 4-8-4 pattern. Another teacher might be in the habit of asking a question, eliciting an open-ended student answer; then the teacher praises the student for the quality of the answer, builds on what the student has said, and initiates a new question. This is a 4-9-2-3-4 pattern.

As teachers are exposed to interaction-analysis data on their classroom teaching, their verbal behavior patterns are likely to become more complex and varied. They also become more aware of how their verbal behavior affects student learning.

Which is better—an indirect or a direct teaching style? As we explained in Chapter 3, research on interaction analysis suggests that use of an indirect teaching style is associated with more positive student attitudes and higher student achievement. But this does not mean that a direct style is necessarily poor teaching. Flanders suggests that there are occasions when the teacher needs to be direct, as in presenting new content to students and giving directions. When using direct teaching, though, there often is opportunity to use some indirect verbal behaviors. For example, the teacher might be giving an extended series of directions for doing an experiment (category 6). While doing this, the teacher might consider pausing to praise or encourage the students for their efforts and success in following directions (category 2).

A similar situation can occur in indirect teaching. For example, the teacher might be moderating a discussion in which students are encouraged to state their own opinions on an issue (category 9). The teacher might acknowledge students' ideas (category 3), encourage silent students to talk (category 2), and verbalize awareness of the feelings that underlie students' opinions (category 1). All these are indirect verbal behaviors. At some point in the discussion, though, the teacher might discover that students are misinformed about a particular issue and so decide to interrupt the discussion temporarily to provide information (category 5) and direct students to do homework reading (category 6). Thus, the teacher has interspersed direct teaching into a predominantly indirect, student-centered lesson.

This is only a brief introduction to the Flanders Interaction Analysis System. We trust that it is enough to help you understand why these classroom observation categories have captured the attention of educators worldwide and why the system has been used extensively in teacher supervision.

Timeline Coding Procedures

In describing interaction analysis, we stated that it has two main features. The preceding discussion concerned the first feature, namely, the ten categories for coding verbal behaviors. The other distinguishing feature is the use of the timeline method for coding behaviors.

Figure 12.8 presents examples of timelines used in conjunction with the Flanders Interaction Analysis System. (Observers used a matrix-coding approach for many years until the timeline method was developed.) The first thing to notice about a timeline is its columns. Each column represents a 3-second interval. The 3-second interval is long enough that the observer need not become preoccupied with recording data. In most lessons there usually are several periods of time lasting a minute or more when only one interaction category is being used. (These are usually categories 4, 5, or 6.) The observer can relax during these time intervals until the pace of interaction increases again.[9]

The timelines shown in Figure 12.8 have 30 columns for recording 30 discrete observations. Because an observation is made every 3 seconds, each timeline covers about $1^1/_2$ minutes of classroom interaction.

The other salient feature of an interaction-analysis timeline is the rows. Each row represents one or two categories. The middle row is for teacher questions (category 4), which often are a stimulus for a series of interactions between teacher and students. Categories reflecting an indirect teaching style (1, 2, and 3) are above the middle row, as is the category reflecting open, student-initiated responses (category 9). Categories that indicate a direct teaching style (5, 6, and 7) are below the line, as is the category for structured, restricted student responses (category 8).

Category 10 (silence or confusion) is not represented by a discrete row. Tallies for this category are made below the timeline. Several categories (1 and 2, 6 and 7) share the same row in order to conserve space. Observers can use different tallies in the cells to differentiate 1 from 2 or 6 from 7, or they can simply change the timeline form by adding two rows so each category has its own row.

The organization of the interaction-analysis categories on the timeline helps the supervisor and teacher detect verbal patterns that occurred during an observed lesson. For example, a majority of tallies above the middle row indicates that the lesson was indirect in style. A majority of tallies below the middle row indicates that the lesson was direct in style. These patterns can be detected much more quickly than by playing back a video or audio recording of a lesson. A timeline usually can be interpreted in less than 2 minutes, whereas the time required to interpret a video or audio recording of a lesson will take longer than the elapsed time of the lesson.

The first timeline in Figure 12.8 is characterized by alternating 4s and 8s. This pattern suggests that the teacher was engaged in a rapid question-and-answer interchange with students, with the level of discourse probably focused on fact recall.

The second timeline in Figure 12.8 suggests a richer, more indirect dialogue. The teacher starts by giving some information on a curriculum topic. Then students are invited to offer their own ideas on the topic. After each student response, the teacher takes care to acknowledge the student's idea and, in some instances, to praise it.

When teachers first become exposed to interaction analysis, they often find that they use a few simple patterns in interacting with their students. As they see these patterns recorded on a timeline, they likely will wish to explore how they can become more flexi-

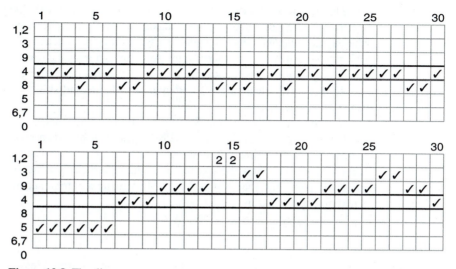

Figure 12.8 Timelines.

Source: Copyright 1974, Far West Laboratory for Educational Research and Development, San Francisco, California. Published by Paul S. Amidon & Associates, Inc., 4329 Nicollet Avenue South, Minneapolis, Minnesota 55409.

ble in their use of verbal behavior. Sometimes, but not always, this involves a shift from a more direct to a more indirect style of teaching.

Our discussion of timelines has focused on its application to the Flanders Interaction Analysis System. Timelines are a generic recording device, however. With a bit of creativity on your part, you can imagine other behaviors that can be inserted in place of the interaction-analysis categories.[10] Also, the 3-second interval represented by the columns of the timeline can be varied.

The recording procedures that we described above are fairly efficient, considering their "paper-and-pencil" basis. Kent Crippen and David Brooks have described how greater efficiencies and capabilities are possible with computer technology.[11] For example, a PalmPilot, which is a lightweight, unobtrusive computer device, can be used to record interaction analysis data and other categories of teacher–student behavior (including the categories described in Observation Technique 17).[12] The supervisor can make a hard-copy transcript of the data recorded on the PalmPilot and use it when conferencing with the teacher. Because the data are in electronic form, the supervisor also can send the transcript to the teacher as an e-mail attachment before the conference. If the teacher also has a PalmPilot, the data can be transferred directly to it from the supervisor's PalmPilot using the device's built-in infrared data transfer system.

OBSERVATION TECHNIQUE 17: THE STALLINGS OBSERVATION SYSTEM

This method of timeline coding was developed by Jane Stallings and colleagues. It has been used in research,[13] inservice education,[14] and preservice education.[15] It can be used at any grade level and with any subject area, and it can be adapted for observing special situations.

The Stallings Observation System is similar to the Flanders Interaction Analysis System in its coding procedure and emphasis on observable classroom behaviors. However, whereas the Flanders system measures ten aspects of teacher and student behavior, the Stallings system measures sixty-four. Another difference is that the Flanders system is based on group-process theory and research, whereas the Stallings system is based on research on effective teaching of academic knowledge and skills. (See Chapter 3 for a review of this research.)

The Stallings Observation System has two components: (1) the classroom snapshot and (2) the five-minute interaction (FMI). The snapshot data show how the teacher and students spend their time during a lesson and the types of activities in which they engage. The FMI data show how the teacher and student verbally interact with each other during a lesson. Together the snapshot and the FMI provide a comprehensive picture of what happened during the lesson.

Snapshot Data

These data are collected at five evenly spaced intervals during a lesson, and FMI data are collected at another five evenly spaced intervals during the same lesson. It is recommended that three lessons be observed to get a stable picture of the teacher's instruction, but one lesson—if it is typical—should be sufficient for the purposes of clinical supervision.

In collecting snapshot data, the observer takes a sweep of the classroom and quickly marks the categories that correspond to what he or she sees on a scantron sheet (a special type of checklist that can be scored mechanically) or computer with appropriate software. When the next interval for collecting snapshot data occurs, this process is repeated. In effect, the observer has taken a series of "snapshots" of the teacher's lesson.

Table 12.1 shows an example of a teacher profile that can be created from snapshot data. The left column lists the aspects of instruction that are recorded by the snapshot. The "criterion" column lists the optimal amount of time that should be spent on each aspect of instruction, as determined by research on effective teaching.[16] Because these criterion percentages are not always appropriate for every age and subject, they can be adjusted as the situation requires. The third column shows the actual percentage of observed time that the teacher (Betty) and her students spent on each aspect of instruction.

To understand Table 12.1 better, let us consider how Betty spent her time monitoring student work. This aspect of instruction is reflected in the top two rows, "Monitoring silent reading" and "Monitoring written work." Looking at the two columns of time-use percentages, we find that Betty used less time (0 percent) than considered optimal (15 percent) in monitoring silent reading, but more time (36 percent) than considered optimal in monitoring written work (20 percent). Looking now at the student activity rows, we find that students read silently (2 percent) less than considered optimal (15 percent), and they spent much more time doing written assignments (55 percent) than considered optimal (20 percent). We also note that while students spent 55 percent of their time on written assignments, Betty only spent 36 percent of her time monitoring them. This is probably because she spent a substantial amount of her time working by herself (18 percent is recorded in the row labeled "Organizing—teacher alone").

These data suggest two goals for instructional improvement as part of the clinical supervision process. First, the teacher should consider providing more interactive instruction

Table 12.1   Snapshot Profile of a Teacher Lesson

Observation variables	Percent of time spent	
	Criterion	Betty's class
Teacher involved in		
Monitoring silent reading	15.00	.00
Monitoring written work	20.00	36.00
Reading aloud	6.00	.00
Instruction or explanation	25.00	10.00
Discussion or review assignments	10.00	13.00
Practice drill	4.00	.00
Taking test or quiz	5.00	.00
Classroom management with students	2.50	.00
Making assignments	10.00	20.00
Organizing—teacher alone	2.50	18.00
Social interacting with students	.00	.00
Student uninvolved	.00	.00
Providing discipline	.00	3.00
Students involved in		
Reading silently	15.00	2.00
Written assignments	20.00	55.00
Reading aloud	6.00	.00
Receiving instruction or explanations	25.00	26.00
Discussion or review	10.00	12.00
Practice drill	4.00	7.00
Taking test or quiz	5.00	6.00
Social interaction	.00	14.00
Student uninvolved	.00	12.00
Being disciplined	.00	3.00
Classroom management	5.00	.00
Receiving assignments	10.00	10.00

Source: Adapted from Figure 2.4 in K. K. Zumwalt (Ed.). (1986). *Improving teaching.* Alexandria, VA: Association for Supervision and Curriculum Development, p. 24.

and spending less time working alone. Second, she should consider assigning more silent reading and less written work.

Five-Minute Interaction

The FMI involves a different data collection procedure than the classroom snapshot. The codes of the FMI were based on naturalistic observations in classrooms. Frequently occurring behaviors were identified and developed as codes for the system. The observer records all teacher and student verbal communications that occur during a 5-minute period. The data can be recorded on a scantron sheet or computer.

The scantron sheet consists of a series of rectangular boxes, as illustrated in Figure 12.9. In the first column of each box, the observer fills a bubble to indicate whether the communication was in a language other than English (NE); it was a repeat of the same communication pattern as recorded in the preceding box (R); or the observer made an error and wishes to cancel what he coded in the box (Ca). The other parts of the box are used to code who was talking (e.g., teacher, student, visitor, aide); to whom the person talked; what the person said (e.g., a command, literal question, response to a question or command); and how the communication related to the lesson (e.g., academic, organizing, behavior management).

An FMI box is coded approximately every 5 seconds during the 5-minute period, and there are five such time periods during the lesson. Therefore, a typical FMI for a lesson consists of 300 coded boxes (12 codings per minute × 5 minutes × 5 time periods).

You will note that the FMI method of coding is similar to the timeline coding in the Flanders system in two ways. First, the emphasis is on teacher and student communication behaviors. Second, observers do not need to write their observations. All observations are in the form of filling in bubbles on the scantron sheet or typing a single letter code on the computer.

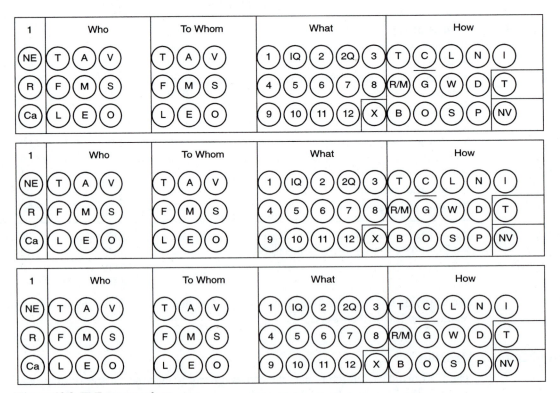

Figure 12.9 FMI scantron sheet.

Table 12.2 Five-Minute Interaction (FMI) Profile of a Teacher's Lesson.

	Observation variables	Percentage of time spent	
		Criterion	Betty's class
001	All academic statements	80.00	65.28
002	All organizing or management statements	15.00	30.76
003	All behavior statements	3.00	3.83
004	All social statements	2.00	.00
005	Total for discrete variables	100.00	100.00
006	Teacher instructs or explains	12.00	15.45
007	Teacher asks direct questions or commands	10.00	4.00
008	Teacher asks clarifying questions	3.00	.13
009	Teacher asks open-ended questions	3.00	.79
010	Student asks academic questions	2.00	1.32
011	Teacher calls upon new students (academic)	6.00	5.02
012	Students respond academically	15.00	5.00
013	Student shouts-out or initiates remarks	.00	7.39
014	Student doesn't know answer	1.00	.13
015	Student refuses to answer	.00	.00
016	All praise	8.00	2.00
017	Teacher praises or supports academic responses	6.00	2.00
018	Teacher praises behavior	2.00	.00
019	Teacher corrects academic responses	6.00	4.35
020	Teacher corrects with guidance	4.00	.00
021	Teacher corrects behavior	2.00	3.03
022	Teacher monitoring academic work	6.00	10.96
023	All written work	.00	.00
024	Students read aloud	10.00	4.62
025	Teacher reads aloud	1.00	2.24
026	Teacher working alone	3.00	6.00
027	Intrusions	.00	3.14
028	Teacher involved with visitor	.00	2.20
029	Positive interactions	4.00	.52
030	Negative interactions	.00	1.50
031	Teacher touching	5.00	.00
032	Teacher movement	3.00	1.12
033	All activity-related comments or action	16.00	9.77
034	Student organizing comments	1.00	.13
035	Student academic comments	3.00	.13
036	Teacher organizing comments	5.00	1.98
037	Students' academic discussion	7.00	7.66
038	Students' cooperative group academic discussion	5.00	.00
	Total Number of Interactions for Teacher: 905		

Source: Adapted from Figure 2.5 in K. K. Zumwalt (Ed.). (1986). *Improving teaching.* Alexandria, VA: Association for Supervision and Curriculum Development, p. 25.

Table 12.2 illustrates the type of display that is created from FMI data. Some of the observation variables represent particular behaviors (e.g., "008—Teacher asks clarifying questions"), whereas others are groups of behaviors (e.g., "001—All academic statements").

The display is for the same lesson as that shown in Table 12.1. By comparing the two exhibits, you can see how the FMI complements and expands on the picture of classroom teaching produced by the snapshot. Also, you will note that both displays use the same format.

The Stallings Observation System is complex, but has the virtues of being comprehensive and focused on important aspects of effective teaching. If you wish to learn how to use this instrument, you will need to receive instruction from a certified trainer.[17]

NOTES

1. Goldhammer, R. (1969). *Clinical supervision: Special methods for the supervision of teachers*. New York: Holt, Rinehart & Winston, pp. 288–289.

2. Many other checklists are described and presented in: Borich, G. D., & Martin, D. B. (1999). *Observation skills for effective teaching* (3rd ed.). Upper Saddle River, NJ: Merill. See also: Borich, G. D., & Madden, S. K. (1977). *Evaluating classroom instruction: A sourcebook of instruments*. Reading, MA: Addison-Wesley.

3. A copy of the full instrument appears in: Veldman, D. J., & Peck, R. F. (1963). Student teacher characteristics from the pupils' viewpoint. *Journal of Educational Psychology, 54,* 346–355.

4. These checklists are called Teaching Analysis Guides by Bruce Joyce and colleagues. They are included in a set of three books: Weil, M., & and Joyce, B. (1978). *Information processing models of teaching*. Englewood Cliffs, NJ: Prentice-Hall; Joyce, B., & Weil, M. (1978). *Social models of teaching*. Englewood Cliffs, NJ: Prentice-Hall; Joyce, B., Weil, M., & Kluwin, B. (1978). *Personal models of teaching*. Englewood Cliffs, NJ: Prentice-Hall, 1978. See also: Borich & Martin, *ibid;* Borich & Madden, *ibid.*

5. This research is reviewed in Flanders, N. A. (1970). *Analyzing teaching behavior.* Reading, MA: Addison-Wesley.

6. Advance organizers, concept maps, and graphic organizers are described in various sources, including: Hyerle, D. (1996). *Visual tools for constructing knowledge.* Alexandria, VA: Association for Supervision and Curriculum Development; Erickson, H. L. (1998). *Concept-based curriculum and instruction: Teaching beyond the facts.* Thousand Oaks, CA: Corwin.

7. Tomlinson, C. A. (1999). *The differentiated classroom: Responding to the needs of all learners.* Alexandria, VA: Association for Supervision and Curriculum Development.

8. Instruction in using the Interaction Analysis System can be found in: Flanders, N. A. (1970). *Analyzing teaching behavior.*

Reading, MA: Addison-Wesley. See also: Acheson, K. (1989). *Another set of eyes: Techniques for classroom observation* (video and trainer's manual). Alexandria, VA: Association for Supervision and Curriculum Development.

9. When a simple interaction category occurs for any length of time, the observer can abbreviate the record-keeping process. For example, if the teacher launches into an extended explanation of a concept, the observer may place a few tallies in the row designated by category 5, and then draw a short arrow with a note indicating approximately how many minutes or seconds this category of verbal behavior was used.

10. For an example of how the Interaction Analysis System can be adapted, see: Sakaguchi, H. (1993). A comparison of teaching methods in English-as-a-Second-Language conversation courses and reading courses in Japanese universities. *Dissertation Abstracts International, 54* (10A), 3692. (University Microfilms No. AAG94-05220)

11. Crippen, K. J., & Brooks, D. W. (2000). Using personal digital assistants in clinical supervision of student teachers. *Journal of Science Education and Technology, 9,* 207–211.

12. Crippen and Brooks describe a software system for the PalmPilot, *Learner Profile*, that can be used to record various classroom behaviors.

13. Sirotnik, K. A. (1983). What you see is what you get—Consistency, persistency, and mediocrity in classrooms. *Harvard Educational Review, 53,* 16–31.

14. Stallings, J. A. (1986). Using time effectively: A self-analytic approach. In K. K. Zumwalt (Ed.), *Improving teaching* (pp. 15–27). Alexandria, VA: Association for Supervision and Curriculum Development.

15. Freiberg, H. J., & Waxman, H. C. (1990). Reflection and the acquisition of technical teaching skills. In R. T. Clift, W. R. Houston, & M. C. Pugach (Eds.), *Encouraging reflective practice in education* (pp. 119–138). New York: Teachers College Press.

16. This research is reviewed in: Stallings, J. (1980). Allocated learning time revisited, or beyond time on task. *Educational Researcher, 9(11),* 11–16.

17. Information about training in the Stallings Observation System can be obtained at this Web address: http://www.coe.tamu.edu/~cclc/stallings.htm

Name Index

Subject Index